D1562979

The Structure of
Long-Term Memory
A Connectivity Model of
Semantic Processing

The Structure of Long-Term Memory

A Connectivity Model of Semantic Processing

Wolfgang Klimesch
University of Salzburg

LAWRENCE ERLBAUM ASSOCIATES, PUBLISHERS
1994   Hillsdale, New Jersey   Hove, UK

Lawrence Erlbaum Associates, Inc., Publishers
365 Broadway
Hillsdale, New Jersey 07642

Cover design by Kate Dusza

A portion of this volume was originally published as *Die Struktur und Aktivierung des Gedächtnisses* by Hans Huber Verlag, Berne, Switzerland.

Library of Congress Cataloging-in-Publication Data
Klimesch, Wolfgang.
    [Struktur und Aktivierung des Gedächtnisses. English]
    The structure of long-term memory : a connectivity model of
semantic processing / Wolfgang Klimesch.
        p. cm.
    Includes bibliographical references and index.
    ISBN 0-8058-1354-3
    1. Memory—Philosophy. 2. Connectionism. 3. Psycholinguistics.
4. Human information processing. I. Title.
    [DNLM: 1. Memory. 2. Nerve Net. 3. Semantics. 4. Models,
Psychological.   BF 371 K65s 1993]
BF371.K54 1993
153.1'3—dc20
DNLM/DLC
for Library of Congress   93-16293
                                                                 CIP

Books published by Lawrence Erlbaum Associates are printed on acid-free paper, and their
bindings are chosen for strength and durability.

Printed in the United States of America
10 9 8 7 6 5 4 3 2 1

To my wife Therese and my daughter Christine

Contents

9.4 The Connectivity Model and Empirical Findings on the Typicality Effect: Evaluating Assumption I   *148*
9.5 The Connectivity Model and Empirical Findings on Traditional Word Norms   *152*
9.6 The Connectivity Model and Empirical Findings on Case 1: Searching Two Codes that Share Common Features   *158*
9.7 The Connectivity Model and Empirical Findings on the Preactivation of Semantic Features   *162*
9.8 The Connectivity Model and the Encoding of Pictures   *168*

10 THE SIMULATION PROGRAM CONN1   174

10.1 Arguments for Modifying Assumptions   *174*
10.2 The Spread of Activation in CONN1   *177*
10.3 CONN1 and Spreading Activation in a Simple Semantic Network   *183*

11 REPRESENTATIONAL ASSUMPTIONS AND THEIR POSSIBLE NEURAL BASES   187

11.1 Basic Principles of Neural Information Processing   *189*
11.2 The Connectivity Model as a Neural Model   *195*
11.3 On the Localization of Memory Processes   *199*

12 CONCLUDING REMARKS   203

12.1 The Connectivity Model and Connectionist Approaches   *204*
12.2 Representational Assumptions and Their Importance for the Future of Cognitive Psychology   *206*

REFERENCES   207

AUTHOR INDEX   223

SUBJECT INDEX   229

Preface

The purpose of this book is to describe a new theory about long-term memory, the connectivity model for semantic processing (chaps. 8 and 9). In addressing the question of the way that complex semantic codes are represented, searched, and retrieved, the model tries to answer the following key problem. Which are the representational assumptions that allow us to predict that complex knowledge stored in long-term memory does not slow down activation and search processes in a systematic way? When the principles of the connectivity model were first published in 1987, my primary concern was the experimental evaluation of the model within the domain of semantic memory. During a research visit at the University of California in Davis, I worked on this topic together with Professor Neal E. A. Kroll. In the following years he has carried out a series of well-designed experiments in order to test several crucial assumptions and predictions of the model (see the brief summary of this work in section 9.7). I am grateful for his contributions, suggestions, and the many enlightening discussions we had together.

The basic logic and procedure which led to the foundations of the connectivity model is characterized by the attempt to define representational assumptions as explicitly as possible and to evaluate their plausibility or empirical validity whenever feasible (chaps. 1–5). Thus, it was a logical consequence to focus also on the implementation of the model. I wish to thank F.G. Winkler who wrote the simulation program CONN1. His work has led to important new insights which are discussed in chap. 10.

When pursuing the representational problem, it gradually became clear to me that the issue of how information is encoded in the brain must also be considered. The more I focused on the elaboration of a connecting bridge between theoretical and neurophysiologically based representational assumptions (chap. 11), the more I became convinced that the future of cognitive psychology lies in the further development of cognitive neuroscience. I am grateful to Professor Jaak Panksepp (from Bowling Green State University, Ohio, where I stayed during a research visit in 1991) for his encouragement to follow-up this approach and for the valuable suggestions he made when reading parts of the manuscript. Chapters 10 and 11 are additions to the English edition which were not included in the original German publication.

Last but not least, I wish to thank Patrick O'Mahony who has translated the German edition into English. His skills and collaborative mind have been invaluable in the prompt completion of the English manuscript.

ACKNOWLEDGMENTS

Parts of this research were funded by the Austrian Fonds zur Förderung der wissenschaftlichen Forschung (FWF), Project S4904, and by the Austrian Forschungsgemeinschaft (ÖFG), Project 06/1064.

Introduction

An important but controversial issue in memory research concerns the way in which the complexity of semantic structures influences processing time and memory performance. Traditional memory theories such as HAM, ACT, or ACT* assume that memory load increases and processing time slows down as more semantic components are processed. This assumption amounts to what is known as the paradox of retrieval interference: The more information is stored in memory, the slower it works. Chapters 6 and 7 give an extensive review of this issue. Chapter 8 includes the mathematical basis for a new, nonconnectionist memory model, the connectivity model, which refutes the paradox of retrieval interference. The basic assumption here is that — in contrast to conventional computers — the speed of search processes in human memory increases as the complexity of interconnected knowledge increases. This prediction, which contradicts all presently existing memory models, explains a variety of different memory phenomena that are discussed in chap. 9. A simulation program is presented in chap. 10. This program allows for a better understanding of the complex predictions of the connectivity model. Neurophysiological evidence is also in close agreement with the predictions of the connectivity model. This issue is addressed in chap. 11, where it is shown that the well-known properties of postsynaptic signal transmission lead to the conclusion that converging neural activity speeds up processing time, and that the stronger a neural signal is, the faster it can be transmitted. Besides other evidence, this fact is also confirmed through reaction time experiments, which show that reaction times decrease as stimulus intensity increases. Finally, chap. 12 gives a brief summary and addresses how the connectivity model differs from connectionist approaches.

One of the fundamental principles on which the connectivity model is based is the assumption that any comprehensive memory theory must explicitly define the format of a code. If explicit representational assumptions are avoided, misleading and contradictory theories about memory or cognitive processes emerge. After a brief historical review about the representational problem in chap. 1, this argument is developed and explained in chaps. 2, 3, and 4. Here, theories and experiments about forgetting show why misleading representational assumptions are responsible for the failure of traditional memory theories. In chap. 5, those theories that define the format of a code explicitly are shown to assume a hierarchical structure. The chapters that follow demonstrate that the assumption of a hierarchical coding format is at the core of retrieval interference. It is argued that only the suggested connectivity model is capable of overcoming this paradox.

1 The Representational Problem: A Historical Perspective

Those who concern themselves with the history of experimental psychology will no doubt conclude that the topics this discipline has dealt with in the last 100 years have not changed much (cf. with this the synoptic works of Boring, 1950; Flugel, n. d.; Lück, Miller, & Rechtien, 1984). In cognitive psychology, for example, there are many experimental paradigms and theoretical concepts that have been dealt with in similar fashion, but under different titles, over many historical periods. Consider the cognitive-psychological concept of a limited capacity of short-term memory (STM). James McKeen Cattell had already carried out studies on the attention span at the Leipzig Institute of Wilhelm Wundt and observed that in a simultaneous, tachistoscopic display of several stimuli only 4 to 6 units — be they lines, letters, or words — could be understood and remembered (Flugel, n. d., p. 157). The terms *capacity of STM* and *attention span* (cf. Ebbinghaus, 1885) refer to one and the same empirical phenomenon. Where they differ is in their historical context and in the ways in which they happen to be embedded in overlapping theoretical relations (e.g., Bahrick, 1985). There is a long list of historical concepts and empirical phenomena that have been redeployed. Here, however, we content ourselves with a few references and, in doing so, recall the historical relations between the following concepts:

- the similarity between Donder's "subtractive procedure" (Donders, 1868; cf. Massaro, 1975, p. 44; Sanders, 1971, p. 17) and the experimental paradigms in cognitive psychology (Posner, 1978; Posner, Boies, Eichelman, & Taylor, 1969);
- the importance that reaction time paradigms have assumed in

experimental psychology ever since Wilhelm Wundt conducted his extensive experiments at the Leipzig Institute;

- the continued importance of verbal association paradigms, which have been an important feature in memory psychology since Ebbinghaus (1885; e.g., McGeoch, 1942; Slamecka, 1985a, 1985b);

- the experimental documentation concerning the superiority of visual memory over verbal memory, which has been known since Kirkpatrick (1894) and Calkins (1898), and not just since Shepard (1967) or Paivio (1971);

- and, within the confines of cognitive psychology, the "rediscovered" findings — dating back to Cattell (1886) — that words can be identified more quickly than images (Potter & Faulconer, 1975).

Seen in this light, it is not surprising that critical voices continually claim that little, if any, scientific progress is being made in our discipline. We attempt to show that this view is misleading because it ignores important recent developments. It can be seen from the comparison of the most important historical approaches that it is the specific preoccupation with the representational problem that is in fact the new contribution of cognitive psychology as it emerged in the Anglo-American sphere. Only the explicit consideration of the representational problem can build a foundation on which to arrive at a consistent interpretation of memory phenomena. Chapters 2, 3, and 4 consider this question in greater detail.

The name *cognitive psychology* has often led to misunderstandings about the actual concerns of this comparatively young field of research. A more precise and specific description would be "the psychology of information processing." Those critics who claim that the "cognitive trend" will soon turn into an "action trend" (Graumann, 1983, p. 68) or "emotional trend," are not taking into consideration the specific contribution made by cognitive psychology. Its task is to examine how information is encoded, represented, and processed. The type of information involved — whether "cognitive," "emotional," or "action relevant" — has no immediate impact on the study of the representational problem. Cognitive psychology is not the counterpart of an "emotional" or "action" psychology. Nevertheless, it emphasizes the cognitive content, because for methodical reasons emotional processes are much more difficult to examine empirically than cognitive processes.

The next section considers the fundamental concepts needed to explain and elucidate the representational problem. Subsequent sections are then devoted to the historical development of the representational problem. Based on these sections, we show that the consideration of the representational problem leads to new and important discoveries.

1.1 DEFINING THE REPRESENTATIONAL PROBLEM: CODE, CODING, AND THE CODING FORMAT

Which processes enable sensory information to be recognized, stored, and recalled? This is the main research topic in cognitive psychology, and characterizes what is generally understood by the encoding or representational problem. *Encoding* or *coding* is the transformation of sensory information into a certain format of a memory representation, resulting in the formation of a memory code. The form, composition, and structure of the internal representation, on the other hand, is known as the coding format. It is precisely this interest in how information is "represented" (i.e., how information is stored in memory) that has led to the preeminent position of memory research in the field of cognitive psychology. Because coding is considered a process of transformation — reflecting different stages of information processes, such as perception, recognition, and selective attention — it becomes clear that memory can be described only if empirically validated assumptions regarding the entire information-processing system are made. This idea of a close interdependence between the properties of the encoding format and the structure of the entire information-processing system is discussed in chap. 4.

The description of the elementary properties of codes is crucial here. Consequently, memory research is the main focus of the following historical survey.

1.2 MEMORY RESEARCH: A HISTORICAL PERSPECTIVE

It is worth noting that Ebbinghaus, as the founder of empirical memory research, had no interest in representational assumptions. Following his description of the "Mangelhaftigkeit des Wissens über das Gedächtnis" (The inadequate knowledge about memory), Ebbinghaus (1885) wrote:

> And because all our knowledge is so uncertain and imprecise, it has remained unfruitful for an understanding of a theory of memory, recall, and association processes. In our ideas on its physical basis, we use different metaphors such as stored images, imprinted ideas, and encarved traces etc., of which we only know that one thing is certain that they are not correct. (p. 7)

Ebbinghaus could hardly have expressed his rejection of the representational problem more clearly. Nevertheless, it would be wrong to assume that memory psychology could have managed without representational assumptions in its early stages. These were more implicit than explicit in nature and were based on the fundamental conceptions of associationism, which was the predominant psychological trend in the second half of the 19th century. Ebbinghaus saw the goal of his work not as an attempt to empirically examine associationistic representational assumptions, but rather to substantiate the scientific claim of his experimental approach in psychology. The status of implicit and explicit representational assumptions within memory psychology is discussed in chaps. 2 and 3.

In order to evaluate the importance of Ebbinghaus' work, we must consider the historical factors that influenced it. Two factors need to be taken into consideration: On the one hand, there was the dismissive attitude toward psychology as an experimental science and, on the other hand, the limited prospect of ever arriving at an empirically validated theory of memory. Ebbinghaus, like other empirical psychologists of his day, was primarily concerned with showing that mental processes — like physical and biological processes — could also be examined and understood using scientific methods. His approach to the problem was therefore primarily one of method as opposed to content. It consisted of the classical scientific procedure of proving what effect the specific variation of one or more independent variables has on one or more dependent variables. The dependent variable was memory performance or the extent of forgetting. Among the most important independent variables were the number of repetitions and the retention interval (i.e., the time that elapses between presentation and test), as well as the nature and amount of material to be learned. Ebbinghaus arrived at a series of rules governing the examined variables, whereby the rule governing the length of the retention interval and memory performance, known as the "forgetting curve," is only one of the better-known examples.

From the perspective of the then-dominant school of thought, these results were a sweeping success. Ebbinghaus was now able to prove that the study of higher mental processes was also possible for a psychology using scientific methods. Thus, together with Wilhelm Wundt, Ebbinghaus made a significant contribution toward the founding of a scientifically and experimentally oriented psychology. It is interesting to note, however, that Wundt had a negative attitude toward the study of higher mental processes — as they represented memory performance — and seven years after first publishing *Philosophische Studien* (the journal founded by Wundt in 1890) Ebbinghaus published *Zeitschrift für Psychologie und Physiologie der Sinnesorgane*, which to a certain extent provided a forum for independent researchers outside of the Wundtian School (Boring, 1950; Flugel, n. d., p. 167).

Müller, Jost, and Pilzecker (Jost, 1897; Müller & Pilzecker, 1900) followed a procedure similar to Ebbinghaus, but even this was completely derived from associationism (e.g., Müller, 1917). The first 30 years of empirical memory research are thus essentially characterized by two factors: on the one hand, by the methodical-scientific orientation that predominates, and, on the other hand, by simple associationistic conceptions of memory. As a result, one finds a wealth of important rules that up to now remain untouched in applied memory psychology. What was missing, however, were approaches to general, overlapping memory theories. Therefore, within the framework of classic memory psychology, it was not the investigation of representational assumptions that predominated, but in effect only the question of how associations develop between memory contents.

After this first classical period of memory research, the emphasis of scientific research shifted from Germany to the Anglo-American sphere. Even there the focus remained for a long time—up to the early 1960s—within the framework of associationism and behavioristic approaches. There were, however, a few important exceptions. For example, F. C. Bartlett, then a Cambridge psychologist, was among the first to introduce the concept of a mental "schema" into memory psychology. Bartlett (1932) assumed that sensory information is structured and stored alongside these mental schemas, which are themselves represented in memory. Schemas, which are derived by means of abstraction, represent the essential characteristics of a whole class of stimuli. The similarity to the Gestalt concept, but also to Rosch's (1975) "typicality concept" in the area of concept formation, should not be overlooked. According to Bartlett, the associationistic viewpoint of memory as a passive store was abandoned, and the active, structuring character of memory came to the fore. Bartlett assumed that schemas are of crucial importance for perception and thinking as well as memory. Thus it became clear that memory could not be studied and understood in isolation from other phenomena of the human mind.

Oldfield joined others in adopting Bartlett's schema concept, which Evans and his colleagues (Evans, 1967; Evans & Arnoult, 1967; Evans & Edmonds, 1966) subsequently applied in the area of concept formation (Homa & Cultice, 1984). Seen from our perspective, Bartlett's works occupy a special position, because they were among the first ideas that—after 50 years of empirical memory research—started out with clearly drawn representational assumptions. It was all the more surprising, therefore, that these important ideas—apart from those exceptions mentioned earlier—did not receive widespread attention.

In the late 1940s, Shannon's information theory and Wiener's cybernetics theory stimulated new interest among researchers in psychology and in other scientific disciplines (see Wiener, 1968). In the hope of a promising and fruitful approach to the study of perception, memory, and thinking, information theory and cybernetics were frequently introduced into psychology with a lack of critical insight. The number of works relating to the concept of information theory, above all in the Anglo-American sphere, soon became vast (Garner, 1962). One of the best-known experiments was carried out by Miller (1956) on the "magical number seven." He was able to show that the human "channel capacity" lies within a range of two and three bits. Thus, STM can store at maximum between four and eight unrelated information units. If this capacity limit is exceeded, information stored in STM is lost. Miller, however, emphasized that his results were closely related to Külpe's, which were reported at the first Congress of Experimental Psychology in Gießen in 1904 (which was, incidentally, inaugurated by Ebbinghaus). Miller failed to mention that similar experiments had already been conducted by James McKeen Cattel and Wilhelm Wundt, who came to the conclusion that the immediate attention span comprises approximately four to six different units.

Psychological research, based on information theory, was often accused of merely altering the names of already well-established results and concepts. This criticism is certainly justified. Information theory was inadequate for psychological resarch because it neither led to a better and deeper understanding of results already known, nor contributed to the discovery of new experimental paradigms. It therefore comes as no surprise that the significance of information theory began to wane by the mid-1960s.

It may seem paradoxical to assume that, in spite of its negative effects, information theory was an essential precursor to cognitive psychology. In order to explain this notion, we must deal separately with the negative and positive influences of information theory.

Its negative influence can be seen in the fact that its concepts—though useful for describing the stimulus material (Garner, 1962; Klimesch, 1974; Miller, 1956) or measuring the amount of information transferred from input to output (cf. choice reaction time experiments and the concept of "channel capacity")—were inadequate in defining representational assumptions for human information processing. The application of information theory in psychology, therefore, stood (whether intended or not) in the best behavioristic tradition.

Information theory also had a positive influence. For the first time in the history of psychology there was a model to describe basic principles of information processing. It was only after the advent of cybernetics that psychologists began to see a parallel between the technical, machine-related, and the human or, generally speaking, biological information processing. Thus, it was only a small step toward the development of a new system, namely that of artificial intelligence and later of cognitive science. Within the framework of this discipline, which developed somewhat later than cognitive psychology and maintained close connections with it, the representational problem was of crucial importance from the outset (J. R. Anderson & Bower, 1973; Newell & Simon, 1972).

Toward the end of the 1960s, there was a "cognitive revolution," or an abrupt renunciation of the formal, descriptive approach of information theory toward the special interest shown in "opening the black box," left in the wake of behaviorism. Opening the black box made it necessary to make assumptions about the internal structure of information processing. Thus, representational assumptions became the central concern of cognitive psychology. Four works can be regarded as milestones in this new development: Neisser's *Cognitive Psychology* (1967), which was, from a historical standpoint, probably the most important work (J. R. Anderson, 1985a, p. 9; Bahrick, 1984); Atkinson's and Shiffrin's work (1968) on an overlapping theory of memory; the introduction into human information processing by Lindsay and Norman (1972); and the epoch-making *Human Associative Memory* by J. R. Anderson and Bower (1973). The importance of this new trend was soon noticed and recognized in the German-speaking area (Wimmer & Perner, 1979).

1.3 REPRESENTATIONAL ASSUMPTIONS IN HISTORICAL APPROACHES TO THE PSYCHOLOGY OF PERCEPTION AND THINKING

Psychology of perception and thinking confronted representational assumptions long before memory psychology. The reason for this is obvious: In contrast to memory processes, certain structures and principles governing perception and thinking are to some extent more accessible to self-observation and can thus be detected more easily.

Thus, for the Würzburg School, the question of how the contents of consciousness are structured and of what elements they consist were among the most important research topics (cf. Messer, 1924, p. 24). By analyzing the contents of consciousness, which could either be conducted by experimental methods or by the method of systematic self-observation, an attempt was made to classify its elements. These examinations led to differentiation between two types of consciousness elements: sensations and intentional acts (cf. the excellent review in Humphrey, 1963; Munzert, 1984). In order to distinguish their approach from that of elementaristic psychology, they introduced an important restriction: Perception and thought, for example, could not be explained by a decomposition into individual elements. The exclusive preoccupation with phenomena accessible to self-observation, as well as the assumption that consciousness processes could, in principle, not be explained by a knowledge of their elements, were the obvious reasons why access to explicit representational assumptions was denied the Würzburg School. Chapter 4 discusses why a general understanding of perception, memory, and thought processes is impossible without assumptions regarding the unconscious course of information processes in their early stages.

For Gestalt psychology, the situation was fundamentally different. Like Bartlett's concept of *schema*, the concept of *Gestalt* was also used as a structuring and ordering principle that commanded importance beyond the well-described principles of perception (see Wellek, 1955, for a review). Hence, it also played a central role in thought processes, as can be seen in Wertheimer's well-known nine-point task. Perception and thought processes were—as in the case of cognitive psychology—closely related phenomena. What connected both can be seen in the common structuring principles expressed in various Gestalt laws and that, from our present standpoint, can be regarded as explicit representational assumptions. As in Gestalt psychology, explicit representational assumptions were also key concepts in cognitive psychology, enabling an understanding of the close interdependence of perception, thought, and memory processes. Another important link between Gestalt psychology and cognitive psychology is the lack of focus on consciousness processes.

The importance of representational assumptions in Gestalt psychology is reflected in the physiologically oriented assumptions known by the term *isomorphism*. From our present perspective, however, isomorphism belongs to the one of the drawbacks of Gestalt psychology. There was a reliance on physiological assumptions without the necessary or appropriate background knowledge, which is just now becoming available (see chap. 11).

The Würzburg School and, above all, Gestalt psychology came very close to the current understanding of the representational problem. In the Würzburg School it was the strict focus on consciousness processes; in Gestalt psychology, on the other hand, it was the premature transition to a physiological explanation and the rejection of an elementaristic approach that hampered a more sophisticated investigation of the representational problem.

1.4 CONCLUSIONS

This short historical review of the representational problem was intended to show how, during the founding period of memory psychology, interests other than the specific examination of representational assumptions stood in the foreground. These important assumptions did not appear until the 1930s, roughly 50 years after the advent of empirical memory research, and remained virtually unnoticed for another 35 to 40 years. On the other hand, the psychology of perception and thinking (which dealt with structuring processes far earlier) came very close to the "cognitive understanding of the problem." Gestalt psychology, above all, made an essential contribution in this area. However, it was still impossible—even for Gestalt psychology—to carry further the representational problem.

The view that the explicit recognition of the representational problem is, in fact, the new contribution of cognitive psychology—although a divided issue among important representatives of cognitive psychology (J. R. Anderson, 1985a, 1985b; Kintsch, 1985)—is by no means widely accepted (e.g., Slamecka 1985a, 1985b). As an example, there are still psychologists who see behavioristic approaches in cognitive psychology (Bruder, 1984). J. R. Anderson (1985b), in referring to the acquisition of word lists, provided a good characterization of the current situation: "Slamecka's (1985a) discussion . . . misses the great thing that we have learned in modern cognitive psychology (not to deny it was known before): Lists are hierarchically organized in chunks. . . . Without recognizing that structure there is a multitude of uninterpretable data" (p. 436). But there are other reasons why Anderson's quote serves as a "guide" through this present volume. Although we agree with Anderson regarding the importance of the representational problem, we attempt to show in chap. 5 and thereafter that the general validity of the assumption regarding hierarchical coding structures is in fact false.

2 Traditional Theories of Forgetting

Memory performance and forgetting are concepts that appear to complement each other. For example, consider the following simple memory experiment: If subjects are required to remember 20 different words, and if during the test they are capable of recalling 15 words, then the 5 words not recalled have, by definition, been forgotten. But what does "forgetting" mean?

Mental representations must exist for those words that have been recalled. But which representational assumptions are valid for the forgotten words? Have the forgotten words decayed, or does forgetting only mean that stored information can no longer be retrieved? Even everyday experience shows us how, for example, a name has "escaped" us, even though we can effortlessly remember it at a later date. This situation is known as *retrieval failure* and is most likely due to processes interfering with the retrieval of the sought-after memory content. The question of whether or not forgetting can be explained by retrieval failure or by the loss of stored information is examined in this chapter.

The causes and effects of forgetting are first discussed on the basis of experiments and theories of traditional—primarily associationistic—memory research, which do not put forward any explicit assumptions concerning the encoding format (G. R. Loftus, 1985; Slamecka, 1985c; Slamecka & McElree, 1983). Chapters 3 and 4 show that, in order to arrive at a consistent explanation of forgetting, explicit representational assumptions are required.

2.1 THE MOST IMPORTANT CAUSES OF FORGETTING: INTERFERENCE OR PASSIVE DECAY?

In memory psychology, there are two competing theories of forgetting: decay theory (J. Brown, 1958; Reitman, 1974; M. J. Watkins, O. C. Watkins, Craik, & Mazuryk, 1974) and interference theory (Postman & Underwood, 1973; Runquist, 1983; Shiffrin, 1970a, 1973; Spring, 1968; Underwood, 1964; see also the overviews in J. R. Anderson, 1985a; Klimesch, 1979a, 1979c; G. R. Loftus & E. F. Loftus, 1976; Stern, 1981). Decay theory assumes that forgetting is caused by a time-dependent autonomous process that becomes increasingly effective the more time elapses and finally leads to the complete loss of stored information. Interference theory, on the other hand, assumes that there are processes that impede or halt the retrieval, perhaps also the storage. Pro- and retroactive interferences of memory contents (L. R. Peterson & M. G. Peterson, 1959), context effects (S. M. Smith, 1982, 1984; S. M. Smith, Glenberg, & Bjork, 1978), or a continuing "unlearning" of stored codes (cf. the classic work by McGeoch, 1932) are regarded as possible interference processes. Figure 2.1 summarizes the most important assumptions and predictions of both theories.

The Brown–Peterson paradigm (J. Brown, 1958; L. R. Peterson & M. G. Peterson, 1959), in particular, and the variants derived from this (e.g., Reitman, 1971; Roediger, Knight, & Kantowitz, 1977) were used to test the predictions of interference and decay theory. The experimental design consists of several individual trials and is shown in Fig. 2.2. Each trial starts with the presentation of a trigram (i.e., a group of three items), which is

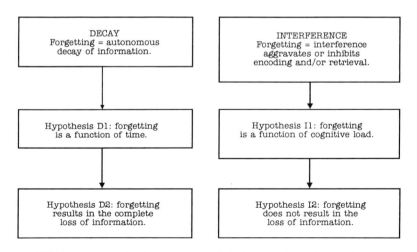

FIG. 2.1. Comparing the hypotheses of the decay and interference theory.

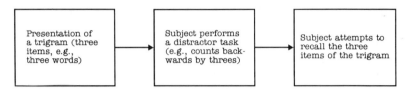

FIG. 2.2.   A single trial in a Brown-Peterson paradigm.

followed by a distractor task and a free-recall task. The distractor task prevents the subjects from memorizing the presented items.

2.1.1 Forgetting as Passive Decay: Empirical Evaluation of Hypothesis D1

The application of the Brown–Peterson paradigm led to some surprising results. First of all, it could be demonstrated that within a retention interval of only 18 s, memory performance dropped to chance-level (L. R. Peterson & M. G. Peterson, 1959). The percentage of correctly reported items lay at a little over 10%. Considering the unexpectedly rapid decline in memory performance (being only a matter of seconds), the assumption that a passive decay process was the cause of forgetting appeared justified (J. Brown, 1958; L. R. Peterson & M. G. Peterson, 1959). Figure 2.3 shows a result typical of a decay theory: the more time elapses, the greater the increase of forgetting.

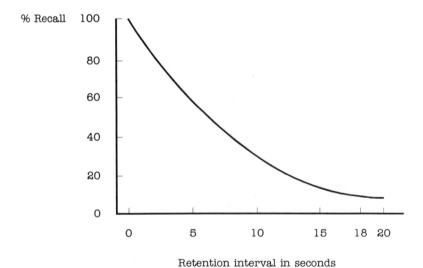

Retention interval in seconds

FIG. 2.3. Idealized results of the Brown–Peterson paradigm. Each data point represents the average of all trials for a certain retention interval.

The results depicted in Fig. 2.3 may create the misleading impression that the extent of forgetting is only a function of the length of the retention interval. However, this is because only the average of all trials is displayed. Keppel and Underwood (1962) pointed to this fact and showed that a separate evaluation of each trial presents a completely different picture, as shown in Fig. 2.4.

Keppel and Underwood's results (1962) demonstrated that time is by no means the only factor that determines the extent of forgetting. There is also a dramatic decline in memory performance with an increase in the number of trials. This effect is known as *proactive interference*. If time were the only factor determining forgetting, and if the length of the retention interval were kept constant, a passive decay theory would predict constant recall probabilities, as demonstrated by Fig. 2.5.

The hypothetical results of Fig. 2.5 demonstrate that every item in each trial is subject to the same autonomous decay process. Consequently, for a given retention interval, recall probabilities are of equal magnitude. But as we know from Fig. 2.4, this is not the case.

Thus far, we relied on the classic findings of J. Brown (1958), L. R. Peterson and M. G. Peterson (1959), and Keppel and Underwood (1962) in our empirical evaluation of Hypothesis D1. However, their findings on pro- and retroactive interference are experimentally safeguarded to such an extent (see also Melton & Martin, 1972) that they are outlined in many standard textbooks (also, e.g., J. R. Anderson, 1985a, p. 155), so we can forego any further description of more recent studies.

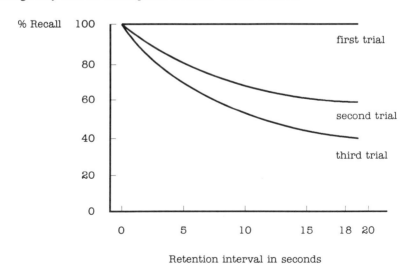

FIG. 2.4. Idealized results of the Brown–Peterson paradigm. Averaging was done separately for the first, second, and third trials.

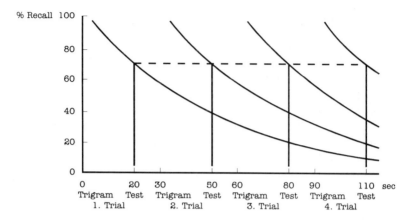

FIG. 2.5. Hypothetical results which are to be expected if autonomous decay is the only cause of forgetting. In this case, recall performance (dashed line) depends solely on the length of the retention interval. The probability of intrusions from preceding trigrams depends on the degree these items have decayed.

2.1.2 Forgetting Caused by Interference: Empirical Evaluation of Hypothesis I1

Decay theory assumes that forgetting is a function of time, but interference theory assumes it is just as much a function of the number of trials carried out. Both variables are responsible for lowering memory performance. According to interference theory, it is the number of trials that are conducted, which lead to a cumulative increase in cognitive load and, as a consequence, to a decline in memory performance. However, the two variables — increasing time and increasing cognitive load — are intertwined and thus experimentally inseparable.

This basic dilemma is illustrated in Fig. 2.4. The two variables — time and interference — cannot be viewed in isolation from each other. The longer the retention interval, the sooner decay processes can become effective. On the other hand, if the retention interval is increased, then the effectiveness of distractor activity as well as interference increases. If the distractor task would be omitted, subjects may repeat the items and remember them perfectly. In this case, the Brown–Peterson paradigm would become an unsuitable method with which to examine forgetting.

In addition to the length of the retention interval and the amount of distractor activity, item similarity is yet another powerful factor influencing memory performance: Memory performance declines with increasing similarity. According to interference theory, two different processes affect the availability of items in a Brown–Peterson paradigm: Whereas cumulative cognitive load operates to decrease the availability of the most recently presented items, spontaneous recovery operates to increase the availability of older items from earlier trials. As a result, these two effects lead to a confusion of older and more recently presented items. Item similarity is an additional factor increasing this tendency to confuse items (Keppel & Underwood, 1962).

The detrimental effect of item similarity on memory performance is documented by a number of different experiments (cf. the review in Melton & Martin, 1972). The most impressive results were those of Wickens (1970, 1972), arrived at with the *release-of-proactive-interference* technique (see also Kroll, Bee, & Gurski, 1973). In this version of the Brown–Peterson paradigm, item similarity is the most important experimental variable. For example, consider the experiment shown in Fig. 2.6: Here, letters are presented during the first three trials and numbers are presented in the remaining three. This constitutes the experimental group. Within the control group, however, letters are presented in all the trials. A comparison of the two groups shows that the "shift trial" (that trial, after which the "new" items — here numbers — are presented) leads to a removal of proactive inhibition. The decrease in item similarity leads to an increase in memory performance.

This result, shown schematically in Fig. 2.6, confirms the validity of interference theory: Forgetting is not only dependent on the extent of an increasing cognitive load (here, the number of trials), but is equally dependent on the type of cognitive demand (here, the remembering of

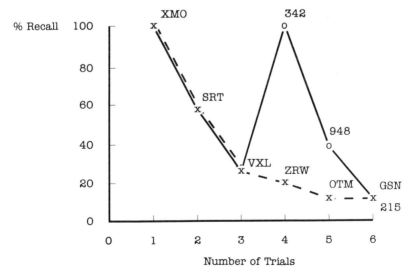

FIG. 2.6.   Idealized results of the release of proactive inhibition paradigm. In contrast to the control group (x), the use of a different type of trigram in the 4th trial (shift trial) leads to a release of proactive inhibition in the experimental group (o).

similar or dissimilar items) that occurred before the critical reproduction attempt (cf. Hypothesis I1 in Fig. 2.1). The results of the release-of-proactive-interference paradigms support Keppel and Underwood's view that forgetting is due to a tendency to confuse items.

The direction of interference is by no means only confined to future events, as is the case in proactive inhibition. Numerous experiments show that previously learned contents can just as easily be disturbed by an interference effect appearing later in time (see the review in Klimesch, 1979a). This is known as *retroactive interference* or *retroactive inhibition*. Both proactive and retroactive inhibition represent different aspects of one and the same phenomenon. Moreover, both can be examined by means of the same experimental group, as shown in Table 2.1. The decisive factor here is whether it is the first or second list that is tested for memory performance. This determines which list must be presented to the control group.

As convincing as these results may seem, there are still important arguments questioning the validity of interference theory. One of these arguments refers to the experimental design: It points out that distractor activity does not necessarily prevent rehearsal. Roediger et al. (1977) listed two conditions to be met to guarantee that distractor activity fulfills its purpose:

1. Care must be taken that the distractor task leads to a complete distraction of attention.
2. It must be guaranteed that rehearsal actually draws on a subject's limited attention capacity and cannot be performed automatically.

The authors discovered that the cognitive load imposed by distractor activity does not influence memory performance. Consequently, they arrive at the conclusion that the aforementioned conditions are not met in interpreting experiments on forgetting. Either the distractor task does not fulfill its purpose and does not lead to a complete distraction of attention, or it must be assumed that no interference exists between the distractor and memory task. This brings us to another objection to the use of distractor

TABLE 2.1
Method for Testing Proactive (PI) and Retroactive Inhibition (RI)

Experimental Design	Sequence of Lists		Subjects Are Tested for
Experimental group	List 1	List 2	List 1
RI:			
Control group	List 1	-------	List 1
Experimental group	List 1	List 2	List 2
PI:			
Control group	-------	List 2	List 2

tasks in experiments on forgetting: The decline in memory performance is due to the fact that the limits of attention capacity are exceeded. This leads to a situation in which new information cannot even begin to be encoded or stored.

Recent examinations of the "next-in-line" effect confirm this interpretation and show that information on which a subject is not concentrating is stored only partially or not at all (Bond, 1985; Bond & Kirkpatrick, 1982). However, information not stored cannot be "forgotten."

The release of a proactive inhibition, when it is caused by a rapid change in similarity, can be explained either by a lessening of confusion or by a shift in attention. If, for example, numbers suddenly appear instead of words after a series of tiring tasks, the result will be an increase in the subject's level of attention and an improvement in memory performance.

2.1.3 Result of the Empirical Evaluation of Hypotheses D1 and I1

Up to now the discussion has focused on the causes of forgetting and has demonstrated that it is actually impossible to distinguish between the predictions of interference and decay theory. On the one hand, there is the fact that the two variables — increasing time and increasing interference — are confounded, and, on the other hand, there is the controversy surrounding the effect of the distractor task on the limited attention capacity. On the basis of these fundamental difficulties it is not surprising that recent research no longer includes experiments on forgetting.

As we have shown, one of the failures of the various theories of forgetting is due to methodical difficulties. Closer inspection, however, reveals that the representational problem is the real reason for the difficulties discussed earlier. As mentioned in the introductory remarks to this chapter, items that can be recalled must be stored in memory. Consequently, there is no obvious motivation to inquire after their precise nature of representation. The crucial question here concerns how to deal with forgotten information. This questions opens up a whole new field of inquiry into the nature of internal representations. Does a code stored in memory decay? If so, what exactly does inhibition or interference mean? What is to be understood by attention, and so forth? Chapters 3 and 4 consider the general importance of the representational problem in greater detail.

2.2 DOES FORGETTING RESULT IN THE FINAL LOSS OF INFORMATION? DISCUSSION OF HYPOTHESES D2 AND I2

Hypothesis D2 clearly states that forgotten information is irretrievably lost from memory. Interference theory, however, focuses on two distinct memory processes: encoding and retrieval. Interference processes can have just as much of an effect on the storage of new information as on the recall of already stored information. As long as recall processes are affected, one speaks of search or retrieval failures and simply assumes that, even though the sought-after information cannot be found, it is, nevertheless, still present in memory. If, on the other hand, storage processes are affected, then it must be expected that interference will block the encoding of new information. However, information that has not been stored cannot be said to have been "forgotten."

There is, however, another major difficulty in examining Hypotheses I2 and D2. This difficulty is due to the fact that a final loss of information can only be examined indirectly and only under certain controlled conditions. Without these controlled conditions, it will be impossible to reject the claim that forgetting is nothing other than the inability to find and/or retrieve stored information. The experimental control of search processes is a crucial prerequisite for the examination of Hypotheses D2 and I2.

These considerations clearly show that interference and decay theory refer to very distinct aspects of memory processes. Whereas interference theory refers to the process of retrieving a code, decay theory (Hypothesis D2) focuses on processes operating within a code.

2.2.1 Forgetting and Hypermnesia

Everyday experience shows that information that appears to have been forgotten can sometimes be remembered at a later date. A well-known example of this is the "tip-of-the-tongue" phenomenon (R. Brown & McNeil, 1966), in which case the memory contents are temporarily unavailable (cf. the "Poetzel-Phenomenon", Poetzel, 1917). This phenomenon is known under various terms, including: *trace storage versus trace utilization* (Melton, 1963); *availability versus accessibility* (Tulving & Pearlstone, 1966; Roediger, 1974); *retrievability versus availability* (Bower, 1970) or *cue dependent versus trace dependent forgetting* (Tulving, 1974); *hypermnesia* (M. H. Erdelyi & Becker, 1974); and *reminiscence* (Madigan, 1976). In more recent research (Payne, 1986, 1987; Roediger & Payne, 1985), the term *hypermnesia* is used when referring to a situation in which a subject's free recall performance increases with the number of attempts made. *Reminiscence* means that a certain item, forgotten at some earlier test date, can be remembered again at a later point in time. Both concepts, therefore, refer only to different aspects of one and the same phenomenon, as illustrated in Table 2.2. It goes without saying that the experimental investigation of hypermnesia or reminiscence requires that subjects do not receive any feedback during the test.

Credit is due to Erdelyi and his collegues (M. H. Erdelyi & Becker, 1974;

TABLE 2.2
Four Different Types of Results in a Multiple Recall Test

		Test 2	
		Recalled	Not Recalled
Test 1	Recalled	Remembering	Intertest forgetting
	Not recalled	Reminiscence	Forgetting

M. Erdelyi, Buschke, & Finkelstein, 1977; M. H. Erdelyi & Kleinbard, 1978; cf. the review in M. H. Erdelyi, 1982) whose research made hypermnesia a well-established phenomenon (Roediger & Payne, 1982, 1985; Roediger & Thorpe, 1978). The extent of hypermnesia depends on how often free recall is tested and which type of stimulus material is used. M. H. Erdelyi and Kleinbard (1978) discovered that in the first test following the presentation of 40 pictures (slides of simple objects), on average, only 19 pictures were remembered. After Test 18 − 80 hours after the first test − the number of pictures remembered increased to 33, but did not undergo any further increase in the following six tests. This corresponds to a hypermnesia effect, that is, a relative increase in memory performance of 74% with respect to the first testing! The strength of hypermnesia is due not only to the number of repetitions, but also to stimulus modality and the way items are encoded: Pictures exert a more powerful hypermnesia effect than words, and words with imagery instructions, in turn, exert more powerful effects than words not provided with imagery instructions (M. H. Erdelyi, Finkelstein, Herrell, Miller, & Thomas, 1976).

Hypermnesia is an interesting phenomenon in memory psychology. It demonstrates that memory performance increases with the length of the retention interval. This phenomenon allows for two different interpretations. On the one hand, it may be assumed that the repeated recall attempts allow for a reconstruction of partially decayed codes. Or it can also be assumed that in the course of testing, subjects learn to use elaborated search or retrieval strategies that allow them to enlarge the relevant search area from one test to the next.

Proof of the existence of hypermnesia is only relevant in evaluating Hypotheses D2 and I2, if it can be ruled out that the unavailability of an item is due to an incomplete search. In attempting to explain search strategies in free recall tasks, one generally starts out from the assumption that retrieval is based on two different processes. In attempting to retrieve an item, a subject first generates possible alternatives that are then recognized as previously stored (J. R. Anderson & Bower, 1972; Shiffrin, 1970a, 1970b). Because subjects rarely make intrusion errors (i.e., subjects rarely report items that were not learned), these "generate-recognize" theories assume that subjects use very strict "recall criteria" in selecting correct responses. If the threshold of the recall criteria can be lowered by using appropriate instructions, it should be possible—at the cost of intrusions—to expand the search area and to increase the extent of hypermnesia effects.

Roediger and Payne (1985) addressed this question by providing different recall instructions. Subjects in one group received the usual instructions for free recall tasks, which consist of writing down as many words as possible in any order whatsoever, without guessing. Subjects in the second group were asked to guess, whereas a third group received an additional instruction to list at least 50 words and, while doing so, to guess as often as necessary. Each group was shown the same 65 words.

The results in Table 2.3 indicate that guessing does not have any significant effect on memory performance. If we start out from the plausible assumption that guessing enlarges the search area, then we come to the interesting conclusion that hypermnesia is not due to an increased efficiency of search processes. More importantly, however, this means that hypermnesia can only be explained by certain characteristics of the coding format. It could, for example, be only a matter of enhancing the accessibility of a code that increases with the number of recall attempts. But it seems just as plausible to assume that partially decayed codes can be "reconstructed."

These findings support the view that forgetting does not neccessarily mean the final and irretrievable loss of information. Another interpretation in support of this view can be traced to Ebbinghaus, who claimed that forgotten information can be learned more quickly than new information (see also T. O. Nelson, 1978). However, this interpretation is valid only in proven instances of reminiscence or hypermnesia. In contrast, instances of "intertest forgetting" may be seen as an indication of the loss of memory

TABLE 2.3
Hypermnesia, Search Area, and Guessing

Type of Task	Mean Number of Recalled Words			% Hypermnesia
	Test 1	Test 2	Test 3	
Free recall without guessing, Search area not extended	25.1	26.6	28.2	12.4
Free recall with guessing, Search area extended	24.3	26.4	28.4	16.9
Forced recall with guessing, Search area strongly extended	25.1	26.0	27.4	9.2

Note: Data from Roediger and Payne, 1985, *Memory and Cognition*, *13*, p. 4. © 1985 by Psychonomic Society, Inc. Reprinted with permission.

information. An independent evaluation of each of the four cases shown in Table 2.2 is, therefore, another important prerequisite in assessing both Hypotheses D2 and I2.

2.2.2 Controlling the Search Area

The search area for free recall tasks can be controlled only with difficulty and, at best, indirectly. Paired-association paradigms present one possibility of assuring that the contents of the search area remain the same during all stages of testing. In this type of task, each item consists of two parts, a "stimulus" and a "response," which subjects must associate. An exact definition of the search area is thus made possible by presenting the subject with the stimulus part. This, in turn, provides a clue as to how to retrieve the correct response.

This method was used in the following four-part experiment by Klimesch (1979b), which included a learning stage, a first recall test, a distractor task, and a second recall test. In the first part of the experiment, the subjects were asked to remember an appropriate label for six different histograms, each consisting of seven columns. After a 100% learning criterion had been attained, the first recall test was carried out using the labels to retrieve the appropiate histogram. Subjects were then asked to draw the outlines of the histogram on a grid with seven columns and nine lines. Between the first and the second recall test, on average, a 36-min distractor task was carried out. This task consisted of comparing new but similar patterns with those already learned. During the second recall test immediately following the distractor task, subjects had to proceed in the same way as in the first recall task.

This experiment was designed in an attempt to ensure that identical search areas could be used in both recall tests. Based on this procedure it may be assumed that memory performance reflects only the accuracy of the coding format but not the efficiency of the search processes.

The accuracy of recall is measured by the extent to which the copy of a pattern differs from its original. Statistical analyses were carried out separately for each of the six patterns and for each of the 68 subjects and are based on a comparison of recall accuracy between the first and second test. Thus, $6 \times 68 = 408$ individual comparisons were carried out by using polynomial distributions. Based on the recall parameters estimated in the first test, it was then tested whether these corresponded to the distribution of recall errors in the second test. The results showed that an improvement in accuracy can be observed in 73 of the 408 comparisons. Thus, with respect to these 73 cases, there is a highly significant improvement in memory performance from the first to the second test. As a result, the assumption is confirmed that reminiscence also occurs if the contents of the search area remain the same during both recall tests. However, the results also show that in 43 cases there was a highly significant decrease in recall accuracy.

The evaluation of Hypothesis D2 (i.e., forgetting means the final loss of information), therefore, results in a paradox: Whereas Hypothesis D2 is contradicted by the 73 cases of reminiscence, it is confirmed by 43 cases of intertest forgetting. The findings, therefore, do not enable us to arrive at a general conclusion regarding the validity of decay theory. A similar argument — albeit with reversed signs — can be applied when evaluating interference theory. As the search areas were kept constant during both recall tests, interference processes do not adequately explain either reminiscence or intertest forgetting. However, in order to explain intertest forgetting, interference theory must rely on the hypothesis of altered search areas. The reason for this can be found in the basic assumptions underlying interference theory, whereby information once stored is never lost. Consequently, intertest forgetting observed in identical search areas clearly supports decay processes.

2.2.3 Result of the Empirical Evaluation of Hypotheses D2 and I2

The results described earlier illustrate a dilemma: Both forgetting theories can be partially confirmed and partially refuted. The cases of reported reminiscence at first appear to support the validity of interference theory. Closer examination, however, reveals that interference theory can explain reminiscence only if different search areas can be assumed. However, this assumption is not generally valid, as reminiscence has, in fact, been detected when search areas were kept constant (Klimesch, 1979b). The cases of intertest forgetting, on the other hand, appear to confirm decay theory, which, in turn, stand in total contradiction to the likewise confirmed cases of reminiscence. As in the discussion of Hypothesis D1 and I1 it once again becomes clear that neither of the two theories can be confirmed.

3

The Failure of Traditional Forgetting Theories: Misleading Representational Assumptions

Chapter 2 focused on the difficulties that arise in trying to test the predictions of decay and interference theory. We were able to demonstrate the paradox that forgetting theories can be partially confirmed and partially refuted. It is not surprising, therefore, that forgetting theories are seldom considered in recent research. Obviously, one is so convinced of their ineffectiveness that modifications of the existing approaches are not even attempted. The contradictions outlined previously are of such a fundamental nature that we can only conclude that the basic assumptions underlying interference and decay theory are wrong.

But the question must still be asked: What assumptions are responsible for the failure of traditional memory theories? In our historical survey (see chap. 1) we suggested that the absence of explicit representational assumptions may be responsible for the poor success of traditional memory psychology. Does this argument also apply to forgetting theories? Is the absence or the insufficient consideration of representational assumptions also the reason for the contradictions outlined?

3.1 REPRESENTATIONAL ASSUMPTIONS UNDERLYING TRADITIONAL FORGETTING THEORIES: THE TWO-PARAMETER MODEL OF MEMORY

In examining which representational assumptions underly both forgetting theories, it becomes apparent that there are only vague notions regarding the structure of these assumptions, and these notions are exclusively

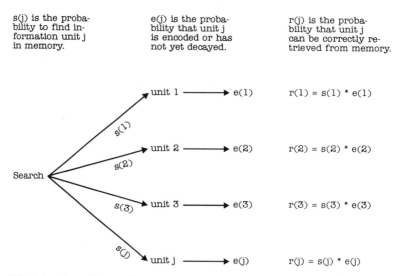

s(j) is the probability to find information unit j in memory.

e(j) is the probability that unit j is encoded or has not yet decayed.

r(j) is the probability that unit j can be correctly retrieved from memory.

FIG. 3.1.   According to the two-parameter model, memory performance is the product of two probabilities, the search and encoding probability.

concerned with a differentiation between the contents of memory and search processes. Interference and decay theory can, therefore, be reduced to a two-parameter model of memory, in that the extent of memory performance depends only on the efficiency of search processes and the accuracy of storage. Only these two factors have been of overriding concern to us so far and are pictured in Fig. 3.1. The question of how memory codes are stored and structured is addressed neither by interference nor decay theory. Figure 3.1 demonstrates that, as a result of the basic distinction between search processes and memory contents, the extent of memory performance must be regarded as the product of two probabilities: search probability and the probability that the sought-after content has not yet decayed. The multiplication of both probabilities clearly shows that accuracy of search and storage are independent processes.

3.2 THE TWO-PARAMETER MODEL IS BASED ON THE IMPLICIT ASSUMPTION OF HOLISTIC CODES

It is the lack of explicit representational assumptions about the coding format that characterizes the two-parameter model. As a result, implicit assumptions were adopted, which in this case focus on the assumption of holistic codes.

The significance of this claim can best be demonstrated by considering the ways information is retrieved from memory. What type of information does a search process use to access a specific memory content? Basically, there are two possible ways. A search process either can use parts of a memory code (i.e., a "probe") or a specific address to retrieve a code. In the first case we speak of a content-addressable search, in the second case of a location-addressable search. However, a content-addressable search can be defined only if there are explicit assumptions regarding the structure and/or elements of memory codes. A content-addressable search requires explicit assumptions about the way a match is defined between the search probe and the sought-after code. A location-addressable search, on the other hand, does not require explicit representational assumptions about the format of a code. However, it requires that the address of the location for the sought-after information be known before the search process begins. Consequently, the search process can be successful only if a code is characterized by a specific address. The crucial conclusion here is that a location-addressable search treats a code as a holistic unit. This fact is responsible for the implicit assumption of a holistic coding format.

Because of the lack of explicit representational assumptions, the two-parameter model allows only for location-addressable search processes. This failure to draw explicit representational assumptions leads to certain restrictions: First of all, there is the implicit assumption of holistic codes that, in turn, makes it necessary to distinguish between "accuracy of search process" and "accuracy of storage." Another important restriction is the independence of both parameters. *Independence* here means that the coding format cannot exert any influence on the search process. Within the context of the two-parameter model we arrive at the implausible conclusion that the high efficiency of human memory can be explained only by the characteristics of search processes, not, however, by the way information is represented. Finally, all questions regarding the composition and structure of memory merge into assumptions regarding search processes.

This discussion is reminiscent of the distinction made between distributed and nondistributed memory storage. There is some resemblance between the concepts of *holistic codes* and *nondistributed memory storage* on the one hand and between *component codes* (see section 3.5) and *distributed storage* on the other hand. Chapter 11 refers to these issues within the context of connectionism and recent physiological approaches to memory.

3.3 THE TWO-PARAMETER MODEL AND THE COMPUTER METAPHOR

A comparison of the two-parameter model with the computer metaphor shows the similarity between both concepts. It turns out that the search parameter corresponds to the term *address*, whereas the encoding parameter corresponds to the term *location*. The address has the function of discovering that information which is stored in a particular location. The sought-after information can only be found if the address is known. The characteristics of the address are thus independent of the format by which information is stored at a certain location.

Consequently, search processes are completely independent of the structure of codes and the characteristics of their format can in no way influence the search process. In conventional computers, search processes function according to an "all-or-nothing" principle, that is, either the address is known and the sought-after information is found, or the address is not known and the sought-after information is not found.

3.4 DEFINING THE TERM HOLISTIC CODE

Thus far, we have discussed some interdependences between assumptions regarding search processes and the encoding format. It was emphasized that, whenever explicit representational assumptions are missing, the search process is independent of the characteristics of the encoding format, and, therefore, holistic codes must be assumed by default. The computer metaphor is a good example to demonstrate the interdependence between the type of search process and coding format.

These considerations show clearly that, once holistic codes are assumed, addresses must be defined. Without an address, it is impossible to find the sought-after content. Thus, the following definition applies to holistic codes (Klimesch, 1986a, 1986b): The term *holistic code* is used whenever specific representational assumptions are not considered, or if the explicit assumption concerning a format that cannot be decomposed is drawn.

In adopting holistic codes, we encounter the following restrictions:

1a. The search process is independent of the format of a code.

1b. As a result of (1a), the search process is also independent of the content represented by a code.

1c. As a result of (1a) and (1b), search processes rely on well-defined addresses.

1d. As a result of (1c), a memory search follows an "all-or-nothing" principle, that is, if the address is known, then all information stored at that particular location can be recalled. It is impossible to access parts of a code directly.

1e. If forgetting is understood as a kind of decay, we must assume — if additional assumptions are not taken into account — that all contents of a code decay at the same rate.

However, there are further consequences arising out of the aforementioned restrictions. For example, on the basis of restrictions (1a) and (1b) it follows — as emphasized earlier — that the structure and efficiency of memory can be explained only by assumptions concerning search processes, but not by those concerning the coding format. As a result of restriction (1d), on the other hand, all the information stored in one code must be available as soon as the code is retrieved. It is inconceivable that only parts of a code can be retrieved. This is because it is only the availability of the address that is important in a successful search.

It is interesting to see how the avoidance of explicit representational assumptions inevitably leads to a number of implausible restrictions and prevents a better understanding of human memory. The next section considers component codes that are the converse of holistic codes and provides the basis for a considerably less restrictive and more plausible theory of memory.

3.5 DEFINING COMPONENT CODES

In contrast to holistic codes, the definition of a component code is more in line with our considerations of the representational problem. The term *component code* is used whenever explicit representational assumptions determine that the coding format consists of a structure of components.

The information stored in a component code is thus represented not only by the components themselves, but also by a specific structure or relation between them. In contrast to holistic codes, the definition of component codes makes clear that assumptions regarding their format must consider the following two aspects: the components themselves and their structure.

In contrast to holistic codes, component codes lead to different restrictions. They enable assumptions (or predictions) that would have led to contradictions, had holistic codes been adopted. The following assumptions are, for example, only compatible with component codes:

2a. The search process depends on the coding format.
2b. As a result of (2a), the search process also depends on the type and content of information represented by a code.
2c. As a result of (2a) and (2b), addresses need not be specified.
2d. As a result of (2c), search processes do not follow an all-or-nothing principle: It is thus possible to have immediate access to any part of a component code.
2e. If forgetting is due to a process of decay, it becomes clear that different components can decay at different rates.

Assumptions (2a), (2b), and (2c) reveal a close interdependence between the coding format and search processes. For example, let us consider the case in which interference processes make some parts of a component code less accessible. Now, assumptions (2c) and (2d) allow for the possibility that even when no information has decayed and the search process has led to the discovery of the correct memory content, only parts of and not the entire information stored in the code may be available.

The different conclusions arising out of the definition of holistic and component codes make it clear that assumptions regarding the coding format have an immediate impact on the properties of the entire information-processing system. Theories not considering these restrictions run the risk of relying on contradictory assumptions.

3.6 HOLISTIC CODES: CONTRADICTORY EXPERIMENTAL FINDINGS

The type of coding format can only be inferred, if the predicted effects of a holistic or component code are empirically tested. In attempting to test all predictions for both holistic and component codes, exact definitions regarding the coding format are of fundamental importance. However, this attempt is successful only if complex representational assumptions are considered within the framework of network models (chaps. 5–9). Otherwise, it is impossible to grasp the interdependence between search processes on the coding format.

This section considers only those findings that refer to forgetting. In doing so, it becomes obvious that search processes do not follow an all-or-nothing principle (restriction 2d), and that the components of a code may decay at different rates (restriction 2e). The experiments relevant to this question are basically derived from the study of three different areas: multirate forgetting, the "tip-of-the-tongue" phenomenon, and hypermnesia.

In an experiment on *multirate forgetting*, Jones (1979) showed his subjects a series of color slides, each of which pictured an object of a particular color and spatial position. Subjects were asked to remember not only the form these objects took, but also their color and spatial position. The following recognition task examined which of the three object components (form, color, or spatial position) were best remembered. The results confirm assumption (2e) and show that the subjects forget different components of a code at different rates. Jones discovered that the color and position components are forgotten twice as fast as the form components. This finding, therefore, clearly argues against the assumption of holistic codes.

The "tip-of-the-tongue" (TOT) phenomenon is a good example with which to demonstrate that memory search does not follow an all-or-nothing principle. If, for example, individuals wish to remember the name of a friend, knowing exactly where and when they last met, then they also know that it would be possible to immediately identify the name provided it is related to them. R. Brown and McNeill (1966) studied the TOT phenomenon and discovered that it was possible for the subjects to give accurate details of the sought-after name (see A. S. Brown, 1991, for a more recent review). Most subjects were in a position to give the first and last letter as well as the number of syllables. It is also important that all subjects knew the meaning (semantic information) of the word. These results support prediction (2d). They enable us to infer that components of a code can be accessed directly.

Studies on hypermnesia show that stored information may be temporarily unavailable, and that situations may arise in which more is remembered at a later test date than an earlier one. As we have emphasized, the phenomenon of hypermnesia (see section 2.2.2) is only relevant for our discussion, if it can be shown that different search areas are not the cause of improved memory performance. The results arrived at by Klimesch (1979b) show, however, that hypermnesia also develops when identical search areas are provided in all of the different recall attempts. Thus, this result also supports prediction (2d). It documents that even if none of the information has decayed and the search process has led to the discovery of the correct memory content, all the information stored in the code need not be available, as is postulated in prediction (1d). This phenomenon can be explained by the assumption that individual components of a code are temporarily unavailable, but can be recalled at a later date.

3.7 THE ASSUMPTION OF HOLISTIC CODES IS RESPONSIBLE FOR THE FAILURE OF TRADITIONAL FORGETTING THEORIES

The aim of this chapter was to show that interference and decay theory are based on the same implicit representational assumptions, which can best be described by a two-parameter model of memory. According to this model, memory performance depends on two independent parameters, the accuracy of search and storage (see Fig. 3.1).

In a subsequent step, we demonstrated that the two-parameter model is based on the assumption of holistic codes. We can conclude this because codes are treated as functional units. Consequently, representational assumptions are meaningless within the framework of the two-parameter model. In all cases in which the predictions of an information-processing model are completely independent of the coding format, holistic codes must be assumed by default.

Both forgetting theories are based on the two-parameter model and are therefore also based on the implicit assumption of holistic codes. Empirical results reported up to now have shown, however, that the conclusions and predictions arising out of holistic codes cannot be confirmed. We are, therefore, inclined to accept that the assumption of holistic codes and other misleading representational assumptions about the format of memory codes are at the core of the failure of both theories. Arguments put forward in the next chapter provide further evidence for such an interpretation.

4 STM Codes: Their Structure and Decay

The assumptions underlying the encoding format command a key position in cognitive psychology, because they are of primary importance for the understanding of cognitive processes. If explicit assumptions are not taken into consideration, theories are put forward that rely solely on the implicit assumption of holistic codes, and are thus identical with either the two-parameter model or some variant of it.

This chapter is concerned with the structure of short-term memory (STM) codes and starts out from the basic observation that assumptions on the coding format must be guided by the most important characteristics of the entire information-processing system. The next section, therefore, begins with a discussion of some of the most fundamental principles of information processing. Following this, we want to show that the format of STM codes reflects basic characteristics of the entire information-processing system.

4.1 FUNDAMENTAL PRINCIPLES OF HUMAN INFORMATION PROCESSING

From the very beginning, cognitive psychology was concerned with the study of different stages of information processing. These studies led to the important discovery that before a stimulus can be recognized it must undergo a complex sequence of perceptual encoding processes. Thus, at different levels of processing, different coding formats must be assumed; these are featured in the model outlined in Fig. 4.1. This model is based on

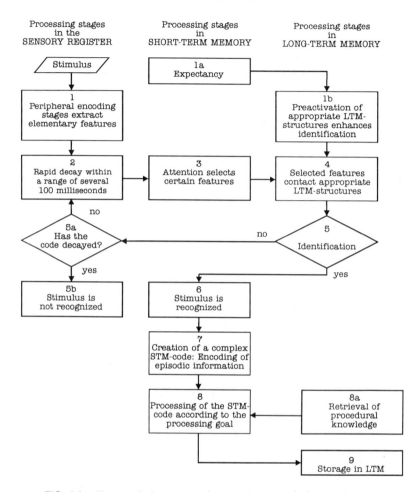

FIG. 4.1. Hypothetical sequence of processing stages in human memory.

the idea that basic aspects of human information processing can be explained by an interaction of three different memory systems: the sensory register, STM, and long-term memory (LTM).

The flow chart in Fig. 4.1 may, however, give rise to two misleading impressions. The first refers to discrete "encoding stages," which are most likely continuous in nature. The second refers to the way in which these stages are connected: Instead of the linear-hierarchical structure suggested by the flow chart, an interconnected structure is to be assumed. These misleading impressions are due to the form of presentation and are not inherent in the ideas underlying the model. Although we have to accept them for the sake of simplicity, we must not confuse them with assumptions intending to explain human information processes.

Peripheral encoding stages have been studied intensively, especially in the area of visual information processing (cf. Breitmeyer, 1984, on masking experiments; Marr, 1982, on simulation approaches). It is the general consensus that their task is to extract elementary features, such as line segments and contures (encoding stage 1 in Fig. 4.1). The results of Hubel and Wiesel's work are especially impressive because they show that in the visual cortex the orientation of line segments is encoded as an elementary feature enabling a first draft of a visual code (e.g., Hubel, 1988; Hubel, Wiesel, & Stryker, 1978). Peripheral processing stages are generally viewed as running parallel as well as being autonomous (Broadbent, 1958; Duncan, 1985; cf. Kahnemann, Treisman, & Burkell, 1983; Schneider & Shiffrin, 1977; Shiffrin & Schneider, 1977, 1984; LaBerge, 1981). Even the notion that the result of peripheral coding stages is held for a short period in a special store (encoding stage 2 in Fig. 4.1) is generally accepted. In visual modality, this store is referred to as "iconic memory" (Sperling, 1960) or generally as "sensory register" (Atkinson & Shiffrin, 1968, 1971). The most important tasks of the sensory register are to coordinate the analysis of sensory information carried out at different rates, and to allow higher cognitive processess to have access to the results of these early encoding processes.

The sensory register is characterized by two important features: an especially high storage capacity and an extremely short storage duration of roughly 200 ms to 300 ms. These features were examined using the partial-report technique introduced by Sperling (1960) and Averbach and Coriell (1961). It requires the tachistoscopic presentation of a series of stimulus pairs consisting of a display of stimuli arranged in the form of a matrix, and a marker that appears after a well-controlled interstimulus interval. The marker indicates a certain position of a stimulus in the previously shown display. The exposure times for both the display of stimuli and the marker are extremely short, and lie within a range of about 50 ms. The subject's task is to name the marked stimulus. This task can be conducted almost perfectly even for very large stimulus matrixes. The only prerequisite is that the marker appears within the limits of the storage duration of the sensory register (Chow, 1985; Coltheart, 1980; Crowder, 1978; Long, 1980).

This result argues convincingly for the assumption that only those contents of the sensory register can be identified on which selective attention is focused (cf. encoding stages 2, 3, 4, 5, 5a, 5b). STM and selective attention are subject to massive limitations in capacity, and, therefore, only a small part of the information stored in the sensory register can continue to be processed. The results derived from the whole-report technique support this notion. Here, in contrast to the partial-report technique and under otherwise identical conditions, no marker is presented.

The subjects have the task of reporting as many stimuli as possible, but now are capable of recalling only approximately five stimuli, regardless of the size of the stimulus matrix. These and similar findings confirm the notion that it is the limited capacity of STM that is responsible for this result. Expectancy (encoding stage 1a) and selective attention (encoding stage 3) decide, within the limits of STM, which stimuli can be recognized and remembered.

The focus on the transition from peripheral processes to those controlled by selective attention has been central to cognitive psychology since the classic works of Sperling (1960). The differences between peripheral processes (cf. encoding stages 1 and 2) and those controlled by selective attention (Schneider & Shiffrin, 1977; Shiffrin & Schneider, 1977, 1984; Sternberg, 1969) have been well-documented. Recent research, however, deals more with the principles on which attention processes are based (Allport, Tipper, & Chmiel, 1985; Duncan, 1985; Kahneman et al., 1983; Shiffrin & Schneider, 1984; Treisman, 1986a, 1986b; Treisman & Gelade, 1980; Treisman & Kahneman, 1985; Treisman & Paterson, 1984). Treisman and her colleagues were able to show, for example, that those processes extracting elementary visual features (e.g., the color and angle position of lines) run parallel and without capacity limitations. However, complex stimuli made up of elementary features are quite capable of making demands on processing capacity and can thus probably only be identified serially.

Which encoding processes lead to the identification and recognition of stimulus information? In answering this question, we start from the notion that it is the knowledge stored in our LTM that allows us to identify and recognize sensory information (cf. encoding stages 1a, 1b, 4, 5). According to this notion, there are certain structures stored in LTM that enable us to identify and recognize stimuli (cf. encoding stage 4). Shiffrin and Geisler (1973) made this very clear: "The process of encoding is essentially one of recognition: the appropriate image or feature is contacted in LTM and then placed (i.e., copied) in STM" (p. 55).

This view of coding as a process of recognition is of fundamental importance. It leads to the conclusion that this process runs primarily between the sensory register and LTM, but not between the sensory register and STM. Sensory information received and stored in the sensory register is compared to structures (schemas and prototypes) that are stored in LTM (encoding stage 4). The result of this comparison (encoding stage 5) is transferred to STM (encoding stage 6), and it is not until this point that there is a conscious awareness and recognition of the stimulus. There is a prerequisite for this, however. The stimulus must have been presented long enough and the extent to which a stimulus matches the corresponding LTM structures must be sufficiently large. If we neglect for the moment the selectivity of attention and expectancy as well as capacity limitations, then it becomes clear that STM is not directly involved in the identification of a stimulus. Only the result of this process is made available to STM. From this stage onward the subject has full control over how to proceed with the recognized stimulus (encoding stage 8 and 9).

The following four characteristics are important in describing STM: its limited capacity (Baddeley, Scott, Drynan, & J. C. Smith, 1969; Broadbent, 1958, 1975; Brown, 1958; MacGregor, 1987; Miller, 1956; Murdock, 1964), its primarily serial way of processing (cf. the "conveyor-belt model" by Murdock, 1974, 1980), its importance as temporary-working store (Baddeley, 1981; Daneman & Carpenter, 1980), and its control processes (Atkinson & Shiffrin, 1968; Baddeley, 1981). One important control process of STM is the encoding of episodic information (cf. encoding stage 7 and Fig. 4.1). Although the question of whether or not episodic information is stored separately from semantic information is controversial, the importance of the distinction between these two types of information (cf. Tulving, 1983, and the tri-code theory in J. R. Anderson, 1983a) is well accepted. It should be noted that episodic information is not always stimulus-related as it is with emotional and mood-related information. In the framework of our model, their importance lies primarily in the control processes of STM (Klimesch, 1989).

4.1.1 Interactions Between Sensory Processing and the Structure of LTM

The model outlined in Fig. 4.1 is based on the important assumption that structures stored in LTM are used to identify sensory information. As a result of this close interaction between LTM and the sensory register, it is to be assumed that sensory codes and those LTM structures used in stimulus identification must have a compatible encoding format. This does not, however, mean that their format is identical. The findings on the sensory register already discussed have shown that the sensory codes rich in information decay extremely quickly, and that it would, therefore, be wrong to equate them with LTM codes. Sensory codes are the result of several processing stages. The necessity for a compatible coding format arises only at the transition between the sensory register and LTM.

The close interaction between sensory processes and the structure of LTM has been pointed out repeatedly (Finke, 1980; Shepard & Podgorny, 1978; Weber, Hochhaus & W. D. Brown, 1981). Not only theoretical considerations support this notion, but so do experimental findings gained from studies on the *symbolic-distance effect* and mental rotation and imagination tasks.

As is well known from psychophysics, a logarithmic function describes the relationship between the perceived and physically defined intensity or magnitude of a stimulus. Surprisingly, experiments on the symbolic-distance effect showed a similar logarithmic relationship, if stimuli were not physically present, that is, were not displayed, but instead had to be compared in mind (cf. Moyer & Landauer, 1967, and the review in Shepard & Podgorny, 1978). For example, in an experiment conducted by Moyer (1973), pairs of animal names were presented and subjects asked to indicate as quickly as possible which of the two animals is in reality the larger one. In a subsequent rating experiment, subjects had to estimate the actual size of the animal. The results show that the reaction time in judging the size difference was shorter, the more pronounced the size difference was in reality. In addition, Moyer (1973) showed that the distribution of reaction times — as a function of size difference between animal pairs — coincided with a logarithmic relationship, as is known from psychophysics (cf. Fechner's law and, more recently, Welford, 1960). These and similar experiments demonstrate that those laws originally found to describe sensory processes can also be applied even when the stimuli to be judged are not physically present, but must be recalled from LTM.

A similar conclusion can be drawn from experiments on mental rotation and imagination. Experiments have repeatedly confirmed that mental operations, in which the stimuli are only imagined, are essentially con-ducted as if the stimuli were physically present (cf. the review by Kosslyn & Shwartz, 1981, as well as Finke, 1986).

These results point to the important fact that the term *coding* is by no means only valid for perception. Even processes that run without sensory input, as for example the mental-rotation or size-comparison tasks, lead to the construction of codes in LTM. Coding is, therefore, an elementary process that is not only significant for perception. On the contrary, coding, perception, memory, and thought processes are phenomena that interact directly and cannot be described or understood independently of each other.

4.2 THE ENCODING FORMAT OF STM CODES

The discussion of our model in Fig. 4.1 has shown that the format of a code formed on the receptor level is changed in subsequent encoding stages. It is thus plausible to assume that the format of a STM code reflects important processing principles of the entire system. Therefore, representational assumptions can also be regarded, in a wider sense, as assumptions underlying the structure of the information-processing system.

Now consider the question of the structure and elements of STM codes. A simple means of arriving at an answer is the concept of levels-of-processing by Craik and Lockhart (1972). According to this view, the processing of stimuli runs through a series of hierarchically ordered processing (coding) stages ranging from sensory to semantically abstract processes (cf. Broadbent, 1977).

Based on this concept and according to the model described in the previous section, the format of a STM code is assumed to reflect these coding stages. Each component of the code being created is the outcome of a coding stage. The number of coding elements is a function of demands placed on attention and on the capacity of STM. The more attention and the more capacity of STM contribute to the perception of a stimulus, the more (a) encoding stages are addressed, (b) components will be created, and (c) exact the memory representation will be. We can now assume the format of the code reflects the structure existing between the processing stages. If, for example, a code is created by a hierarchically ordered sequence of processing stages, then the format of the resulting code will also consist of hierarchically structured coding components. The coding format is, therefore, a result of that particular cognitive structure that determined the run of information processing during encoding. This definition shows very clearly that a code depends not only on the physical characteristics of the stimulus, but is equally dependent on the processing principles of the cognitive system. Figure 4.2 shows a hypothetical example of a component code representing a word.

Other important characteristics of a component code can be discerned in Fig. 4.2: The individual components refer to different aspects and are to a great extent redundant. The word code can be reconstructed out of the semantic code, the letter code can be reconstructed out of the word code,

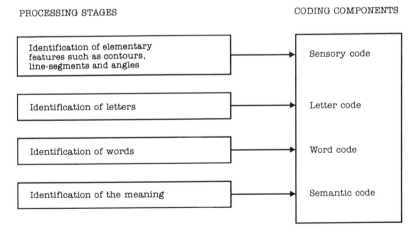

FIG. 4.2. Processing and encoding a visually presented word. The result of each processing stage is an element of the respective code, created in STM.

and the sensory code can be reconstructed out of the letter code. As long as all components of a code are available and each component is directly accessible, then — even if individual components are already decayed — they can be reconstructed.

The following assumptions state more precisely what is understood by the structure and the elements of a component code in STM:

1. The components are the outcome of different encoding stages.
2. The structure of the code arises out of the structure that also connects the processing stages with each other. In other words, the structure of a code is the same as the cognitive structure that was already active in processing the stimulus.

In the first chapter, coding was understood to be the process of transformation of a stimulus into a certain format of a memory representation. Now we are in a position to state this more precisely. The transformation of sensory stimuli occurs by means of a structure of particular processing stages, and the format of the code is a copy of that particular structure of processing stages that might vary according to certain demands. This expanded definition makes clear that an understanding of the elementary characteristics of a code can only be achieved, if the structure of the entire information-processing system is taken into consideration.

4.3 THE COMPONENT DECAY MODEL: AN ATTEMPT AT A CONSISTENT INTERPRETATION OF THE CAUSES UNDERLYING FORGETTING

If one accepts the notion that storage is as economical as possible, then it would be undesirable to store all and, on top of that, redundant components of a code. It is significant, however, that each piece of relevant information is preserved for a longer period. That which is relevant and important is determined by the processing goal. For example, if someone reads a text, conture elements, letters, and words have to be identified in order to understand the meaning of a text. Thus, with respect to the processing goal "understanding a text," the desired level or "depth" of encoding is the semantic level that is the "deepest" in this case. Hence, that which is to be remembered are not contures, letters, and words, but rather the semantic information derived from these. The opposite holds true for the processing goal "proofreading," in which shallow processing stages are focused on in order to detect spelling errors. In both examples the same sort of sensory code must be formed, but less components will be created at the level of STM in the case of proofreading than in the case of normal reading. It is, therefore, also to be expected that the proofread text will be forgotten much more quickly than a text read normally.

We assume that a code in STM is subject to an autonomous decay process and "shallow" coding components decay faster than "deep" ones. The example cited earlier is designed to underscore the plausibility of this assumption: The sensory word code decays very quickly, the semantic code, on the other hand, is preserved the longest. If a component code is retrieved, then it appears obvious to assume that the search process starts at the deepest level. The assumptions discussed here are depicted in Fig. 4.3 in the example of a "coding vector" comprising n components.

The component decay model is not only in a position to explain the predictions of traditional decay theories but also those of traditional interference theories. Its uniqueness lies in the fact that interference processes can be described as a consequence of decay processes. Consequently, it is possible to combine the two contradictory Hypotheses I1 and D2 into a single hypothesis. More components decay with the passing of time, and, therefore, the interference and confusion tendency in the retrieval of the code also increases. The effect of item similarity can also be explained very easily within the framework of the component decay theory: The more alike two stimuli are, the more alike are the components of the code. As long as none of the components have decayed, it is possible to differentiate between the two codes without difficulty. With the beginning of decay, however, it becomes increasingly difficult and finally impossible to differentiate between both codes.

Because shallow codes decay faster than deep ones, predictions can also be made with regard to the type of similarity. The two words *hat* and *rat* show partially identical components on the comparatively shallow phonemic-graphemic coding level. A single letter indicates the word in question. However, on the semantic level the two codes do not share a single component: The one word describes an article of clothing, the other an animal. Now, if the processing goal consists of recognizing the meaning of a word, then the phonemic-graphemic similarity of the words should not

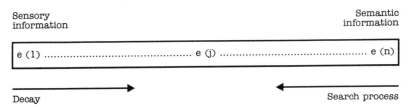

FIG. 4.3. Decay and search processes operate in opposite directions. Sensory information decays faster than semantic information. On the other hand, semantic information can be retrieved faster than sensory information.

lead to any errors of confusion: The sensory code may have already decayed, but the semantic code completely suffices in order to differentiate between both memory representations.

Finally, let us address the issue as to how the component decay model deals with the question of whether or not forgetting means the final loss of memory (cf. Hypotheses D2 and I2 in chap. 3). In the first place, one would think that our model only agrees with the traditional decay theories and not with the interference theories. However, this view is wrong because, on the one hand, it can be assumed that a partially decayed component code can be reconstructed, and, on the other hand, that deeply encoded components are to the greatest possible extent decay resistant.

It should be noted that the process of reconstruction is only conceivable if component codes are assumed. The components as well as the structure contain the redundancy necessary to reconstruct parts of a code. Assume, for example, that someone wants to remember a name and the following components are at various stages of decay: (a) the sensory and letter code have completely decayed, (b) the word code to a great extent, and (c) the semantic code only partially. It is still possible to remember the first and last letters, the approximate length of the word, and that the sought-after word describes a city in Northern Germany. These clues may suffice in order to reproduce the sought-after name.

If parts of a holistic code are lost, then – if no additional assumptions are drawn – there is no way of reconstructing lost information. The format of a holistic code does not contain any redundancy that could be used in the reconstruction of lost contents. Consequently, decay means the final loss of information in this case. Component codes, on the other hand, allow decayed information to be reconstructed. Here then, decay does not necessarily mean the final loss of memory contents.

We have to emphasize that the aforementioned conclusions are only valid if no external information is available for reconstruction, as is, for example, the case in a recognition task. Here, if a pairwise presentation is conducted during testing, subjects are allowed to compare their memory trace with a target. A partially decayed representation of the target may be reconstructed by matching the pattern of the partially decayed code with the physically presented target. In this particular case even a holistic code could be reconstructed to some extent. In contrast to holistic codes, however, component codes can be reconstructed even in a case in which no additional external information is available.

We thus arrive at the important conclusion that it is the format of a code that determines whether decay results in the final loss of memory contents. This underscores the crucial status of representational assumptions. Within the framework of traditional forgetting theories, it would have been impossible to state that decay does not inevitably lead to a loss of information.

5 Networks Theories: Basic Assumptions on the Structure of LTM

In chap. 4 we focused on the interdependence between information processing and the formation of STM codes. It was assumed that the processing results of individual encoding stages are the components of STM codes, and the structure that determined the sequence of the encoding stages during the processing of the stimulus is also the structure that interconnects the individual components of a STM code. This view was discussed using the model represented in Fig. 4.1.

This chapter is concerned with the way in which information is stored in LTM. Thereby, we have to differentiate between two aspects, one concerning the structure and the other the type of information stored. Network models refer in their assumptions almost exclusively to the structural aspect, whereas those aspects regarding content are, with few exceptions, only dealt with in passing. One exception is J. A. Anderson's (1983a, p. 45) tri-code theory. It assumed that knowledge representation in LTM is based on three different types of codes: (a) temporal strings that record the run of events, (b) spatial images that represent—above all, but not exclusively—visual knowledge, and (c) abstract propositions that serve to represent semantic knowledge. This chapter is primarily concerned with the structural aspect, so a clarification of the types of information distinguished in LTM is useful.

In chap. 4, when dealing with STM codes, we were concerned with different levels of coding stages. In LTM, however, we focus exclusively on the deepest level, that is, the semantic level. The reason is obvious. Consider the process of perception. It is always directed toward a certain processing goal, which in virtually every case is the comprehension of perceived information and, therefore, the semantic level. Semantic encoding must not be understood as a marginal process or a special case alongside other encoding processes. Here we are concerned with a form of representation that allows us to integrate and understand information from the various sources of sensory information. According to this view, semantic encoding is the deepest form of encoding in human information processing. Therefore, it is plausible to assume that knowledge stored in LTM is essentially structured alongside semantic dimensions.

In this sense, "semantic information" is synonymous with the "deepest" level of encoding in memory and corresponds to E. E. Smiths (1978) definition: "At the broadest level, semantic memory is assumed to be our store for meaningful material, be it our permanent knowledge of the meaning of words or our transient memory of a particular sentence that was presented to us in a laboratory experiment" (p. 1). According to this vague definition, all network theories can be described as semantic memory theories. However, there are more restrictive definitions, two of which have gained an important influence. On the one hand, there is the differentiation between semantic and episodic information (Tulving, 1972, 1983, 1984, 1986) and, on the other hand, there is the notion that only the meaning of concepts should be referred to as semantic information (e.g., Kintsch, 1980).

According to Tulving, semantic information comprises our permanent knowledge on language and all different aspects of general knowledge. Episodic information, on the other hand, refers to autobiographical knowledge structured according to context and time (c. f. the "temporal strings" of J. R. Anderson, 1983a). This definition is more restrictive than the one suggested earlier. Semantic information, in the sense of the deepest form of encoding, is more general and less specific than Tulving's term *semantic information*. The narrowest and most restrictive definition is the one equating semantic with conceptual information. Figure 5.1 outlines the relation between three different definitions of semantic information.

The next sections demonstrate that the network models rely heavily on the assumption of a hierarchically structured coding format.

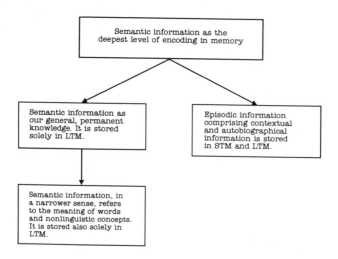

FIG. 5.1. Different meanings of the term *semantic information.*

5.1 BASIC CONCEPTS

Network theories are based on two different types of assumptions: structural and processing. Structural assumptions refer to the geometric characteristics of memory networks. They specify how information is stored or represented in memory. Processing assumptions describe how information is retrieved and recalled. Both assumptions rely on each other. It is possible to point to the interaction that exists between them only when both are explicitly defined (cf. the definition of holistic and component codes in sections 3.4 and 3.5).

Processing assumptions and their interaction with structural assumptions are discussed within the framework of different network theories. Before doing this, however, we must define some basic terms concerning structural assumptions.

5.1.1 What Are Memory Networks?

Memory networks are inferred structures designed to explain how information is stored and recalled. They are built on two different classes of elements: nodes and connecting links. Both elements form a structure known as the *memory network*. Its graphic representation is by no means a defining feature for network theories. Complex structures can also be described using a mathematical calculus or by a simulation language. However, as most network models allow for a clear and easy graphic representation, this is the form of representation we favor here.

In a network, information is represented by links as well as nodes. The question of whether links or nodes store redundant information depends on the coding rule. For example, consider the Huffmann tree depicted in Fig. 5.2. This well-known binary coding structure is a good example of a

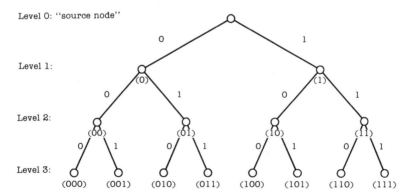

FIG. 5.2.   The Huffman tree as an example for a binary and strictly hierarchical network.

redundant network: The links leading from a node carry information which is also represented in that particular node.

In the binary network of Fig. 5.2, there are two types of links: those carrying the information "zero" and those carrying the information "1." Each node represents a different number. The structure is hierarchical, so the more encoding stages are encountered, the more complex is the information that can be represented. Only binary numbers can be represented on Level 1, but by Level 3 octal numbers can be stored.

Although psychological theories are no longer based on a binary coding format (cf. Human Associative Memory [HAM] by J. R. Anderson & Bower, 1973), the example in Fig. 5.2, nevertheless shows all the essential characteristics of a memory network. It demonstrates that information can be represented both by nodes and links, and that networks become more complex as more information is stored in them.

The principle of hierarchical coding, as pictured in Fig. 5.2, forms the elementary basis of computer languages. The extent to which psychological memory theories are oriented toward this principle can be seen in the example of Anderson's Adaptive Control of Thoughts (ACT) theory (J. R. Anderson, 1976). ACT, as a modified version of HAM (J. R. Anderson & Bower, 1973), is concerned with the question of how propositions are represented and processed as basic knowledge units in human memory. Complex linguistic propositions are used in examining ACT; an example is given in Fig. 5.3. A comparison of Figs. 5.2 and 5.3 reveals two essential differences: The coding principle in Fig. 5.3 is neither binary nor redundant.

ACT is based on the assumption that sentences are represented by subject–verb relations. The node connecting the subject link with the predicate link is the fact node. It represents the fact that is expressed by a sentence. The verb—here represented by the predicate node—is further

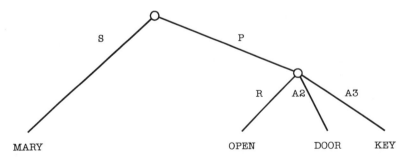

FIG. 5.3. Memory network for the sentence "Mary opens the door with a key." From *Language, Memory, and Thought* (p. 161) by J. R. Anderson, 1976. © 1976 by Lawrence Erlbaum Associates. Adapted with permission.

specified by argument links (cf. the argument links R, A2, and A3 in Fig. 5.3). In the simulation of ACT, fact nodes correspond to a function with the two arguments "subject" and "predicate." The verb, itself an argument of the fact function, is represented by a function comprising a certain number of arguments, their exact number being determined by the meaning of a sentence. In our example, argument A2 refers to the object ("door"), A3 to the instrument ("key"), and R to a specific relation existing between the subject and the object (here the subject "opens" the object).

As this example indicates, the graphic representation of a network can also be used to illustrate the structure of a simulation program. A node in the graphic representation corresponds to a function in the simulation program, whereas a link corresponds to an argument of the function.

5.1.2 Memory Networks, Codes, Coding Format

The term *coding* — at least in the way it has been used up to now — may have created the impression that codes are units independent of each other. However, in network theories it can easily be shown that codes are not only closely interrelated, but also partly overlapping structures. Depending on the processing goal, codes may be assembled from different parts of a complex memory structure.

Consider the code of the sentence: "Mary opens the door with a key" in Fig. 5.3. The code of the sentence can, in turn, be part of a more complex memory structure. There may be further propositions — for example, about "Mary" (what kind of job she has, where she lives, etc.) or about "key" or "door" — which are connected with the code. Conversely, however, the code representing the sentence is based on a number of other codes that may refer to the lexical and semantic information of the words appearing in the sentence. Which of these codes (i.e., which parts of the network) are searched depends exclusively on the goal of the search process.

Codes can be regarded as parts of a memory structure. Of which parts they consist is determined by the type of cognitive operations that take place in memory. The given structure within a code is referred to as the *coding format*.

5.1.3 Limiting Spreading Activation and Search Area

Network theories describe a memory search by a process of spreading activation. This assumption, however, evidently so plausible, leads to a fundamental problem unavoidable by any memory theory: How can it be explained that spreading activation is confined to the relevant part of the network? Or, put another way: Which assumptions prevent a search process from triggering off an "epileptic seizure" in memory? There are essentially two ways of handling this problem: One can proceed from the assumption of either "local" or a "central" control of spreading activation.

Most network theories (e.g., ACT or even ACT*—a revised version of ACT—J. R. Anderson, 1983a, 1983c) assume that spreading activation is controlled by two factors: (a) the assumption that the strength of activation decreases the more links and nodes have been activated, and (b) the assumption that, with the passing of time, activation of each node decays. Thus, the search process loses activation as the length of the activated path increases. The explanation of very complex search processes, which must activate large parts of the network in order to retrieve the sought-after information, is unlikely to be based on these mechanisms.

A more interesting explanation lies in the assumption of control mechanisms that refer to the concepts of *preactivation* and *inhibition*. Preactivation means that before a search process is initiated, relevant parts of the network are already in a state of increased activation. Inhibition stands for the opposite effect: Those parts of the network irrelevant to the search are in a state of decreased activation. Preactivation and inhibition can explain how the search process is controlled and directed. The problem here is how the search process provides feedback to a central monitoring device (chap. 11). Information can be retrieved as soon as intersecting pathways are found. But how is the intersection fed back, and how is the search process terminated? Chapter 8 deals with this problem in greater detail. In doing so it becomes clear that the issue of control mechanisms (assumption C3 in sections 8.6.2 and 8.6.3) is one of the more neglected aspects of memory theories.

5.2 DIFFERENT CLASSES OF MEMORY NETWORKS

Given the unlimited possibilities that exist in constructing networks, it is surprising to see how few of them are used in memory psychology. Those that do exist are outlined here.

5.2.1 Strictly Hierarchical and Linear Structures

Strictly hierarchical structures can be defined by the relationship existing between the number of nodes and links. Thus for example, the structure in Fig. 5.2 shows a total of 15 nodes and 14 links. In Fig. 5.3 there are 6 nodes and 5 links. Let n be the number of nodes and m be the number of links. For a strictly hierarchical structure, then, it always holds that: $m = n - 1$.

Linear structures can be regarded as a special instance of strictly hierarchical structures. They are created when a single link emanates from a node at each hierarchical level (Fig. 5.4c). Thus, the same equation ($m = n - 1$) holds true for linear structures. Strictly hierarchical and linear networks are, therefore, defined by a fixed relationship between the number of nodes and links (Fig. 5.4).

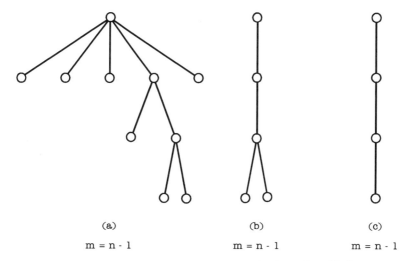

(a)   (b)   (c)

$m = n - 1$ $m = n - 1$ $m = n - 1$

FIG. 5.4. A linear structure (c) is a special case of strictly hierarchical structures shown in (a) and (b).

5.2.2 Nonstrictly Hierarchical Structures

Although they essentially show the same characteristics of a hierarchical structure, *nonstrictly hierarchical networks* do not correspond to the equation $m = n - 1$. Structures that are not strictly hierarchical emerge when additional links are inserted either within or between different hierarchical levels (Fig. 5.5a, b).

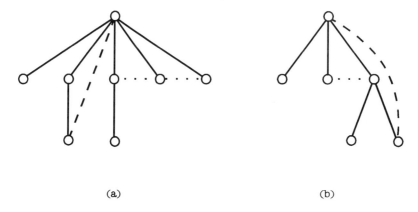

(a)   (b)

FIG. 5.5. Examples of nonstrictly hierarchical structures. This type of network emerges if additional links are inserted between nodes of different hierarchical levels (dashed lines) or between nodes of the same level (dotted lines).

5.2.3 Interconnected Structures

Interconnected structures represent a new class of network. They show none of those features characteristic of hierarchical structures. The "nesting" principle is missing, and the number of links exceeds the number of nodes ($m > n$ for $n > 3$). Figure 5.6 offers an example of an interconnected structure (each node is connected to every other node) and two examples of partially interconnected structures ($m > n$ is still valid, but each node is not connected to every other node).

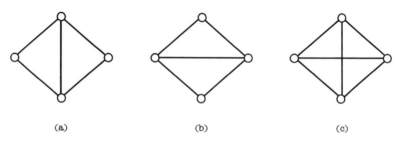

(a)   (b)   (c)

FIG. 5.6.   Examples for partially (a, b) and completely interconnected structures (c).

5.3 TWO TYPES OF NETWORK MODELS WITH STRICTLY AND NONSTRICTLY HIERARCHICAL STRUCTURES

Network models may be classified according to very different criteria, such as whether they focus on semantic or episodic information (Tulving, 1983), or on modality specific (Bleasdale, 1983; Paivio, 1971) or nonmodality specific information (J. R. Anderson, 1978; Kosslyn, 1981). Here, however, we only wish to draw attention to the fact that the vast majority of network models assume strictly hierarchical structures. This is also the case for well-known and influential models such as J. R. Anderson and Bower's (1973) HAM model, J. R. Anderson's (1976) ACT model and to a large extent J. R. Anderson's (1983a) ACT* model, the model by the LNR research group (Norman & Rumelhart, 1975), and Collins and Quillian's model (1969, 1970). The following chapters show that hierarchical coding structures lead to very restrictive memory models incapable of explaining a series of important findings.

  Why then do hierarchical network theories enjoy such great popularity? One reason for this may lie in the fact that hierarchical structures offer a very efficient ordering principle that is found not only in many natural languages (e.g., in the form of superordinate and subordinate relationships), but also in many scientific classification systems. However, there is another — and for our purposes more interesting — reason: Network models are, from the outset, either conceived as simulation models or have at least been strongly influenced by them. The format of (traditional) simulation languages is hierarchical in nature and thus invites the adoption of hierarchical structures in memory psychology. Hierarchical networks originate in "nesting" computer functions, that is, functions contain arguments that in turn are then used as functions. When representing a geometric structure, each function refers to a certain hierarchical level, whereas its arguments refer to the complexity, that is, the number of branches at that level.

This makes it clear that hierarchical network models proceed from representational assumptions most likely derived from computer languages. It is, however, questionable whether these assumptions offer suitable explanations for human information processing. Nevertheless, the following chapters show that by assuming hierarchical structures some important characteristics of search processes can be determined. Figure 5.7 gives an overview of strictly and nonstrictly hierarchical memory models.

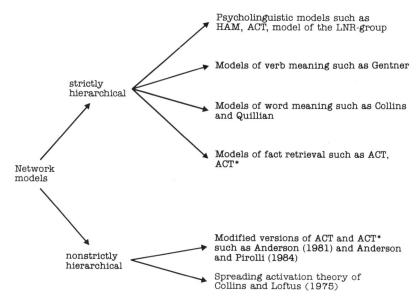

FIG. 5.7. Memory theories, classified into strictly and nonstrictly hierarchical models.

Network theories have been well-documented elsewhere (Kintsch, 1980; E. E. Smith, 1978; E. E. Smith & Medin, 1981; Wender, Colonius, & Schulze, 1980). The following chapters consider those theories that meet the following two criteria: On the one hand, they must be directly relevant to the distinction made between strictly and nonstrictly hierarchical structures and, on the other hand, must enable predictions regarding the speed of memory processes. Psycholinguistic theories are, on the basis of these criteria, not immediately relevant to our question, because they cannot be fully tested. In addition, there is hardly another area in memory psychology in which the idea of strictly hierarchical structures is so strongly accepted (cf. Bierwisch, 1977). Models on fact retrieval and semantic memory, however, do meet the aforementioned criteria. They refer to strictly as well as nonstrictly hierarchical structures and, in addition, their predictions can be tested in elaborated experimental paradigms. The next two chapters are devoted to the discussion of these theories.

6 Strictly and Nonstrictly Hierarchical Models of Fact Retrieval

How structural and processing assumptions interact, and how the speed of search and activation processes is influenced by the different forms of memory structures, is the central issue of recent memory research and is discussed here and in the following two chapters. This chapter focuses on experiments on fact retrieval, whereas the next chapter is concerned with experiments on word meaning. Chapter 8 introduces a network model designed to overcome the inadequacies of strictly and nonstrictly hierarchical models.

The following discussion is based on the assumption of component codes. Here, as well as in chap. 3, we confront the issue as to how the search process is influenced by the characteristics of the encoding format. This problem, by its very nature, is complex and difficult. Both theoretical considerations and the adequacy of the experimental procedures are important here. The representational assumptions of the different models only make sense within the context of a particular experimental procedure, thus it is necessary to discuss these procedures in a more detailed manner. Accordingly, we first discuss the experiments and then go over to explain the theoretical framework.

6.1 STRICTLY HIERARCHICAL MODELS OF FACT RETRIEVAL

The following models were developed within the confines of HAM and ACT. Their representational assumptions refer to the simplest hierarchical structure imaginable — the fan. A fan is a network in which there are various links leading from a single node termed the *concept node*. Those nodes accessed by the links are referred to as *fact nodes*.

In fact retrieval experiments subjects are always expected to study a set of sentences. Each sentence expresses a fact about a particular concept X or Y. Sentences may take the form of "A person (concept X) is in location (concept Y)." The sentences are compiled in a way that the concepts X or Y are linked to one or several facts expressed by a sentence. Consequently, a fan is assumed to represent the facts learned about a concept. Results have repeatedly shown that the more facts (sentences) there are to be learned, the longer the search process lasts (cf. the review in J. R. Anderson, 1983b). This result became known by the term *fan effect*, or retrieval interference (cf. Sternberg, 1969, for similar results).

6.1.1 The Experimental Paradigm and the Most Important Results

The paradigm of fact retrieval has its origin in sentence verification experiments used in evaluating HAM and ACT. Fact retrieval experiments can be regarded as a specific variant of sentence verification experiments in which the syntax of the sentences remain constant, whereas the number and type of facts expressed in the sentence varies. The experimental procedure is pictured in Table 6.1, Part A and Part B. It consists of three different stages: (a) The acquisition of a series of sentences that express different facts about a concept, (b) a test in which subjects have to recall the facts about a concept, and (c) a recognition test in which subjects have to distinguish similar sentences (distractors) from those learned.

The most important experimental variable is the number of facts stated about a certain concept. For example, consider the concepts "firefighter" and "park," which are used in Table 6.1. Whereas "firefighter" appears only once as a concept, "park" occurs three times. There is, therefore, only one fact that refers to "firefighter," but three facts that refer to "park." In a series of experiments (J. R. Anderson, 1974, 1975, 1981; J. R. Anderson & L. M. Reder, 1987; King & J. R. Anderson, 1976) it was generally discovered that reaction times for yes and no responses in the recognition test were dependent on the number of facts. The more facts that were learned, the longer were the reaction times (cf. the results in Table 6.1). This increase in reaction time, which is a function of the number of facts learned, is known as the fan effect.

6.1.2 Structural Assumptions Underlying the Fan Effect

According to the traditional explanation of this effect, activation decreases as the number of links leading from a node increases. Consider the

TABLE 6.1
An Example of a Fact Retrieval Experiment

A. Experimental Design

Sequence of Tests

1. Learning	2. Recall Test	3. Recognition Test
Presentation of a list of sentences. Each sentence expresses a fact about a person and a location.	Learning performance is checked by a recall test: For each person subjects must recall the corresponding location(s) and for each location the corresponding person(s).	Subjects have to distinguish between the learned target sentences and new distractor sentences. Distractors use the same set of persons and locations but in different combinations.

B. The Design of the Recognition Task

Examples of Target Sentences

A doctor is in the bank.	(1-1)[a]
A firefighter is in the park.	(1-3)[a]
A lawyer is in the church.	(2-1)[a]
A lawyer is in the park.	(2-3)[a]
A captain is in the park.	(1-3)[a]

Examples of Distractor Sentences	Correct Response	Number of Associated Facts about	
		a Person	a Location
A lawyer is in the bank.	"No"	2	1
A doctor is in the bank.	"Yes"	1	1
A lawyer is in the park.	"Yes"	2	3
A firefighter is in the church.	"No"	1	1
A captain is in the park.	"Yes"	1	3

C. Mean RTs (ms) in the Recognition Task

Number of Facts		Targets Persons				Distractors Persons			
		1	2	3	Mean	1	2	3	Mean
Locations	1	1,111	1,174	1,222	1,169	1,197	1,221	1,264	1,227
	2	1,167	1,198	1,222	1,196	1,250	1,356	1,291	1,299
	3	1,153	1,233	1,357	1,248	1,262	1,471	1,465	1,399
	Mean	1,144	1,202	1,267	1,204	1,236	1,349	1,340	1,308

Note: [a] The first number in parentheses refers to the frequency with which a person appears in the list of sentences; the second number refers to the frequency for a location. Data from *Language, Memory, and Thought* (p. 255) by J. R. Anderson, 1976. © 1976 by Lawrence Erlbaum Associates.

following example from Fig. 6.1: "A firefighter is in the park." According to ACT, the search process starts at the concept nodes "firefighter" and "park." It is at these nodes that the search process encounters fanlike structures. Because there are three sentences in which park is used as a concept, three (experimental) links lead from the concept node "park." There is only one sentence concerning "firefighter." Thus, there is only one (experimental) link leading from that concept node.

The concepts "firefighter" and "park" have different meanings for different subjects. As a result, the preexperimental knowledge about these concepts varies between the subjects. Because storage efficiency requires that any given concept be stored in only one particular location in memory, several preexperimental links will have already existed before subjects take part in an experiment. Consequently, preexperimental knowledge will enlarge the fan and, according to ACT, will lead to a deceleration of reaction times just as with the number of facts learned in the experiment. In Fig. 6.1 experimental links are represented by continuous lines, whereas preexperimental links are represented by dash-dotted lines. The two dotted arrows indicate where the search process originates.

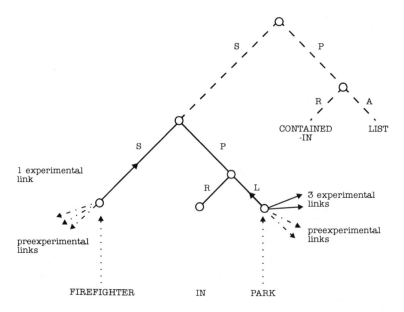

FIG. 6.1.   ACT representation of the sentence "A firefighter is in the park." The fact node of this sentence is connected to another proposition (dashed lines) which states explicitly that this sentence is contained in the list of learned sentences. The search process spreads from FIREFIGHTER and PARK (dotted line). From *Language, Memory, and Thought* (p. 262) by J. R. Anderson, 1976. © 1976 by Lawrence Erlbaum Associates. Adapted with permission.

6.1.3 Processing Assumptions Underlying the Fan Effect

According to ACT, a search process originates at the concept nodes for "person" and "location" and aims at finding an intersecting pathway. An intersection will be found only if a sentence connecting "person" and "location" is learned and can still be remembered. In this case the intersection is the fact node that represents the learned sentence. Detecting an intersection is the necessary criterion for a yes response. If no intersection is found, the result will be a negative response. According to ACT, the learned sentences are also connected to propositions that state explicitly whether or not a particular sentence is contained in the study list. This latter assumption, however, has no bearing on the explanation of the fan effect.

As complicated as ACT might appear, there is only one crucial factor in explaining the fan effect: the interaction between the number of links and the amount of activation. The more links there are leading from a concept node, the longer reaction time will be for yes as well as for no responses. Figure 6.2 contains a schematic depiction of that section of Fig. 6.1 relevant to explaining the fan effect.

Activation $a(i)$ spreading along link i depends on the strength $s(i)$ of link i and the sum S of the combined strength of all the links leading from the concept node ($S = \Sigma s(i)$; $i = 1, \ldots n + k$; all $n + k$ links leading from

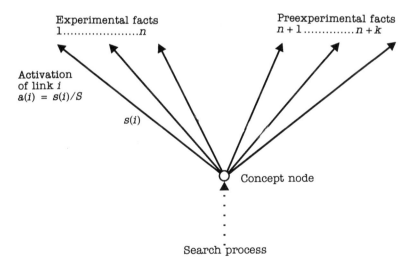

FIG. 6.2. A simple strictly hierarchical structure called a "fan," underlies the explanation of the fan effect. Summing the strengths $s(i)$ of all links i gives S, which can be considered the total strength of the search process.

the concept node; cf. Fig. 6.2). Thus, according to ACT (cf. J. R. Anderson, 1976, p. 263), activation is defined as:

$$a(i) = s(i)/S. \tag{6.1}$$

The time $t(i)$ needed to activate the link is the reciprocal value of $a(i)$:

$$t(i) = S/s \; (i). \tag{6.2}$$

Equation 6.1 reveals an important fact: The sum of all outputs $a(i)$ leading from a node is equal to the input received by that particular node. In other words, the links emanating from a node literally divide the activation received by the concept node.

Given the case that all links are of equal strength [$s(i) = 1$], activation $a(i)$ depends only on the number of links.

$$a(i) = 1/(n + k). \tag{6.3}$$

Consider, for example, a fan with two links of equal strength, and assume that input activity is $I = 1$. Then, activation $a(i) = \frac{1}{2}$. Thus, the sum of all outputs [$O = \frac{1}{2} + \frac{1}{2} = 1$] equals input activity, and hence $I = O$.

This explanation of the fan effect enables a clear prediction: The more facts that are learned, (a) the less activation $a(i)$ will spread to the fact node, and (b) the more time $t(i)$ will be needed to access the fact node. Provided that all links are equal in strength, activation time $t(i)$ is:

$$t(i) = n + k. \tag{6.4}$$

The reaction time for retrieving a sentence will increase, the greater the number of facts learned. As it is assumed that the search process emanates from the concept nodes, regardless of whether or not the nodes intersect, ACT predicts comparable effects for yes and no responses.

Less convincing is the assumption that the number of preexperimental facts k will slow down the search process to the same extent as the number of facts learned during the experiment. A more obvious assumption would be that the subjects are capable of focusing on that search area containing the facts learned in the experiment. If preexperimental knowledge, which varies to a considerable degree among subjects, does in fact have as great an influence as Anderson (1983a, 1983b, 1983c) assumed, then it is surprising that the fan effect can be replicated so easily.

6.2 A MODEL OF STRICTLY HIERARCHICAL SUBSTRUCTURES: FOCUSING ON THE RELEVANT SEARCH AREAS

The explanation of the fan effect offered so far leads to a paradox. Because it is assumed that all of the links must be searched, regardless of number, we arrive at the paradoxical conclusion that the more knowledge is stored in memory, the slower it works.

E. E. Smith, Adams, and Schorr (1978) pointed out this paradox and emphasized that the interpretation of the fan effect in many cases contradicts our everyday experiences. Compare the knowledge of an expert who knows many facts about a certain subject with that of a novice who only knows a few facts. Then, according to ACT, it should be assumed that it would take the expert much longer to retrieve a fact than it would the novice. Our everyday experiences show, however, that in fact the opposite is the case. It is more plausible to assume that the expert's knowledge is better structured and the expert is, therefore, faster than a novice at retrieving relevant facts.

But what does an "efficient structuring" of the facts stored in memory mean? McCloskey and Bigler (1980) conducted a number of very convincing experiments on this issue. They were able to show that subjects group together those facts containing a similar content, and the speed with which a fact is retrieved is by no means only dependent on the total number of facts learned for one concept—as would be expected according to ACT.

6.2.1 The Experimental Paradigm

McCloskey and Biegler (1980) used sentences like "The (person) likes (object)." The most important experimental variables were the number of objects and their affiliation to semantic categories. The objects belonged either to the category "animals" (Category A) or to the category "countries" (Category B). Some persons learned only one fact from Category A (sentences of Type 1A-0B); others learned five facts from Category B and only one fact from Category A, and so forth. The structure of this experiment and the most important results are represented in Table 6.2.

TABLE 6.2
Experimental Design and Results of Experiment 1

A. Types of Target and Distractor Sentences		
Target Type 1A-0B[a]	The architect likes elephants	
Distractor Type 1-0[b]	The architect likes wolves	
Target Type 1A-5B		lions
		Portugal
	The editor likes	Italy
		Canada
		England
		Brazil
Distractor Type 1-5	The editor likes bears	
Distractor Type 5-1	The editor likes Mexico	

(continued)

TABLE 6.2 *(continued)*

Target Type 6A-0B		wolves
		rabbits
	The lawyer likes	bears
		tigers
		pigs
		dogs
Distractor Type 6-0	The lawyer likes elephants	

B. Results, Mean RTs (ms) in the Recognition Task

Sentence Type	Targets	Distractors
1-0	1,202	1,382
1-5	1,312	1,620
5-1	1,570	1,801
6-0	1,617	1,876

Note: [a]A denotes category "animal," B denotes category "country."
[b]First number stands for the number of relevant facts, second number for irrelevant facts. From McCloskey and Bigler, 1980, *Memory and Cognition, 8,* pp. 253,254. © 1980 by Psychonomic Society Inc. Reprinted with permission.

6.2.2 Structural and Processing Assumptions

If one were to assume that subjects divide the facts for animals and countries into different hierarchical substructures, the result would be a hypothetical memory network of the kind represented in Fig. 6.3, which refers to sentences of Type 1A-5B. The assumption regarding subnodes for objects of Categories A and B enables the prediction that only the facts of the relevant category are searched. For distractor sentences of Type 1-5 (one relevant and five irrelevant facts) one can expect shorter reaction times than for distractor sentences of Type 5-1, where five relevant facts must be considered. The results shown in Table 6.2, Part B support this prediction.

A comparison of the results of sentences of Type 1-0 and of Type 1-5 shows that not only the relevant but also the irrelevant facts play a role. Although only one relevant fact is present under both experimental conditions, the reaction times for sentences of Type 1-5 are, nevertheless, longer than those for sentences of Type 1-0. This result also agrees with the assumption of subnodes. The representation of relevant and irrelevant facts requires a fan, which is missing in Type 1-0. Accordingly, the fact retrieval of these sentences takes place faster than in those sentences in which relevant and irrelevant facts must be distinguished.

It is more complicated to explain why sentences with five relevant facts and one irrelevant fact (Type 5-1 sentences) are evaluated more quickly than sentences with six relevant and zero irrelevant facts (Type 6-0 sentences). If one starts out from the assumption on the equal strength of all links, then

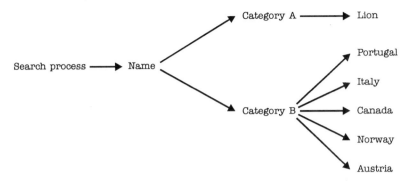

FIG. 6.3.   Sentences of the type 1A-5B in Table 6.2 can be represented by hierarchical substructures.

the opposite result is to be expected. In the network in Fig. 6.3, each subnode representing sentences of Type 5-1 is activated by an amount equal to $\frac{1}{2}$. This amount is divided among the five fact nodes. They receive activation in the amount of $(\frac{1}{2})$ $(\frac{1}{5})$ = 0.1. For sentences of Type 6-0, a fan with six links is to be assumed. Here the activation of each node is equal to $\frac{1}{6}$ or 0.17. Because sentences of Type 6-0 receive greater activation, one could expect shorter reaction times than with sentences of Type 5-1. This, however, is not the case.

Assume that the strength of the link leading to the relevant subnode is greater than the strength of the link leading to the irrelevant subnode. Now, it is possible to explain the difference in reaction times between sentences of Type 6-0 and 5-1. This assumption means that the subject can evaluate and directly influence the path the search process should take. If, for example, the strength of the relevant link is 0.9 and the strength of the irrelevant link is only 0.1, then according to Equation 6.1 there is an activation of 0.9/(0.9 + 0.1) = 0.9 for the relevant subnode. Accordingly, each relevant fact node receives activation in the amount of 0.9/5 = 0.18. This amount is slightly larger than the activation of a node in a fan with six links. The assumption regarding different strengths in links enables us to explain why the search process in sentences of Type 6-0 lasts a little longer than in sentences of Type 5-1.

A reliable verification of the model of hierarchical substructures requires a quantitative prediction of reaction time differences between various sentence types. In making a quantitative prediction, however, one is faced with two problems: On the one hand, it is unlikely that there is a method by which one could estimate the strength of a link, and, on the other hand, it is not only conceivable but also plausible that the strength of a link does not remain constant, but rather varies according to the experimental conditions and the kind of search process.

6.3 NONSTRICTLY HIERARCHICAL MODELS OF FACT RETRIEVAL

The assumption underlying strictly hierarchical memory structures has led to a fundamental problem: The speed of activation and search processes decreases as the complexity of memory structure increases. E. E. Smith, Adams, & Schorr (1978), McCloskey and Bigler (1980), and J. R. Anderson (1981) stressed the problem commonly described as the "paradox of retrieval interference." Even the attempted solution discussed in the previous chapter—the introduction of subnodes (J. R. Anderson, 1983a, 1983c)—is not capable of giving a generally satisfactory explanation of the problem of activation deceleration. Although strictly hierarchical structures with subnodes enable faster search processes compared to structures without subnodes, an increase in the number of subnodes leads inevitably to a deceleration of activation and search processes. In realistic situations a huge number of subnodes is required in order to structure knowledge efficiently. As a result, the paradox of retrieval interference is only passed on from the level of concept nodes to that of subnodes.

The traditional explanation of the fan effect, according to J. R. Anderson (1974, 1976), is put into question not only because of theoretical considerations, but also through a series of experimental findings. It has been shown that under the following conditions no fan effect could be traced:

- In the case of overlearned facts, Hayes-Roth (1977) was able to show that the fan effect disappears as the learning phase is lengthened: After a total of 11 experimental sessions, no fan effect could be discerned.
- In the case of consistency judgments, where subjects must examine the relationship between concepts, a negative fan effect was discovered. This means that reaction time decreases as the number of facts increases (J. R. Anderson & L. M. Reder, 1987; L. M. Reder & Ross, 1983; L. R. Reder & Wible, 1984). However, if subjects are set to the task of recognizing sentences, then reaction time increases with the number of facts learned (positive fan effect).
- In the case of integrated facts, that is, facts that are connected thematically and refer to each other, E. E. Smith et al. (1978), Moeser (1977, 1979), L. M. Reder and J. R. Anderson (1980), J. R. Anderson (1981), and Myers, O'Brien, Balota, and Toyofuku (1984) revealed that the fan effect occurs only when the facts learned are encoded as unintegrated episodes. If the subjects manage to connect the individual facts to an episode, then a fan effect can no longer be observed.

What are the consequences of these results? The negative findings of Hayes-Roth (1977) can easily be explained without rejecting a strictly hierarchical memory structure. It is theoretically sound to assume that the repeated learning of facts leads to an increased strength of experimental links, at the expense of preexperimental links. As a result, the fan effect diminishes to an extent that it can no longer be measured (Equation 6.1 and Fig. 6.2). J. R. Anderson (1983c, p. 266) made explicit reference to this possibility.

A similar interpretation holds true for the negative fan effect discovered in consistency tasks. Here, for example, the subjects had to judge whether or not a concept and a corresponding verb were connected in a grammatically correct manner: The more facts that were learned in relation to a concept, the more often this concept was represented in the learning phase (see the experimental design on fact retrieval in Table 6.1, Part A). With an increased frequency of exposure, concept nodes may be accessed more easily (J. R. Anderson, 1983c, p. 266). Thus, in consistency judgments, those concepts about which many facts were learned are retrieved faster than those on which only few facts were learned (J. R. Anderson & L. M. Reder, 1987).

Why does this not generally lead to a negative fan effect? The answer is surprisingly simple. The search strategy determines whether or not a positive fan effect appears. A positive fan effect can only be observed if the fan is actually activated. With regard to this, it is important to recall that the links of a fan always lead away from concept nodes to different facts (Fig. 6.1). In consistency tasks, however, only concepts — not facts — are retrieved, and as a result there is no reason for a positive fan effect to emerge. If, however, subjects are set the task of recognizing sentences, then reaction times increase with the number of facts learned in relation to a concept. Now the different links leading from a concept node to fact nodes must be activated, which therefore leads to the activation of the fan, which in turn leads to an increase in reaction time, and thus to the creation of a positive fan effect. The negative and positive fan effects can, therefore, be explained by the fact that there are different search strategies in one and the same memory network — as always, this has a strictly hierarchical structure (L. M. Reder, 1987).

In contrast, the results from integrated facts force us to abandon strictly hierarchical memory structures. In the experiments reported in section 6.1, all the facts were thematically independent of each other. There is no thematic connection between the statement "The firefighter is in the park," and the statement "The captain is in the park" (Table 6.1, Part B), apart from the common concept "park." Consequently, it must be assumed that the individual facts are not connected to each other in memory. They are only connected indirectly by a common concept node ("park"), but between them, there is no direct connection (see section 5.2.1). However, in the case of integrated facts, a strictly hierarchical structure is no longer plausible as their relatedness must be reflected by additional links in the memory network. The following experiment by E. E. Smith, Adams, and Schorr, (1978, p. 442) can be used to demonstrate this idea. Consider the following statements about Marty: "Marty broke the bottle" and "Marty did not delay the voyage." Without additional information, no thematic connection may be detected. Thus, a strictly hierarchical structure seems appropriate for the representation of these unrelated facts (Fig. 6.4a). The situation changes, however, when a third sentence is introduced: "Marty had been chosen to christen the ship." Now it becomes clear that the first two facts are also connected: Marty did not delay the voyage (the maiden voyage of the ship), because he broke the bottle of champagne on the bow of the ship, as is the custom. The networks in Fig. 6.4 show a strictly hierarchical structure, as can be assumed for the representation of unrelated facts (Fig. 6.4a), and a nonstrictly hierarchical structure for the representation of thematically connected or integrated facts (Fig 6.4b).

As insignificant as it may at first appear, the assumption of nonstrictly hierarchical codes forms the starting point for a completely new group of network models. Together with nonstrictly hierarchical codes, a new processing assumption becomes effective that would be meaningless in the case of strictly hierarchical structures. As there are no cycles or redundant pathways in strictly hierarchical structures, indirect activation can never be

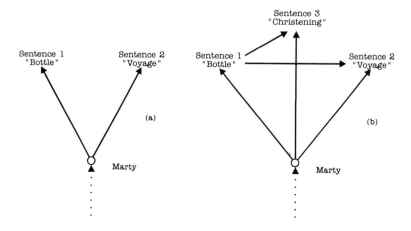

FIG. 6.4.   The representation of unintegrated facts (a) requires a hierarchical structure whereas integrated facts (b) require an interconnected structure. Note that it is Sentence 3 that turns the unintegrated facts into a meaningful episode. Sentence 1: Marty broke the bottle. Sentence 2: Marty did not delay the voyage. Sentence 3: Marty did the christening of the ship. From E. E. Smith, Adams, and Schorr, 1978, *Cognitive Psychology*, *10*, p. 442. © 1978 by Academic Press. Adapted by pemission.

effective. In nonstrictly hierarchical or in interconnected structures, additional links and redundant pathways do exist, allowing spreading activation to follow two different routes: a direct route proceeding from one node to another, and an indirect route that either passes through a cycle or one or more additional pathways. The concept of indirect activation, discussed in detail in Chap. 8, enables us to explain a positive as well as a negative fan effect. Most importantly, however, it allows us to predict that the speed of activation and search processes does not necessarily decrease as the complexity of the network increases, but may instead increase. This principle, more than any other discussed so far, allows us to explain the high efficiency of our memory performance.

The role that indirect activation plays, and how implicitly and unsystematically this assumption has been adopted by the predominantly strictly hierarchical memory models (J. R. Anderson, 1981, 1983a, 1983c), is shown in the next sections.

6.3.1 The Experimental Paradigm: The Effect of Integrated Facts on the Acquisition and Retrieval of New Information

J. R. Anderson (1981) examined the question of how thematically connected facts are integrated with new information. The experimental design of this work corresponds in its basic features to fact retrieval experiments discussed in section 5.4.1. Thus, here too, J. R. Anderson used sentences of the type "The (person) is in (location)." This experiment is novel because subjects receive prior knowledge on the persons mentioned in the sentences, before these are actually acquired (see the experimental design depicted in Table 6.3, Part A).

The amount of prior knowledge was varied at five stages during three different experiments: Under the experimental conditions with the greatest amount of prior knowledge (Condition 1), subjects were given the names of famous personalities (e.g., Benjamin Franklin, Richard Burton, etc.); under the condition with the second largest amount of prior knowledge (Condition 2), subjects received detailed descriptions of different names of fictional characters; under the third experimental condition, a sentence was used to express a fact about each fictional character (Condition 3); under a further experimental condition, the subjects were only given the names of the persons (Condition 4); no prior knowledge was given to the subjects under the controlling condition (Condition 5).

The dependent variables are the number of errors that occur before reaching the learning criterion in the free recall task, as well as the reaction times in the recognition task. The experimental design and the most important results are given in Table 6.3.

TABLE 6.3
Experimental Design and Results of Experiment 2 (Conditions 2–5) and Experiment 3 (Condition 1)

A. Experimental Design

Sequence of Tests

| 1. Learning of prior knowledge about each of a list of persons | 2. Learning of sentences of the type "The (person) is in (location)" | 3. Recall test | 4. Recognition |

The Amount of Prior Knowledge Is Varied in 5 Experimental Conditions

Condition 1: Subjects are presented with the names of well-known personalities, such as Robert Kennedy and Benjamin Franklin.

Condition 2: Subjects are presented with a list of unfamiliar names, but a detailed description of each person is given (e.g., "Carol Norman is a lawyer but owns an antiques shop. Running the antiques shop is her hobby. She owns a beautiful collection of old clocks.").

Condition 3: Subjects are presented with a list of unfamiliar names. Only a brief description of each person is given (e.g., "Henry Caputo buys a ticket for the football game in New Haven.").

Condition 4: Subjects receive only the list of unfamiliar names without any further description.

Condition 5: No prior knowledge is given.

B. Results

	Experimental Condition				
	1	*2*	*3*	*4*	*5*
Errors, recall test					
1 location	.31	.67	.80	1.51	2.55
2 locations	.88	1.71	1.59	1.79	2.54
Means	.59	1.19	1.20	1.65	2.55
RTs, recognition test					
1 location	706	1168	1156	1080	1097
2 locations	939	1326	1324	1277	1342
Fan effect	233	158	168	197	245

Note: Data from J. R. Anderson, 1981, *Memory and Cognition, 9*, pp. 241, 242, 245. © 1981 by Psychonomic Society Inc. Reprinted with permission.

6.3.2 Structural and Processing Assumptions

The crucial representational assumptions in the experiment just described refer to the question of how prior knowledge is structured in memory and how it is connected to the sentences acquired later. Anderson attempted to explain this by using experimental Condition 2 (i.e., a high amount of prior knowledge: detailed description of fictitious characters) and experimental

Condition 4 (i.e., a small amount of prior knowledge: only the names of the persons are given; Table 6.3, Part A).

The prediction for Condition 4 is simple. The appearance of the well-known fan effect is to be expected: The concept node representing the person is connected with either one or two location nodes depending on how many locations have been learned.

In experimental Condition 2, on the other hand, a prediction on the memory structure is more complicated. Not only the representation of prior knowledge (acquired in Learning Phase 1) but also the integration of prior knowledge with the facts (learned in Phase 2) needs to be considered (Table 6.3, Part A). The statements contained in prior knowledge (e.g., "hobby," "old clocks," "antique shop") refer to each other and form a coherent episode, which is used to describe the fictitious character (cf. the example in Table 6.3, Part A). A network of integrated facts is created by these statements. It can, therefore, be assumed that fact nodes are not only connected with the concept node (the person), but also with each other. In Learning Phase 2 the concept node is also connected with one or two location nodes, depending on how many locations have been presented. The more elaborate the prior knowledge, the easier it will be for the subject to integrate the newly acquired facts (locations) into the already existing knowledge. Assume, for example, that in Learning Phase 2 subjects are presented with the statement "Carol Norman is in the bank." It is likely that subjects will attempt to integrate this sentence into the previously learned episode about Carol Norman, that is, to infer that Carol Norman is in the bank to get money in order to purchase an expensive antique clock. This process of integration leads to the formation of additional pathways between the location node and one or more nodes representing prior knowledge (Fig. 6.5).

Now three different predictions can be distinguished: The first prediction relates to the number of errors in the acquisition of locations, the second prediction gives details on the length of reaction times in the recognition task, and the third prediction is concerned with the strength of the fan effect.

Prediction 1.   Anderson started out from the plausible assumption that integrated facts facilitate the acquisition of sentences in Learning Phase 2. The more prior knowledge that is available, the better the new knowledge can be linked with old knowledge, and the more resistant the resulting memory structure is against the loss of information. Even in the case of some nodes or links having been forgotten or not originally encoded, missing information can still be reconstructed on the basis of the existing and thematically connected facts. It is, therefore, to be expected that the number of errors made in reaching the learning criterion decreases with an increase in the amount of prior knowledge. The results presented in Table

(a) Unintegrated facts

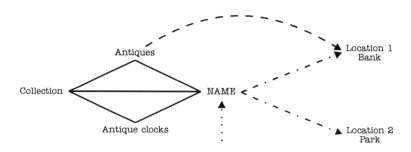

(b) Integrated facts

FIG. 6.5.   Representation of sentences referring to (a) experimental Condition 4 and (b) experimental Condition 2 in Table 6.3.

6.3, Part B are, without doubt, a confirmation of this prediction. Four times as many errors were made under the experimental condition without prior knowledge (Condition 5) as compared to the condition with the highest amount of prior knowledge (Condition 1).

Prediction 2.   The second prediction relates to the question of what influence prior knowledge has on the speed of the search process. Because it emanates from the concept nodes (here the person nodes), one must assume on the basis of the ACT model that its speed decreases to the extent that the number of links leading from concept nodes increases. The more links that lead from a concept node, the more prior knowledge is connected with it. As a result, with an increase in the amount of prior knowledge, there is also an increase in reaction time. Contrary to the expectations of ACT, by far the shortest reaction times were found under those experimental conditions with the highest amount of prior knowledge. J. R. Anderson (1981) was able to show that this effect is not due to the faster coding of the known (in contrast to the fictitious) names. Thus, this result can be regarded as a challenge to ACT. Even the more recent version, ACT* (J. R. Anderson, 1983a, c; J. R. Anderson & Pirolli, 1984), does not provide a satisfactory explanation of this result (section 6.3.2). Only the connectivity model (introduced in chap. 8) provides a basis to explain this and similar findings.

Prediction 3. The third — and for our purposes most interesting — prediction focuses on the fan effect. Here, in contrast to the second prediction, the assumption of indirect activation becomes relevant. The search process starts out at the concept node and spreads in two directions: in that part of the network representing prior knowledge and in that part representing the acquired locations. As these are also connected to the integrated facts of prior knowledge (Fig. 6.5b), they are not only activated primarily by concept nodes (direct activation), but also indirectly through prior knowledge (indirect activation).

In order to describe the quantitative relation between direct and indirect activation, we use Anderson's (1981) notation: Let n be the number of acquired locations, and let s be the strength of each link connecting the concept node (person node) with a location node. The combined strength of all the links of prior knowledge is indicated by K. Thus, the strength of all pathways leading from the concept node is equal to $K + ns$. According to ACT, the total strength of activation S $[S = K + ns]$ is divided among all the links leading from the concept node. Thus the amount of direct activation for a location node is equal to $s/(K + ns)$.

However, location nodes are not only activated directly, but also indirectly by an amount equal to fK (fraction of K). In other words, because the exact geometry of prior knowledge is not known, only rough estimates can be given for fK. Consequently, indirect activation is defined as $fK/(K + ns)$.

Adding direct and indirect activation results in $(fK + s)/(K + ns)$. The time t spreading activation needs to arrive at the location nodes is, therefore (cf. Equation 6.2):

$$t = (K + ns)/(fK + s). \tag{6.5}$$

In order to estimate reaction time (RT), a linear function is assumed, with a and b as regression constants:

$$RT = a + b [(K + ns)/(fK + s)]. \tag{6.6}$$

By converting Equation 6.6, we arrive at the following result:

$$RT = a + bK/(fK + s) + bns/(fK + s). \tag{6.7}$$

The third term $[bns/(fK + s)]$ of Equation 6.7 refers to the fan effect. As n is contained in the numerator, it follows that RT increases with an increasing number of acquired locations. At the same time, it must also be taken into consideration that K is contained in the denominator and that the fan effect, therefore, decreases as the amount of prior knowledge increases.

As the reaction times in Table 6.3, Part B indicate, the previous predictions apply to experimental Conditions 2–5 only. The more prior knowledge that is acquired, the more effective indirect activation becomes, and the smaller the fan effect. However, the results of experimental Condition 1 with the largest amount of prior knowledge contradict the predictions of ACT. Here, the fan effect is almost as large as the one in experimental Condition 5, in which no prior knowledge was represented.

6.4 THE SPEED OF SPREADING ACTIVATION IN ACT AND ACT*

It is one of those rare and exciting events when an established theory—like J.R. Anderson's ACT model, for example—must be modified as a result of a single but decisive experiment. Credit is due to Ratcliff and McKoon (1981) for drawing attention to the problematic nature of one of the central assumptions of the ACT model, namely that the time needed to activate a network link is 50 ms to 100 ms (J. R. Anderson, 1976). Ratcliff and McKoon demonstrated, with the help of a priming experiment, that the time for the spread of activation is so small as to be insignificant and probably accounts for only a few ms per network link.

Because of the great importance of this finding, the experimental procedure deserves a closer look. Before the priming experiment, subjects had to learn linearly structured sentences in which a concept of the first sentence is connected with a concept in the second sentence. This was then connected with one in the third sentence, and so on. The sentences, connected in such a way, resulted in a sequential-linear chain of events, as the following example shows (Ratcliff & McKoon, 1981, p. 455): "The researcher gave the sheriff a dig in the ribs" (N1 V N2). "The sheriff stared at the space ship" (N2 V N3). "The space ship carried a stranger" (N3 V N4). "The stranger pulled out a weapon" (N4 V N5). "The weapon vaporized a mountain" (N5 V N6). The symbols N1 . . . N6 stand for "Noun 1" . . . "Noun 6, " V stands for "verb." These sentences can be represented as a chain of hierarchical structures, as depicted in Fig. 6.6.

After these sentence chains had been acquired, the priming experiment was carried out. Before the target word, another word was presented as the prime, which was either at a great distance from the target (e.g., N1 as prime and N6 as target) or more closely situated (e.g., N5 as prime and N6 as target).

The subject's task was to judge whether or not the target appeared in the list. The most important independent variables were the stimulus-

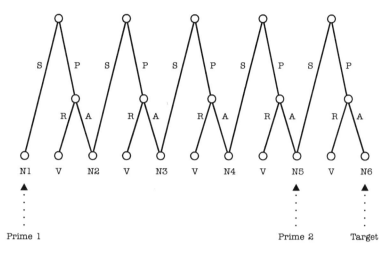

FIG. 6.6. Sentences which are linked by single nouns (N1, N2, . . . N6) create a strictly hierarchical structure. N = noun; V = verb; P = predicate; R = relation; A = argument. From Ratcliff and MCKoon, 1981, *Psychological Review*, *88*, p. 456. © 1981 by American Psychological Association. Reprinted by permission.

onset-asynchrony (the interval between the onset of prime and target) and the distance between the prime and target in the list of sentences. The most important dependent variable was reaction time. The results of these experiments show that priming effects (i.e., a decrease in reaction time caused by the prime) for prime-target pairs that were far away, as well as those that were not so far away, appeared simultaneously and after a stimulus-onset-asynchrony of only 100 ms. In assuming a rather slow activation of network links, the closest prime should become effective much sooner than the one that is further away. This, however, is not the case, as the results clearly show.

In the ACT* model, J. R. Anderson started out from the assumption of a very fast and almost simultaneous spread of activation (J. R. Anderson, 1983a, p. 28, 1983c, p. 265; J. R. Anderson & Pirolli, 1984, p. 792), which can be described by simultaneous linear equation systems (cf. detailed discussion of an example in section 8.4.2). As a consequence of this assumption, reverberating activity becomes effective: Each activated node sends activity back to that node by which it was first activated (e.g., J. R. Anderson, 1983c, p. 266). In addition, reverberating activation helps to strengthen intersections. This leads to a weakening of the fan effect.

Looking back over chap. 6 notice that nonstrictly hierarchical structures (Anderson, 1981) were introduced in order to explain the effects of integrated knowledge. This also holds true for the more recent version of ACT*. But despite the differences between ACT and ACT* (cf. the review in J. R. Anderson, 1983a, p. 22), the arguments discussed up to now remain as valid as ever, mainly because the explanation of the fan effect (according to Equations 6.1 and 6.2) is just as valid for ACT as it is for ACT*. Chapter 8 points out that, in order to overcome the paradox of retrieval interference, the assumption of hierarchical structures and those underlying Equations 6.1 and 6.2 must be rejected.

7 Strictly and Nonstrictly Hierarchical Models of Word Meaning

Models of word meaning and fact retrieval are generally concerned with different types of information. But with regard to representational assumptions, there are notable similarities. The following sections show that whereas the early models of word meaning were strictly hierarchical, such assumptions were abandoned in more recent models. Let us first, by way of comparison, point to the differences between models of word meaning and fact retrieval and then discuss the central issues governing word meaning.

7.1 A COMPARISON OF WORD MEANING AND FACT RETRIEVAL

Models of fact retrieval refer exclusively to those encoding structures that interconnect different concepts and are thus termed *large-scale models of memory* (E. E. Smith, 1978). In contrast, models of word meaning focus on the coding format of concepts. Consequently, they are called *microscale models of memory*. Most models assume that the format of a concept (i.e., the meaning of a word) can be explained by a structure of semantic features. But once this assumption is accepted, the question arises as to how different concepts are connected to each other. Thus, models of word meaning are also concerned with particular relations existing between concepts, such as super- and subordinate relations. Those relations connecting different features within a concept as well as those nonepisodic relations connecting different concepts were summed up under the term *innerconceptual relations* (Klix, 1977a, 1977b; Klix, Kukla, & Klein, 1976). They represent that type of knowledge that, even according to the strictest definition, can be regarded as semantic information. *Interconceptual relations*, on the other hand, refer to a very heterogeneous class of knowledge comprising episodic as well as linguistic and syntactic information. According to Klix's definition, the different types of information the two models refer to can easily be categorized into two groups: Models of word meaning refer primarily to innerconceptual information, whereas models of fact retrieval refer exclusively to interconceptual information.

To some extent this definition is similar to the distinction Tulving made between episodic and semantic information (Tulving, 1972, 1983). However, innerconceptual relations comprise only a small subset of that information that Tulving terms "semantic." Interconceptual relations, on the other hand, comprise not only episodic but also certain linguistic relations and thus semantic information as well. Based on interconceptual relations, models of fact retrieval may thus not be regarded as pure semantic memory models. Fact retrieval experiments always consist of a recognition task. Because this task examines knowledge acquired within a particular experimental context, subjects must retrieve contextual (i.e., episodic) information in order to arrive at a correct answer, that is, they have to judge whether a sentence presented during the recognition task is "old" (i.e., was presented during the preceding learning session) or "new" (i.e., was not presented during this learning session). Without knowing this contextual information (so characteristic of episodic information) it would be impossible to perform the recognition task.

In contrast to models of fact retrieval and regardless of the various definitions of semantic information, all of the different models of word meaning (cf. Fig. 5.1) may be regarded as pure semantic memory models. They are all confronted with the question as to how the meaning of concepts is represented in memory. Concepts form the basis of our permanent knowledge, which is stored exclusively in LTM.

Experimental paradigms for investigating fact retrieval and word meaning also differ fundamentally in the type of memory tasks they employ. Subjects participating in fact retrieval experiments must first learn those items on which they are to be tested later. In a typical experiment subjects are required to reach a 100% learning criterion before their recognition performance is tested. Thus, fact retrieval may not be considered a STM task. Furthermore, in comparison to semantic memory tasks, fact retrieval cannot be considered a pure LTM task. In contrast to semantic knowledge, which is at our disposal our entire lives, the information subjects have learned in a fact retrieval experiment will be forgotten after some time. Memory tasks that can be classified neither as pure STM nor as pure LTM tasks, are usually termed *nonpermanent memory tasks*. Subjects participating in semantic memory tasks are not required to learn the material on which they are being tested. Their task, for example, is to judge whether or not a certain concept (e.g., "eagle") belongs to a superordinate concept (e.g., *bird, animal, being*). What is being tested here is the ability to access information that is at the disposal of every adult. Semantic memory tasks, therefore, represent the purest conceivable form of LTM task.

7.2 CENTRAL TOPICS IN THE EXAMINATION OF WORD MEANING

There are only a few areas in memory psychology as well documented as models of word meaning (Hoffmann, 1986; Hollan, 1975; M. K. Johnson & Hasher, 1987; Johnson-Laird, 1987; Johnson-Laird, Herrmann, & Chaffin, 1984; Kintsch, 1980; McNamara & Sternberg, 1983; Medin & E. E. Smith, 1984; E. E. Smith, 1978; E. E. Smith & Medin, 1981). We can thus forego a description of these models and instead concentrate on some of the crucial issues concerning semantic memory research.

Almost all recent models of word meaning proceed from the basic assumption that the meaning of concepts can be derived from a structure of semantic components (Gentner, 1975). One of the reasons why this assumption, commonly known as the "decomposition of meaning" (or the "atomization of meaning"; Bolinger, 1965), has become so widely accepted may be due to the well-known work of Katz and Fodor (1963). Their theory is based on the notion that words are stored as "lexical items" in a kind of "dictionary," and their meaning can be described in terms of "semantic markers" and "distinguishers": "The semantic markers and distinguishers are the means by which we can decompose the sense of the lexical item into its atomic concepts, and thus exhibit the semantic structure in a dictionary entry and the semantic relations between dictionary entries" (p. 185).

The assumption of decomposition and the distinction between certain types of components are of crucial importance to any semantic memory theory. It comes as no surprise, therefore, that there are as many definitions of the term *semantic components* as there are names to describe it. Collins and Quillian (1969) spoke of "properties," E. E. Smith (E. E. Smith & Medin, 1981; E. E. Smith, Shoben, & Rips, 1974) and Kintsch (1974) of "semantic features," and Rosch (Mervis & Rosch, 1981) used the more general term "attributes." Glass and Holyoak (1975), on the other hand, borrowed the term semantic marker from Katz and Fodor. All of these terms apply to nouns only. The semantic components of verbs have been termed *semantic primitives*.

Different emphases are placed on the various types of semantic components. E. E. Smith et al. (1974) introduced the well-known distinction between defining and characteristic features (cf. McNamara & Sternberg, 1983). Klimesch (1981) distinguished between object (concrete) features, conceptual (abstract) features, and episodic features. Engelkamp (1987, 1991) stressed the importance of motor components and Hoffmann (1986; Hoffman & Zießler 1982) pointed to the differences between sensory and nonsensory features.

In order to remain consistent in our terminology, we employ the more general term *semantic features*. By this we simply mean that the meaning of a word can be decomposed into a structure of features.

When accepting the assumption of decomposition, it becomes clear that semantic codes are actually component codes. Semantic features are the components of semantic codes that represent the meaning of words. According to Assumption 2d in section 3.5, the activation of a component code inevitably leads to the activation of at least some of its components. Thus, within the framework of component codes, the assumption of decomposition is compulsory.

There are different views on whether or not the decomposition of word meaning is obligatory. Kintsch (1974, 1980) rejected this idea and assumed that the meaning of a concept can be retrieved without activating its semantic features. His argument was based on the notion that complex concepts with many features will be processed more slowly than less complex concepts with fewer features. Only if this assumption, which Gentner (1981) termed the complexity hypothesis, can be empirically supported, would Kintsch be inclined to accept that concepts are actually represented by features. Experimental results reported by Kintsch (1974, p. 219), however, suggest that complex concepts are not processed more slowly nor do they require more memory capacity than less complex concepts. Because of this failure to support the complexity hypothesis, Kintsch assumed that the meaning of a word is not represented by semantic features at all.

The debate on the decomposition and complexity hypotheses centers around the question of whether or not semantic information is represented by holistic or component codes. Rejecting the decomposition hypothesis means to neglect assumptions regarding the format of semantic codes and thus to assume a holistic format by default. In this case, the meaning of concepts must be defined by holistic prototypes, schemas, or templates (cf. the example in E. E. Smith & Medin, 1981, p. 130). In accepting the assumption of holistic codes, the complexity hypothesis is rendered meaningless.

By accepting the decomposition hypothesis, on the other hand, one must assume component codes. Now the assumptions regarding the type of semantic features and their structure must be considered. The decomposition hypothesis, however, does not offer a satisfactory answer to this question. If explicit assumptions on the structure of component codes are lacking, then the decomposition hypothesis is left ill-defined and must, by necessity, give way to the complexity hypothesis. The complexity hypothesis is based on the more or less implicit notion of a hierarchical coding structure. Hierarchical structures, however, lead to the prediction that with more complex semantic codes, activation and search processes become slower.

Chapter 8 shows that for interconnected structures the converse prediction holds true. Complex codes can be processed faster than less complex ones. The decomposition hypothesis must, therefore, not be rejected until it is ascertained whether or not the complexity hypothesis is correct. Thus, both hypotheses are interdependent (Fig. 7.1) and cannot be examined independently of each other.

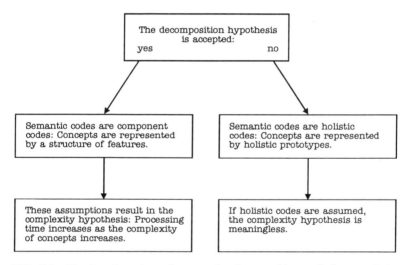

FIG. 7.1. The interdependence between the decomposition and the complexity hypotheses.

The following section demonstrates the apparent persuasiveness of the assumption of a hierarchical coding format for semantic information. Chapter 9, however, shows that even a hierarchy of concepts can be represented by an interconnected structure of semantic features.

7.3 STRICTLY HIERARCHICAL STRUCTURES OF WORD MEANING

Kintsch (1980) correctly pointed out that the assumption of a hierarchical concept structure is more than 2,000 years old. Aristotle (Topika, book 1, chap. 4, 5, 15; in Rolfes, 1918) dealt with the logical definition of words and introduced a semantic hierarchy in which each genus is divided into subgenera. According to Aristotle, the most important feature of a concept is the way it refers to its natural superordinate concept or genus (genus proximum; cf. the interconceptual features of Hoffmann, 1986, or the abstract features of Klimesch, 1981). For example, the concept "man" is best described as belonging to the genus *sensuous being*. The proposition "humans are living beings," on the other hand, is too general, as plants are also living beings.

But Aristotle also distinguished between other important properties that need to be considered in the classification of a concept, namely *Proprium* and *Akzidenz*. Proprium stands for those features characteristic of only one particular concept, but not for other concepts of the same genus. E. E. Smith et al. (1974) termed these features "defining." Thus, for example, the feature "is capable of learning grammar (i.e., reading and writing)" applies only to "human" but not to "bird" or any other member of the genus *living being*.

Aristotle also considered those conceptual properties that do not fall under the strict definition of Proprium and are thus not defining in the narrow sense of the term. The feature "has two legs" distinguishes "human" from "dog" or "hare," but not from "bird." There is an obvious similarity between this proposal and the definition of characteristic features by E. E. Smith et al. (1974). Although characteristic for humans, the feature "has two legs" is not a defining feature, as birds as well as other living beings also have two legs.

Those features summarized under the term Akzidenz are neither a proprium nor a genus and only describe some transitory properties such as "sleeping" or "sitting." Figure 7.2 gives an example of a strictly hierarchical network used by Kintsch (1980) to explain Aristotle's classification hierarchy.

As Fig. 7.2 shows, the meaning of a word is determined by its genus as well as by a variety of specific properties. Aristotle's theory of word meaning can thus be described as a semantic feature theory. It bears an obvious similarity with well-known memory models (Collins & Quillian, 1969, 1970; E. E. Smith et al., 1974).

Katz and Fodor's (1963) semantic theory, which has been so influential in psychological research, is also based on the assumption of a strictly hierarchical structure. The question raised in their theory concerns the meaning of morphemes and the interpretation of different grammatical structures. Katz and Fodor assumed that the meaning of morphemes is stored in a dictionary, and that projection rules guarantee access to the lexical items. Projection rules can, therefore, be regarded as an important link connecting syntactic and semantic information. The term *dictionary*

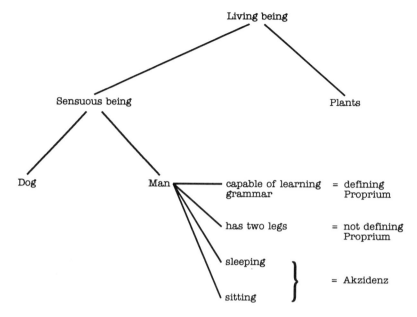

FIG. 7.2. An early feature model of word meaning: The semantic hierarchy of Aristotle. Adapted from Kintsch in *Attention and Performance* (R. S. Nickerson, Ed.), 1980. © 1980 by Lawrence Erlbaum Associates. Reprinted with permission.

refers to what is essentially known as semantic memory. Both terms are often used synonymously. Because each spoken or written sentence must first be analyzed phonemically and graphemically, it can be assumed that each dictionary entry is first analyzed according to syntactic and grammatical characteristics. Thus, at the beginning of the lexical entry, there are so-called grammatical markers indicating the word group (nouns, verbs, adjectives, etc.) to which a certain lexical item belongs. The different meanings of lexical items are represented by two different types of features — semantic markers and distinguishers. Semantic markers are general features common to all lexical items located on any given lower level of the conceptual hierarchy; distinguishers, on the other hand, give a specific meaning to each lexical item that distinguishes it from competing meanings. The famous "bachelor" example in Fig. 7.3 illustrates what is to be understood by grammatical and semantic markers as well as by distinguishers.

We thus see that the well-known and influential work of Collins and Quillian (1969) did not actually introduce the first hierarchical semantic memory model. Theirs, however, was the first model to undergo a systematic experimental examination.

Collins and Quillian's model is, like HAM, ACT, or ACT*, based on a

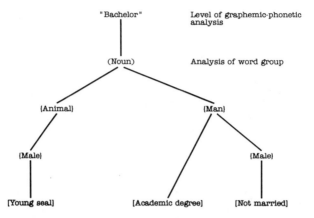

FIG. 7.3. The "bachelor" example,. Different types of parentheses denote grammatic markers ( ), semantic markers { }, and distinguishers [ ]. From Katz and Fodor, 1963, *Language*, *39*, p. 186. © 1963 by Linguistic Society of America. Adapted with permission.

simulation program, the Teachable Language Comprehender (TLC). It exhibits a strictly hierarchical structure surprisingly similar to Aristotle's classification structure. However, Collins and Quillian decomposed the meaning of any concept (even those of abstract superordinate concepts) into features. Each feature is stored only in the highest possible place in the conceptual hierarchy. Figure 7.4, for example, shows that the feature "fly" is stored with "bird" but not with "canary" or "ostrich."

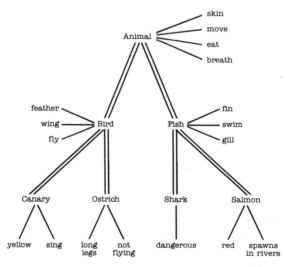

FIG. 7.4. A strictly hierarchical semantic network as suggested by Collins and Quillian, 1969, *Journal of Verbal Learning and Verbal Behavior*, *8*, p. 241. © 1969 by Academic Press. Adapted with permission.

The classic approaches of Aristotle and Katz and Fodor share two important features with Collins and Quillian's model: (a) the strictly hierarchical structure, and (b) the assumption that the meaning of a concept can be defined by a set of features. It is the latter assumption that has often been criticized (cf. Fodor, Garret, Walker, & Parkes, 1980). Chapter 9 deals with these questions in more detail. Here we want to show how strictly hierarchical models succeed in explaining experimental results.

7.3.1 The Experimental Paradigm of the Type "Is X a Y?" and Its Most Important Results

In testing the predictions of semantic memory models, three different types of experimental paradigms are used: (a) sentence verification (e.g., Collins & Quillian, 1969; E. E. Smith et al. 1974), (b) semantic judgment (Klimesch, 1981, 1982a), and (c) priming paradigms (section 9.7). In spite of the differences between these paradigms, there is one essential characteristic common to all semantic memory experiments. They all test relations either between different concepts (such as super- or subordinate relationships) or between a particular concept and its features.

In sentence verification experiments, these relations are expressed in the form of sentences (e.g., "A canary is an animal") and subjects have the task of judging the validity of this semantic relation by responding with "yes" or "no." In semantic judgment tasks, on the other hand, a superordinate concept (e.g., *animal*) is presented first, followed by the presentation of a series of different concepts ("canary," "car," "shark," etc.). An alternative way of presenting this is to show the subjects concept pairs (e.g., "canary" — "eagle," "car" — "shark"). They then have to judge whether or not each concept belongs to the appropriate superordinate concept. In priming experiments, the presentation of stimulus pairs is obligatory. Here, one is not only interested in the effects of semantic relations, but also in the duration of the interstimulus interval separating the presentation of the two stimuli.

Sentence verification paradigms are problematic insofar as not only semantic but also syntactic relations vary. Because only semantic relations are important here, a possible confounding of syntactical and semantic relations is an uncontrollable source of misinterpretations. This is possibly the reason why in more recent research, semantic judgment and priming experiments have been preferred to sentence verification paradigms.

All of the three paradigms focus on semantic relations existing between two concepts or semantic features termed "X" and "Y" in the following. Another characteristic common to these paradigms is that the validity of a semantic relation can be judged only by responding with "yes" or "no". The dependent measure is reaction (verification) time.

Table 7.1 shows the design and the most important results of the well-known experiment by Collins and Quillian (1969), which is of the type

TABLE 7.1
An Example of a Semantic Decision Task of the Type "Is X a Y?"

A. Experimental Design
A set of 224 sentences is presented. Each sentence states a semantic relationship between two concepts X and Y or a concept X and a feature x. For half of the sentences the semantic relationship is true, for the other half false. Subjects respond by pressing a yes or no response key. The dependent measure is RT.

B. Results							
Level in Concept Hierarchy	X		Y	RT (ms)	X		x	RT (ms)
0	Salmon	---	Salmon	1,000	Salmon	---	Spawn	1,305
1	Salmon	---	Fish	1,165	Salmon	---	Gill	1,385
2	Salmon	---	Animal	1,240	Salmon	---	Skin	1,465

Note: From Collins and Quillian, *Journal of Verbal Learning and Verbal Behaviour, 9*, p. 244. © 1969 by Academic Press. Adapted with permission.

"Is X a Y?" The results are straightforward and can easily be interpreted in terms of the memory network, as depicted in Fig. 7.4. An examination of the respective means in Table 7.1 shows that reaction time increases as the number of links that need to be activated in the conceptual hierarchy increases. Therefore, the same rules seem to apply to semantic memory as to fact retrieval: The more complex the memory network, the longer the decision times.

7.4 NONSTRICTLY HIERARCHICAL MODELS OF WORD MEANING

Collins and Quillian's model (1969) was criticized by Rips, Shoben, and E. E. Smith (1973), among others, for not being able to explain why, for example, "eagle" can be recognized and classified more easily as a bird than "penguin." In other words, how can strictly hierarchical networks explain typicality effects?

This and similar objections led Collins and E. F. Loftus (1975) to revise their model and to enlarge the number of assumptions. The most important of the 13 assumptions refers to the structure of semantic representation: "The . . . semantic network is organized along the lines of semantic similarity. The more properties two concepts have in common, the more links there are between the two nodes . . . and the more closely related are the concepts" (p. 411). Here, for the first time, the concept of semantic similarity or relatedness is systematically applied to describe semantic relations, and the notion of hierarchy is pushed into the background.

The Collins and Loftus model is the first connectivity model of semantic encoding. It enables predictions that were denied by the strictly hierarchical model of Collins and Quillian (1969), such as the hypothesis that the more features two concepts share, the faster they can be compared with each other. Collins and E. F. Loftus' (1975) research has led to a new approach that refers to the internal structure of concepts and the relation between different semantic features within a concept. This issue is still of crucial importance in semantic memory research (Johnson-Laird, 1987; Malt & E. E. Smith, 1984; McNamara & Sternberg, 1983; Medin & E. E. Smith, 1984; Rosch, 1978).

Despite its originality and persuasive plausibility, Collins and Loftus' spreading activation theory has not gained nearly as much importance as models of fact retrieval such as ACT. One of the reasons for this is that almost any prediction can be derived from the 13 assumptions underlying this theory. As an example, consider a task of the type "Is X a Y?" in which a subject has to judge a superordinate relationship (e.g., "Is an eagle a bird?"). Assumption 8 in Collins and Loftus' theory states that concepts may be compared on the basis of their features. On the other hand, Assumption 9 postulates that the discovery of a superordinate concept link suffices to make a semantic decision. Both assumptions can, therefore, be arbitrarily interchanged when trying to predict or explain the results of a semantic judgment task.

Chapter 9 deals in detail with the theoretical and empirical foundation of the connectivity model put forward by Klimesch (1987). It shows that the assumption of special superordinate concept links is superfluous and misleading (section 9.2.4).

Distributed memory models are also based on the assumption of inter-connectedness (J. A. Anderson & Hinton, 1981, Knapp & J. A. Anderson, 1984). These models, however, can only be partially applied to semantic memory. Furthermore, and most importantly, they do not enable clear predictions regarding the speed of search and judgment processes in semantic networks (section 12.1).

8 The Connectivity Model

Our discussion of hierarchical network models has shown that the speed of search processes decreases as the complexity of networks increases. This amounts to what is known as the paradox of retrieval interference: The more information stored in memory, the slower it works. However, we have demonstrated that not only theoretical considerations, but also experimental findings (section 6.3; chap. 9) refute the general validity of this notion.

Various suggestions were made on how to overcome the interference paradox. These refer in part to the modification of structural assumptions and to the definition of new processing assumptions. Strictly hierarchical structures were modified and gave way to nonstrictly hierarchical structures (J. R. Anderson, 1981; Collins & E. F. Loftus, 1975). New processing assumptions, those regarding indirect and reverberating activation, were introduced, mainly by J. R. Anderson (1981, 1983a, 1983c). ACT* is based primarily on the concept of reverberating activation. Each activated node reflects back onto the node(s) from which information was received. This principle may explain why nodes with many links (i.e., nodes rich in information) are retrieved faster than nodes with fewer links. This interpretation, however, not only leads to new problems, as is shown in this chapter, but also threatens the empirically well-grounded explanation of the fan effect.

In order to solve these problems, an alternative model already suggested elsewhere (Klimesch, 1987) — the connectivity model — is outlined in this chapter. It is founded on three basic assumptions: on the structural assumption of interconnected codes (see Assumption A, section 8. 2. 1), on the processing assumptions of indirect activation, and on the unlimited capacity of spreading activation (summarized under Assumption B, section 8. 2. 2). The combination of these assumptions results in the prediction that the extent of indirect activation increases with the number of interconnected nodes. Here the basic idea alleges that interconnected structures allow input activation to increase significantly, thereby boosting processing speed. The connectivity model will therefore enable us to explain how processing speed varies as a function of the degree of complexity and the extent of interconnectedness. Both of these factors operate together to reduce processing time.

8.1 STRUCTURAL ASSUMPTIONS: INTERCONNECTEDNESS AS A GENERAL PRINCIPLE FOR THE ENCODING OF SEMANTIC INFORMATION IN LTM

We proceed from the basic assumption that interconnected facts are stored in LTM. By this we mean that each code is represented not in isolation from, but instead in direct relation to, other codes in LTM. The more links there are between codes, the better the information contained in these codes can be integrated into LTM. Integrated facts can best be represented by interconnected structures, whereas nonintegrated (i.e., isolated) facts are best represented by strictly hierarchical structures.

It would be wrong to assume that our memory is constructed exclusively from interconnected codes. The fan effect, which can be explained in terms of strictly hierarchical structures, contradicts this assumption. We can assume, however, that nonintegrated codes or strictly hierarchical structures form an exception to the general principle of integrated storage. ACT proceeded from the exact opposite assumption. Here, the general principle was strictly hierarchical coding, and the nonstrictly hierarchical networks that are similar to interconnected structures were the exception. The assumption regarding strictly hierarchical structures appears to be justified, especially in those cases in which new information—which has not yet been interconnected with existing knowledge or cannot be interconnected or integrated—has been learned. This is precisely the case with subjects participating in a fact retrieval experiment. They must learn new nonintegrated facts that are in no way related to their previous knowledge.

This unusual situation corresponds to what is ordinarily called *rote learning*. In rote learning no emphasis is placed on comprehension, which in our context means interconnecting the acquired items. This comes close to the everyday experience reflected in the following definition of rote learning from the *Oxford English Dictionary*: "Knowledge got by repetition, from unintelligent memory." Here, the loss or forgetting of only one component (a node or link) of the network leads to the loss of stored information. In interconnected structures, on the other hand, there are more links connecting one node with others and thus these structures can be used in reconstruction. Only interconnected but not hierarchical structures bring about the necessary redundancy that enables the reconstruction of lost or forgotten information.

8.1.1 Interconnected Structures and the Inadequacy of the Computer Metaphor

Our criticism of hierarchical network models brings us to almost the same conclusion we arrived at in our criticism of forgetting theories. In chap. 3 it was the implicit assumption of holistic codes that completely agreed with the computer metaphor. A similar conclusion was drawn in chaps. 5 and 6, where we considered hierarchical memory models. In the latter case it was the assumption of strictly hierarchical structures, whereas in the former it was the assumption of holistic codes on which the computer metaphor was based.

Holistic and strictly hierarchical codes are by no means identical, although they do have one important feature in common: In both cases the contents of the codes are isolated, that is, they are not related to each other. Instead, they are only indirectly connected by common links.

If memory were to contain isolated, holistic, and/or strictly hierarchical codes, then it would be a collection of nonintegrated pieces of information. Memory content would be similar to that of computers in that it would be built on clearly distinguishable and nonoverlapping codes, which are not connected to each other except by means of their addresses.

From the very beginning, memory psychologists were puzzled by the phenomenon of association, which is a powerful process enabling us to detect overlapping commonalities, even with facts that appear to be heterogeneous and unrelated. If one had to explain these processes in terms of how conventional computers work, one would be forced to rely on processing rather than on structural assumptions. Once again, this is because the contents of locations are not related to each other. Accordingly, any algorithm designed to explain associative processes must rely on processing assumptions focusing on the means by which addresses are accessed. As we already know, such an algorithm would inevitably lead to the paradox of retrieval interference.

The phenomenon of retrieval interference constitutes a paradox within the context of human memory. However, within the context of the computer metaphor it is a basic principle by which information is processed. Computers with parallel processing capabilities are to some extent an exception (connection machine, Gabriel, 1986; Hillis, 1985). Here, although large amounts of information can be processed without deceleration, there is still no way of explaining why large amounts of information can be processed faster than small amounts.

8.1.2 Interconnected Structures and the Question of an Efficient Storage

E. E. Smith, Adams, and Schorr (1978) were undoubtedly correct in stating that the high efficiency of human memory is due to an especially efficient structuring of the information stored within it. We, however — unlike E. E. Smith et al. (1978) or J. R. Anderson (1976, 1983a) — do not assume that high memory efficiency can be primarily described by hierarchical structures. We do assume that interconnected structures enable the high efficiency and performance of memory.

When the following four criteria have been met there is efficient storage:

1. Each piece of information may only be stored at one location in memory.
2. The information relevant to the goal of the search process must be quickly retrievable.
3. It should be possible either to form connections between relevant pieces of information easily, or these should already exist.
4. The speed of the search process may not systematically decrease with an increasing amount of permanently stored information.

Strictly and not strictly hierarchical models are not capable of meeting Criterion (4) or to a certain extent even Criterion (2). The theoretical analysis in this chapter shows that the assumption of interconnected structures meets the necessary criteria for efficient storage.

8.2 BASIC ASSUMPTIONS AND PREDICTIONS UNDERLYING THE CONNECTIVITY MODEL

The connectivity model is based on three central assumptions: the representational assumption about connectivity, and on the previously mentioned processing assumptions. The central prediction that search processes run faster as more information is stored may generally be derived from these assumptions. By doing this, we proceed from the notion that the duration of search processes depends on the speed of indirect spreading activation. It also depends on the fact that the amount as well as the speed of indirect activation increases with the number of activated nodes or coding components.

In discussing the connectivity model, we distinguish between qualitative and quantitative levels of description. This section deals with the qualitative level and forms the basis for the next section, where we discuss the quantitative approach. Here we focus on the central assumptions about connectivity and indirect activation (Assumptions A and B) in their relation to those assumptions regarding the type and duration of search processes (Assumptions C and D).

It should be emphasized that these four assumptions have not been conceived as an axiomatic system. Instead, their compilation was governed by didactic considerations. This was done in an attempt to give a clear and simple presentation of the connectivity model and to enable an understandable comparison of our assumptions with those of ACT and ACT*. In order to achieve this didactic objective, which is only important for the qualitative description of the model, it is necessary to group several elementary albeit related assumptions into more general assumptions. The four assumptions are to be understood as a guide in the description of the connectivity model. Section 8.3 provides a detailed discussion on the diverse elementary assumptions.

8.2.1 Assumption A: The Structure of Codes in LTM

Assumption A determines that codes stored in LTM are represented by components (chap. 4) and the structure connecting the individual components with each other is not hierarchical but interconnected. The assumption of connectivity contradicts the previously discussed memory theories (ACT and ACT*) and means that the components of a code are stored as integrated and not isolated information components.

The components of an interconnected code are connected to a source node, which may function as an access point for search processes originating in STM. The source node — represented by an "x" in Fig. 8.1 — is part of an interconnected code and is directly connected to all code components by a link. Any node connected to all of the remaining n-1 nodes of the same code may serve as an access node.

8.2.2 Assumption B: Indirect Activation and the Inadmissability of Reverberating Activation

The assumption of indirect activation is derived from Assumption A. It means that activation originating in a source node flows to connected nodes, which in turn send convergent activation back to the the source node. Thus, for indirect activation to occur, the following three criteria must be met: (a) one or more nodes of a network must be activated by convergent pathways; (b) those activation processes leading to convergent activation must stem from the *same* source node; and (c) they must meet simultaneously or almost simultaneously within a critical time span $t(k)$ in order to enable the accumulation of convergent activations (Assumption 2 in section 8.3.3). Indirect activation can only become effective in interconnected structures, but never in hierarchical structures.

Indirect activation should not be confused with reverberating activation or preactivation. Reverberating activation means that activity flows back from each activated node in the opposite direction to the original flow of activation. The assumption of reverberating activation is excluded from the framework of the connectivity model (Assumption 5 in section 8.3.3). The reason for this is a consequence of Assumption C, which indicates conditions under which search processes are terminated.

The term *preactivation*, on the other hand, is used if activation processes meet and intersect with each other, provided they originated from *different* source nodes. Thus, processes of preactivation only play a role when activation processes proceed from two or more source nodes (section 8.6).

8.2.3 Assumption C: The Duration of the Search Process

The search process begins with the activation of one or more source nodes and ends as soon as activation flows back to one of these nodes. How many source nodes are activated depends on the search goal (sections 8.6, 8.7.1). If it consists in searching only one single code, then the activation of a single source node will suffice. However, if common pathways between several codes are to be found, then several source nodes need to be activated. The following section starts with the discussion of simple search processes that spread from one single source node.

If reverberating activation were effective, then the search process would be terminated straight after the activation of the first node: Activation would flow back from this node to the source node and the search process would end even before the first results were in. Consequently, Assumption C and the assumption of reverberating activity cannot be effectively combined with each other.

Indirect activation flowing back to the source node indicates a successful search process, and thus provides evidence of a positive result. The amount of indirect activation corresponds to the amount of positive evidence: the more indirect activation flows back, the greater the "echo" of the search process and thus the greater the evidence that a positive result has been achieved. In the following, let I stand for the extent of indirect activation and $t(I)$ for the length of a search process with a positive result (i.e., the time elapsed, before indirect activation flows back).

If within a critical waiting period $t(wI)$ no activation flows back to any of the source nodes at which the search process originated, this would indicate an unsuccessful search, that is, the sought-after information cannot be found. In this case the search process is terminated after time $t(wI)$ has elapsed.

Now a simple but important conclusion can be drawn from Assumption C: Search processes showing positive results must terminate sooner than comparable search processes showing negative results. Thus, $t(I) < t(wI)$. Only under this precondition can Assumption C be considered consistent.

8.2.4 Assumption D: The Speed with Which the Result of a Search Process Can Be Processed

The cognitive process of retrieval consists not only of the search process, but also of the evaluation of its results. For example, it must be evaluated whether or not the outcome of a search corresponds to original expectations or to other knowledge.

Assumption D assumes that the extent of positive evidence I not only indirectly facilitates the speed of further processing via short search times, but also in a more direct way: The greater the positive evidence I, the faster the result can continue to be processed.

8.2.5 The Most Important Predictions of the Connectivity Model

Assumptions A, B, and C form the basis for the following crucial predictions of the network model. Assumption D will be dealt with in greater detail in section 8.8. This section considers only those predictions referring to the interaction between the complexity of a network and the speed of the search process. We distinguish between two predictions:

Prediction 1. In interconnected structures, the extent of indirect activation (I) increases with the number of nodes or components n.

Prediction 2. In interconnected structures, the speed of the search process increases and time $t(I)$ decreases with the number of nodes or components n.

Just how these two predictions are derived from the assumptions underlying the connectivity model is discussed within the framework of the quantitative description. However, before going into detail, consider an outline of the general procedure shown in the example depicted in Fig. 8.1.

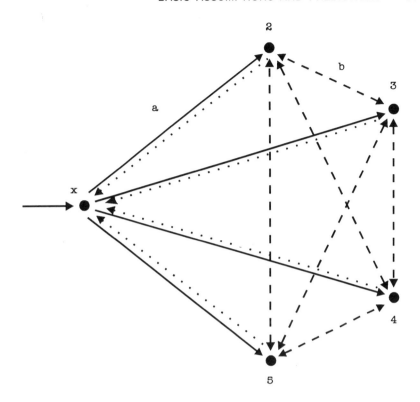

FIG. 8.1. A completely interconnected component code with 5 components, comprising 4 feature nodes (2, 3, 4, and 5) and 1 source node (x). A search process, initiated in STM, has direct access only to the source node (x). From here, activation spreads in three stages. In the first stage (bold lines), activation flows to all of the feature nodes (2, 3, 4, and 5). In the second stage (dashed lines), each feature node sends activation to neighboring feature nodes. Then, in the third stage (dotted lines), activation spreads back to the source node (x).

This example shows a completely interconnected component code with 5 components (nodes) and 10 different links: Each of the five nodes is connected to every other node by a link. Because all nodes are connected with each other, each node can take on the function of a source node (Assumption A). We can, therefore, assume that the search process can begin at any node (indicated by "x" in Fig. 8.1) and from there it can encompass all the other nodes of the network (see the definition of component codes in sect. 3.5). The crucial idea in all subsequent considerations has already been determined by Assumptions B and C: The search process ends with a positive result as soon as indirect activation flows back to that node where the search process originated. In other words, the search process is terminated, if a correspondingly strong "echo" is found in memory.

Now the close interdependence between Assumptions A, B, C, and D becomes clear. Indirect activation occurs only in interconnected, but not in fanlike hierarchical structures. Without indirect activation, however, it is impossible within the confines of our model to determine the duration of a search processes.

This idea can be illustrated using the following examples: If the five components of the code in Fig. 8.1 were not interconnected, then the links represented by dashed lines could be omitted, and only the fanlike structure represented by the continuous links would remain. Although activation originating from the source node x would travel along the continuous links, it would nevertheless terminate at nodes 2-5. In this case—which was already discussed in detail in the framework of ACT—the result (according to Equations 6.2 and 6.4) would be that activation time increases with the number of nodes. Even if we were to allow for the assumption of reverberating activation, it would still be impossible to explain why (according to Prediction 2) activation time should decrease when the number of nodes increases (see the detailed discussion in section 8.4.2). These considerations underscore the importance of Assumption A. However, the situation changes fundamentally if we start out from the assumption of interconnected codes. Now activation spreads out across nodes 2-5 and flows in the form of indirect activation back to the source node.

8.3 THE QUANTITATIVE BASIS OF THE CONNECTIVITY MODEL

The assumptions discussed in the previous section are still too general to enable conclusive predictions. However, this is possible if processing Assumption B is specified in such a way as to allow for a quantitative evaluation of spreading activation. Thus, we set out from the following definitions and processing assumptions:

8.3.1 Definitions Underlying Assumption A: Completely and Partially Interconnected Structures

A structure is completely interconnected, if—in addition to source node x— any one of the n nodes is connected with all the remaining $n - 1$ nodes (cf. Fig. 8.1). The number of links m in completely interconnected structures can be determined according to Equation 8.1:

$$m = [n(n - 1)]/2 \tag{8.1}$$

Thus, a structure is partially interconnected if the source node x is connected via links to all other $n - 1$ nodes, and if each of the $n - 1$ nodes

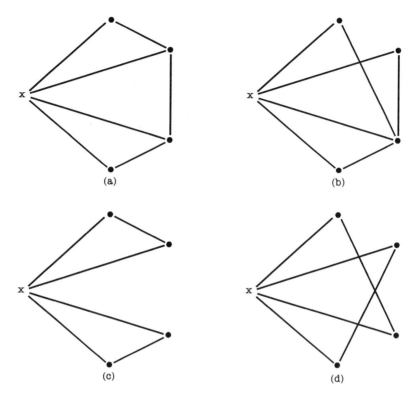

FIG. 8.2. The structure of partially interconnected codes must be closed as in (a) or (b) and must not disintegrate into separate substructures as in (c) or (d) which are not interconnected with each other.

is connected to the remaining $n - 2$ nodes in such a way that a "closed" network is created. The network of a code is closed if all the $n - 1$ nodes are directly or indirectly connected with each other by a pathway that does not pass through x (cf. Figs. 8.2a and b with Figs. 8.2c and d). A code is interconnected if it meets the requirements for partially interconnected structures.

Because we assume that only interconnected codes are stored in LTM, those not corresponding to the previous definition (Figs. 8.2c, d) are excluded from any further consideration. In doing so, we are not proceeding from an arbitrary criterion, but instead from the conclusions derived from the assumptions discussed earlier. This is because Assumptions B and C are only meaningful if the result of a search process is unambiguous and if it is clear in which code indirect activation originated. Structures like those depicted in Figs. 8.2c and d, however, actually consist of two completely interconnected codes that share a common source node. In this case, indirect activation spreading from both codes to the common source node would accumulate, thereby making it impossible to determine the extent of activation of each code. Therefore, each code must have only one source node (Fig. 8.3).

8.3.2 The Connectivity Model and Hierarchical Nodes

Surprisingly, the fact that the connectivity model can also be applied to noninterconnected or even hierarchical structures by no means contradicts the assumptions underlying our model. In order to understand this, it is necessary to keep in mind that the definition of interconnectedness applies only to the internal structure (i.e., the format) of LTM codes. Consequently, this definition in no way determines how different codes are interconnected. Structures interconnecting different codes may well be hierarchical, as can be seen in Fig. 8.3.

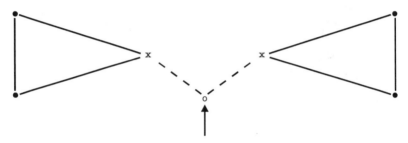

FIG. 8.3. Interconnected nodes may be linked by a hierarchical structure (dashed line). A node which is only linked by hierarchical connections (node o) is termed *hierarchical node*. Hierarchical nodes serve as access nodes for a concept with multiple meanings (cf. the concept *move* in Fig. 10.4).

However, a hierarchical node (like the one depicted in the bottom of Fig. 8.3 or in Fig. 10.4) is considered a passive node, which transmits activation only if it is used as an access node. Activation arriving at a hierarchical node may accumulate there with other activation, but will never be transmitted to other nodes (see section 10.1.4 for an example).

The connectivity model must also be capable of describing search processes that take place between different codes (sections 8.6 and 8.7.1). Thus, it is a necessary precondition that the processing assumptions of the connectivity model apply to all structures, and not only to those that are interconnected.

8.3.3 On the Specification of Processing Assumption B

1. Any activated node can pass on the entire amount of activation to each of the links leading from that node. Therefore, this assumption is

termed the "unlimited capacity of spreading activation." Assumption 1 describes a discrete and discontinuous spreading activation process. The only exception is that hierarchical nodes pass on activation only if they are used as access nodes.

2. A node remains active only within a critical time span $t(k)$. If an activated node does not receive any further activation within $t(k)$, then its activity is set at 0. If activation processes converge at different times but within $t(k)$, we speak of "simultaneous" activation of this node.

3. If a node is activated, then the resulting activation is equal to the sum of the original and newly received activity.

4. Each link can be activated in both directions simultaneously.

5. Assumption 4, however has the restriction that reverberating activity is inadmissable. This means that each link, after it has passed on its activation to another node, cannot be activated by that same node in the opposite direction within time $1/sh$. Let s be the amount of activation transported by this link, and let h stand for an inhibiting ($h < 1$) or disinhibiting ($h > 1$) factor. For simplicity we assume that h equals unity ($h = 1$). In this case the duration of inhibition is reduced to $1/s$.

6. Time $t(i)$, needed to activate a node i, is the reciprocal value of that amount of activation $s(i)$ with which the link leading to this node was activated: $t(i) = 1/s(i)$.

7. All links and nodes show the same strength when in a "neutral" state, that is, in the absence of preactivation and inhibition. Different strengths for both links and nodes are the result of the spreading activation processes.

Based on these assumptions we can show that there are two important rules governing the relationship between the number of nodes n and the amount of indirect activation I. First, the more nodes a code comprises, the more indirect activation I spreads back and, second, the faster it accumulates at the source node x.

8.3.4 On Deducing Prediction 1: The Extent of Indirect Activation Increases with Complexity

In interconnected structures we must differentiate between three different stages of spreading activation. In calculating this process, we once again turn to the example in Fig. 8.1.

8.3.4.1 Activation Stage 1: Completely Interconnected Structures. In the first stage, all $n - 1$ nodes that are directly connected to source node x are — according to Assumptions 1 and 7 — activated by x with amount a (see the boldly drawn links in Fig. 8.1). We thereby assume that a is that amount of activation received by source node x. At the end of the first activation stage, each of the $n - 1$ nodes (nodes 2-5) is activated with a. According to Assumption 6, the duration of the first activation stage is equal to $1/a$.

Because we have rejected the assumption of reverberating activation, no activation returns from the $n - 1$ nodes to x. The reason for this lies in Assumption 5: A link, in passing on its activation to the next node, cannot be activated in the opposite direction by this same node within $t = 1/s$ (here equal to $1/a$). According to Assumption 6, the $n - 1$ nodes are activated after $t = 1/a$. Thus, after this point none of the $n - 1$ nodes is capable of sending activation back to x during an additional time interval of $1/a$.

8.3.4.2 Activation Stage 2: Completely Interconnected Structures. In the second stage, because of Assumption 5, activation flows from each of the $n - 1$ nodes to all $n - 2$ nodes (see the links represented by dashed lines in Fig. 8.1). Now each one of these links is activated in both directions (Assumption 4). We assume that in the second stage the amount of activation equals b. Thus, each of the $n - 1$ nodes is activated by all of the remaining $n - 2$ nodes with amount b. The sum of activation at each of the $n - 1$ nodes is, according to Assumption 3, equal to $b(n - 2)$. Depending on whether or not we consider a dampening function during the course of spreading activation, the value of b will either be equal to a (in the case of the dampening function not being effective) or less than a (in the case of the dampening function being effective). It should be noted, however, that the value assumed by b is of no importance in deducing Predictions 1 and 2 (see the discussion of Equation 8.2). If we assume that the $n - 1$ nodes are still activated with amount a (i.e., that up to now $t(k)$ has not been exceeded; Assumption 2), then this value is added to activation in Stage 2. At the end of the second stage, therefore, activation at each of the $n - 1$ nodes is equal to $a + b(n - 2)$.

Now let us once again consider the role of Assumption 5. As mentioned earlier, after Stage 1 — which lasts for a time span equal to $t = 1/a$ — no activation can flow back to the source node within an additional interval of $1/a$ time units. Thus, only after time $t = 1/a + 1/a$ has elapsed can nodes 2-5 send back activation to x. The time it takes to finish Stage 2 is equal to $1/b$. Consequently, a total of $1/a + 1/b$ time units have elapsed since x passed on its activation. Because $1/a + 1/b$ is greater than or equal to $1/a + 1/a$, the links leading from the $n - 1$ nodes to node x have already been disinhibited by the time the second stage is finished and the third and final stage begins. On the other hand, at the end of the second activation stage, with all $n - 1$ nodes having been activated by the remaining $n - 2$ nodes, no activation can flow back to these $n - 2$ nodes.

8.3.4.3 Activation Stage 3: Completely Interconnected Structures In the third stage an amount equal to $a + b(n - 2)$ flows from each of the $n -$

1 nodes back to source node x. Because two stages have already expired since the beginning of activation, assume that $t(k)$ has been exceeded (Assumption 2) and therefore that node x has in the meantime lost all of its original activation. At the end of the third stage, the source node is indirectly activated by $[a + b(n - 2)]$ $(n - 1)$. In any completely interconnected structure having three or more nodes with $m = [n(n - 1)]/2$ links, the amount of indirect activation I can be determined by the following equation:

$$I = [a + b(n - 2)](n - 1). \tag{8.2}$$

Considering that a and b remain constant and do not vary with n, it becomes clear that I depends only on one variable, the number of nodes: The more components a completely interconnected structure comprises, the more indirect activation I will flow back to the source node x.

Equation 8.2 confirms Prediction 1. At the same time we can also observe that Prediction 1 holds true even if we vary the values for $t(k)$ and b. Although in both cases the absolute amount of I would change, this does not hamper the predicted relationship between I and n.

This relationship is valid for both completely and partially interconnected structures, as is shown in Fig. 8.4. This figure gives an example of a partially interconnected structure in which each feature node is connected with the source node, but with only one of the remaining $n - 2$ nodes. Here, as in the case of completely interconnected structures, we may also distinguish between three different stages of activation.

8.3.4.4 Activation Stage 1: Partially Interconnected Structures. As with completely interconnected structures, all $n - 1$ nodes are activated by amount a at the end of the first stage. Here too, Assumption 5 prevents reverberating activation from flowing back to source node x.

8.3.4.5 Activation Stage 2: Partially Interconnected Structures. In the second stage, however, there are—in contrast to completely interconnected structures—fewer than the possible maximum of $n - 2$ links. In our example, the number of links is reduced to the minimum, that is, a single link. If we assume that in partially interconnected structures the average number of links is reduced by a fraction f, then the number of links in the second stage can be indicated by $f(n - 2)$. At the end of the second stage, therefore, each of the $n - 1$ nodes is activated with the amount $a + bf(n - 2)$.

8.3.4.6 Activation Stage 3: Partially Interconnected Structures. Here, as in the case of completely interconnected structures, activation from all n

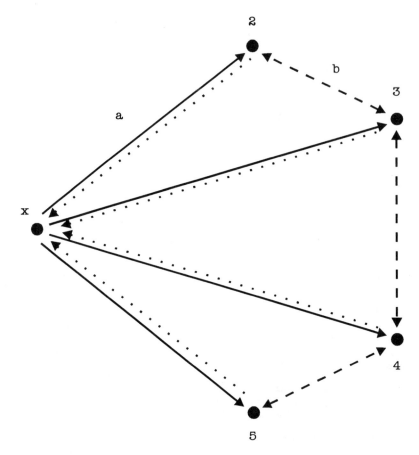

FIG. 8.4.   A partially interconnected code with a minimum number of interconnections.

— 1 nodes flows back to the source node. Node x is indirectly activated with
an amount equal to $[a + bf(n - 2)](n - 1)$.

Equation 8.3 applies to partially interconnected structures:

$$I = [a + bf(n - 2)](n - 1) \qquad\qquad (8.3)$$

where $1 \leq f(n - 2) \leq (n - 2)$.

Equations 8.2 and 8.3 differ only with regard to variable f, which lowers the
extent of indirect activation for partially, as opposed to completely
interconnected codes. Nonetheless, it can also be seen here that I increases
with the number of nodes. This applies even to the case when there is only
one link, $f(n - 2) = 1$. Although the accumulating effect of indirect

activation is weakened, I nevertheless increases by the amount $(a + b)(n - 1)$.

In summary, we find that in both completely and partially interconnected structures there is a positive relationship between the amount of indirect activation I and the number of nodes n. The amount of indirect activation increases with the number of nodes in interconnected structures. Thus, the validity of Prediction 1 holds true for all the cases already discussed.

8.3.5 On Deducing Prediction 2: The Speed of the Search Process Increases with Increasing Complexity

We have assumed that the search process ends with a positive result as soon as indirect activation I flows back to the source node (Assumption C). The speed of the search process, therefore, depends on time $t(I)$. In evaluating $t(I)$, we proceed from Assumption 6, which also underlies other network models (cf. ACT, ACT* or Equations 6.2 and 6.4). It states that time $t(i)$ needed to activate a link is the reciprocal value of activation a. Because we have already determined the amount of activation for Stages 1, 2, and 3, activation time $t(I)$ can easily be calculated. For completely interconnected structures it was found that the amount of activation in the first stage equals a and in the second stage equals b. Up to the end of the second stage the activation process will therefore need only $1/a + 1/b$ time units. It is at this precise moment that indirect activation accumulates at each of the $n - 1$ nodes with strength $a + b(n - 2)$. During the third stage, this amount flows back from each of the $n - 1$ nodes to x. Thus, the duration of Stage 3 is $1/[a + b(n - 2)]$ time units. Accordingly, time $t(I)$ needed for indirect activation to flow back to x can be determined by Equation 8.4:

$$t(I) = 1/a + 1/b + 1/[a + b(n - 2)]. \tag{8.4}$$

In partially interconnected structures the first two stages also require $1/a + 1/b$ time units. At the end of the second stage, however, there is comparatively less indirect activation accumulating at the $n - 1$ nodes, equal to $a + bf(n - 2)$. In the third stage then, this amount flows from all of the $n - 1$ nodes back to the source node. In this case, the duration of search process $t(I)$ is defined by Equation 8.5:

$$t(I) = 1/a + 1/b + 1/[a + bf(n - 2)] \tag{8.5}$$

In Equations (8.4) and (8.5), the number of nodes n only occurs in the denominator. This is why the duration of the search process is shortened with an increase in the number of nodes. Complex codes with many components can, therefore, be searched faster than less complex codes with only a few components. This holds true for both completely and partially interconnected structures, as can be seen by comparing Equations 8.4 and 8.5.

8.4 THE CAPACITY OF SPREADING ACTIVATION

If one compares the processing assumptions outlined earlier with those of ACT or ACT*, then it becomes clear that Assumption 1 contradicts the explanation of the fan effect. Assumption 5, on the other hand, is compatible with ACT, but not with ACT*. This is because ACT* is based on the assumption of reverberating activation. Most other processing assumptions, however, could just as easily have been adopted by ACT and ACT*.

We have already outlined in detail how the explanation of the fan effect is based on the assumption that input activation (that activation received by a node) is equal to the sum of output activations (the sum of all activations spreading from that node). This is expressed by Equations 6.1 and 6.3, which are of crucial importance to ACT and ACT*. However, within the framework of Assumption 1 it is assumed that output activation (as the sum of all activations leaving a node) exceeds input activation. Figure 8.5 illustrates the differences between the two assumptions.

As can be demonstrated by Fig. 8.5, according to ACT and ACT* output activation for a particular link decreases as the number of links increases. This assumption not only leads to a notable weakening, but also to a significant deceleration of spreading activation (Equations 6.2 and 6.4) in ACT and ACT*. In view of this effect, we call the processing assumption, so central to ACT and ACT*, the limited capacity of spreading activation. Within the framework of the connectivity model we proceeded from the

The calculation of output activation according to

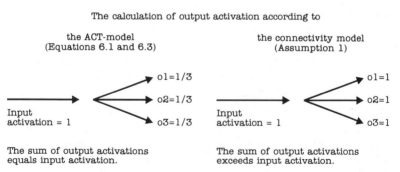

FIG. 8.5.   The calculation of output activation according to ACT and the connectivity model.

assumption of an unlimited capacity of spreading activation (Assumption 1).

In what follows, we show that the predictions of the connectivity model are only valid when the capacity of spreading activation is either not limited or only partially limited. For this purpose, when evaluating a and b for Equations 8.2 and 8.3, we do not proceed from Assumption 1 of the connectivity model, but instead from Equation 6.3 of ACT and ACT*. As a result, it can be seen that neither prediction of the connectivity model is now valid, and search speed $t(i)$ and indirect activation I depend on the capacity of spreading activation.

Once again consider the example in Fig. 8.1: Because during the first activation stage $n - 1$ links lead away from the source node, the amount of activation of nodes 2-5 is, according to Equation 6.3 of ACT, equal to $1/(n - 1)$. Therefore, a equals $1/(n - 1)$. In the second stage, a is "weakened" or divided by $n - 2$ links. For b we get $1/[(n - 1)(n - 2)]$. When adopting these new estimates of a and b for Equation 8.2, we can determine the amount of indirect activation in completely interconnected structures:

$$I = \{1/(n - 1) + [1/((n - 1)(n - 2))] (n - 2)\}(n - 1).$$

Simplifying by $(n - 2)$ and $(n - 1)$ we receive:

$$I = [1/(n - 1) + 1/(n - 1)] (n - 1)$$
and finally: $I = 2.$ \hfill (8.6)

The same relationship also holds for partially interconnected structures, as the substitution of $1/(n - 1)$ for a and $1/[(n - 1) f(n - 2)]$ for b in Equation 8.3 shows:

$$I = \{1/(n - 1) + [1/((n - 1)f(n - 2))] f(n - 2)\} (n - 1).$$

Simplifying by $f(n - 2)$ and $(n - 1)$ the result is

$$I = [1/(n - 1) + 1/(n - 1)] (n - 1)$$
and finally: $I = 2.$ \hfill (8.7)

This surprising result shows clearly that the assumptions of connectivity and indirect activation—if they are combined with the assumption of a limited spreading activation capacity—are by no means sufficient to confirm the predictions of the connectivity model. This demonstrates that Assumption 1 is of central importance for the connectivity model. If we proceed from the assumption of limited capacity, then it can be seen that I no longer depends on the number of nodes n (Equations 8.6 and 8.7). ACT or ACT* is, therefore, not in a position to explain why the amount of indirect activation increases in interconnected structures.

When calculating the duration of the search process $t(I)$ while proceeding from the assumption of limited capacity, the central importance of Assumption 1 can be shown more clearly. The length of the search process in completely interconnected structures can be found by substituting the previously determined values of a and b in Equation 8.4:

$$t(I) = n - 1 + (n - 1)(n - 2) + (n - 1)/2. \qquad (8.8)$$

In determining $t(I)$ in partially interconnected structures, we must start out from Equation 8.5. By substituting the corresponding values of a and b we arrive at Equation 8.9:

$$t(I) = n - 1 + (n - 1)f(n - 2) + (n - 1)/2 \qquad (8.9)$$

According to the structure of Equations 8.8 and 8.9, therefore, an increase in n leads to an increase in search time $t(I)$.

Even if the assumption of a limited spreading activation capacity is combined with the assumptions of connectivity and indirect activation, it is not possible to substantiate the predictions of the connectivity model. This fact underlines the crucial nature of the assumption of a limited spreading activation capacity.

8.4.1 The Assumption of Partially Limited Capacity: Explaining the Fan Effect on the Basis of the Connectivity Model

Processing Assumption 1 contradicts the explanation of the fan effect. Both the assumption of limited capacity (underlying ACT*) and the assumption of unlimited capacity (Assumption 1) signify the final points on a continuous and bipolar dimension. Consequently, it is possible to proceed from the assumption of a partially limited spreading activation capacity. The following section shows that this assumption not only guarantees the explanation of the fan effect, but also supports Prediction 1 of the connectivity model.

The capacity of spreading activation is partially limited if, on the one hand (as with the connectivity model), the sum of output activations increases with the number of links leading from a node, and if, on the other hand (as with ACT and ACT*), the output activation of each separate link decreases with the number of links leading from a particular node. Let $o(j)$ be the strength of the output activation of link j, let O be the sum of all $o(j)$, and let v be the total number of links leading from a node. The following function then satisfies the definition of a partially limited spreading activation capacity:

$$o(j) = \text{(Input activation)} \, [(v + 1)/v]. \qquad (8.10)$$

In order to compare the results of Equation 8.10 with the assumptions of limited and unlimited spreading activation capacity, we have summarized some numerical examples in Table 8.1. Here we can see that, according to Equation 8.10, output activation $o(j)$ decreases with the number of links v leading from a node, but that at the same time the sum of output activations O not only exceeds input activation (which in this example is equal to 1), but is also enlarged by an increase in v.

Is this assumption capable of changing the predictions of the connectivity model? In order to examine this question, let us calculate numerical values for a and b (of Equations 8.2 and 8.3) on the basis of Equation 8.10. In the first stage of activation, v equals $n - 1$ links (Fig. 8.1). Therefore, according to Equation 8.10, $a = n/(n - 1)$, when assuming that input activation equals 1. In calculating b we have to consider the fact that in the second stage of activation input activation equals $a = n/(n - 1)$. In completely interconnected structures $v = n - 2$ links. Therefore $b = [n/(n - 1)] [(n - 1)/(n - 2)]$. When simplifying by $n - 1$, $b = n/(n - 2)$. If we now substitute these values for a and b in Equation 8.2, we discover:

$$I = \{n/(n - 1) + [n/(n - 2)] \ (n - 2)\}(n - 1).$$

Simplifying by $(n - 2)$ and $(n - 1)$ yields:

$$I = n + n(n - 1) \text{ or } I = n^2. \tag{8.11}$$

In partially interconnected structures there are also $v = n - 1$ links in the first stage of activation. In the second stage, v is reduced to $f(n - 2)$. We see again that $a = n/(n - 1)$, but for the second stage we find that $b = [n/(n - 1)] \{[f(n - 2) + 1]/[f(n - 2)]\}$. Substituting these expressions into Equation 8.3 and simplifying by $f(n - 2)$ yields:

$$I = \{n/(n - 1) + [n/(n - 1)] \ [f(n - 2) + 1]\} \ (n - 1).$$

TABLE 8.1
Output Activation o(j) as a Function of Spreading Activation Capacity and
the Number of Links, v, Leading from a Node

Limited (ACT Model)			Unlimited (Assumption 1)			Partially Limited (Equation 8.10)		
v	o(j)	O	v	o(j)	O	v	o(j)	O
2	0.5	1	2	1	2	2	1.5	3
3	0.33	1	3	1	3	3	1.33	4
4	0.25	1	4	1	4	4	1.25	5
5	0.2	1	5	1	5	5	1.2	6
6	0.17	1	6	1	6	6	1.17	7
7	0.14	1	7	1	7	7	1.14	8
8	0.13	1	8	1	8	8	1.13	9

When simplifying by $(n - 1)$ we get:

$$I = n + nf(n - 2) + n. \tag{8.12}$$

In both formulas, an increase in n also leads to an increase in indirect activation I. This shows that Prediction 1 remains unchanged if we adopt the assumption of partially limited capacity.

In order to examine whether Prediction 2 can also be supported, we calculate the duration of the search process $t(I)$, according to Equations 8.4 and 8.5, by substituting the previously determined values for a and b. For completely interconnected structures we find:

$$t(I) = (n - 1)/n + (n - 2)/n + (n - 1)/[n + n(n - 1)],$$

which can be reduced to:

$$t(I) = (2n - 3)/n + (n - 1)/n^2.$$

After determining a common denominator we get:

$$t(I) = (2n^2 - 2n - 1)/n^2. \tag{8.13}$$

For partially interconnected structures we find:

$$t(I) = (n - 1)\{1/n + f(n - 2)/[nf(n - 2) + n] + 1/[nf(n - 2) + 2n]\}. \tag{8.14}$$

In Equations 8.13 and 8.14, n appears in both the numerator and denominator. On the basis of this evidence, therefore, we are not able to judge whether $t(I)$ will increase or decrease with n. Calculating $t(I)$ for some different values of n shows, however, that in both cases activation time increases as the number of nodes increases (Table 8.2).

TABLE 8.2
The Relationship between $t(I)$ and the Number of Nodes n

Equation	$n = 4$	$n = 5$	$n = 6$	$n = 7$	$n = 8$	$n = 10$	$n = 12$	$n = 100$
8.13	1.438	1.560	1.639	1.694	1.734	1.790	1.826	1.980
8.14								
$f(n - 2) = 1$	1.375	1.467	1.528	1.571	1.604	1.650	1.681	1.815
$= 2$	1.438	1.533	1.598	1.643	1.677	1.725	1.757	1.898
$= 3$		1.560	1.625	1.671	1.706	1.755	1.788	1.931
$= 4$			1.639	1.686	1.721	1.770	1.803	1.947
$= 5$				1.694	1.729	1.779	1.812	1.956
$= 6$					1.734	1.784	1.817	1.962
$= 7$						1.788	1.821	1.966
$= 8$						1.790	1.823	1.969
$= 9$							1.825	1.971
$= 10$							1.826	1.973

Thus, the assumption of partially limited capacity supports only Prediction 1, but not Prediction 2 of the connectivity model. Does this mean that the connectivity model – by adhering to its specific predictions – is incapable of explaining the fan effect?

In answering this question we refer to section 6.4. There we pointed to the findings of Ratcliff and McKoon (1981), who were able to show that spreading activation is probably so fast that it is irrelevant for predicting reaction times. As already emphasized, this result has led J. R. Anderson (1983a, p. 95) to use only the amount of activation but not activation time in predicting reaction times.

It thus becomes clear that only Prediction 1 can be effectively used to estimate reaction times as a measure of the duration of search processes. The search process not only consists of the activation process, but also of an examination of the search results (Assumption D of the connectivity model). When focusing on the prediction of reaction times, the connectivity model is capable of giving a simple explanation of the positive as well as of the negative fan effect. If hierarchical structures are searched, then reaction time increases as the complexity of the memory network increases. In searching interconnected structures, on the other hand, reaction time decreases with increasing complexity of the network.

Only one problem remains to be considered. According to the connectivity model, a search process terminates as soon as indirect activation flows back to that node where the search process originated. In a strictly hierarchical structure, activation can never spread back and thus, according to Assumption C, it would be impossible to terminate a search process. This, however, is true in the rather special case of a single hierarchical code being activated. As we know from Assumption A, the connectivity model considers only codes that agree with the definition of interconnectedness. But this does not mean that the structure connecting different codes must not be hierarchical. As Fig. 8.3 shows, interconnected codes might well be connected by a hierarchical structure. In order to demonstrate this idea, consider the strictly hierarchical network in Fig. 6.1. If in this network we would substitute each node by an interconnected code, the connectivity model would be capable of explaining the spread of the search processes starting at "park" and "firefighter." Given this type of structure and the assumption of a partially limited capacity of spreading activation, the connectivity model can easily explain the fan effect. More complex networks containing interconnected as well as hierarchical coding structures are considered in chap. 10 together with the simulation program CONN1.

Finally there is another interesting issue to be considered. There is no plausible reason to assume that the capacity of spreading activation is a constant quantity. Instead, the capacity of spreading activation might vary as a function of a variety of different variables, such as age, degree of elaboration or interconnectedness, and even intelligence. With respect to memory performance, we do know that memory capacity varies considerably between subjects. But why should similar considerations not also apply to processing capacity? There also might be a relationship between these two types of capacity terms in the sense that spreading activation capacity increases with memory capacity. Because we referred exclusively to Assumption A and LTM codes, it makes sense to retain the assumption of unlimited capacity within the framework of the connectivity model. Fact retrieval tasks, which are dealt within the framework of ACT and ACT*, may not be considered pure LTM tasks (Klimesch, Schimke, & Ladurner, 1988), and it therefore appears appropriate in this case to accept the assumption of limited capacity.

8.4.2. ACT* and the Predictions of the Connectivity Model

As compared to ACT, the more recent version of ACT* (J. R. Anderson, 1983a, 1983c) exhibits three fundamental modifications. The first modification refers to the assumption of reverberating activation, the second to a continuous spreading activation, and the third to the assumption of an extremely high activation speed of less than 1 ms per network link. In sharp contrast to this, in ACT activation could only spread in one direction and only in a discontinuous way at a very slow speed of approximately 50–100 ms per link (J. R. Anderson & Pirolli, 1984). The central assumption of a limited spreading activation capacity, however, was adopted by ACT* without any modifications.

Because reverberating activation strengthens the amount of activation each node receives, the question arises whether ACT* is capable of predicting that indirect activation I increases in interconnected structures. Anderson did not confront this problem. He was able to show that an increasing number of converging links leads to an increase in activation at those particular nodes (J. R. Anderson 1983c, p. 286). However, it still remains an open question whether or not more complex networks can in general be activated faster than less complex ones.

In an attempt to answer this question, we apply the processing assumptions of ACT* to interconnected structures. J. R. Anderson (1983c) showed that this assumptions can be described in terms of simultaneous linear equation systems, showing the following general form:

$$a(1) = k(2)la(2) + \ldots\ldots\ldots\ldots k(n)la(n) + A$$

.
.

$$a(i) = k(1)la(1) + \ldots\ldots\ldots\ldots k(n)la(n)$$

.
.

$$a(n) = k(1)la(1) + \ldots\ldots\ldots\ldots k(n-1)la(n-1)$$

Where A = the amount of activation of the source node,
      $a(i)$ = the amount of activation of node i,
      n = the number of nodes, and
      $k(i)$ = a structural coefficient, which must be calculated on
           the basis of the geometric properties of node i.
      l = a dampening factor. Its value may lie between 0 and 1.

As an example, let us calculate $a(1)$ to $a(5)$ for the completely interconnected structure shown in Fig. 8.1. According to ACT*, we proceed from
the following five equations:

$$a(1) = 0.25la(2) + 0.25la(3) + 0.25la(4) + 0.25la(5) + A$$
$$a(2) = 0.25la(1) + 0.25la(3) + 0.25la(4) + 0.25la(5)$$
$$a(3) = 0.25la(1) + 0.25la(2) + 0.25la(4) + 0.24la(5)$$
$$a(4) = 0.25la(1) + 0.25la(2) + 0.25la(3) + 0.25la(5)$$
$$a(5) = 0.25la(1) + 0.25la(2) + 0.25la(3) + 0.25la(4)$$

Coefficients $k(i)$ show a value of 0.25 or $\frac{1}{4}$ because in a completely
interconnected code with five nodes exactly four links lead from any of the
five nodes. Due to the assumption of reverberating activation and the
extremely high rate of spreading activation, all nodes are activated almost
simultaneously. When assuming equal strengths for all links, the activation
is simply divided by the number of links leading from a node.

In order to solve the equation system, we not only require numerical
values for $k(i)$ but also for dampening factor l. In most of his examples
Anderson used a value of 0.8 (J. R. Anderson, 1983c, p. 266, 286). We thus
adopt this value for our example. The last value to consider is A, which
refers to the amount of activation the source node sends into the network.
Table 8.3 lists the results found for the source node $a(1)$ and the remaining
$a(2)$ – $a(n)$ feature nodes in completely interconnected structures with
different complexity and for two different values of l. It should be noted
that a large dampening factor l passes on more – not less – activation. In
summarizing the results of Table 8.3, we find:

1. Activation $a(i)$ decreases as the complexity of the network increases. This holds true for any given node or dampening factor.
2. The extent of this decrease is affected by the size of dampening
   factor l: The larger the dampening factor, the greater the decrease
   in activation.

TABLE 8.3
Activation at the Source Node a(1) and the Feature Nodes a(2)... a(n), Calculated for two Loss Factors l

Number of Nodes (n)	l = 0.8		l = 0.99	
	a(1)	a(2) . . . a(n)	a(1)	a(2) . . . a(n)
4	1.84	1.05	25.54	24.79
5	1.67	0.83	20.64	19.84
6	1.55	0.69	17.36	16.53
7	1.47	0.59	14.47	13.61
8	1.41	0.51	13.21	12.33

3. The larger the dampening factor, the more activity is passed on to the other nodes of the network.

As already emphasized, according to ACT*, the speed with which the information stored in node i can be retrieved depends on activation strength $a(i)$. It thus becomes clear that ACT* is not capable of supporting the predictions of the connectivity model. On the contrary, the predictions of both theories contradict each other. Once again we see that it is the assumption of the limited capacity of spreading activation — here reflected by the way $k(i)$ is determined — that is responsible for the deceleration of spreading activation.

Completely interconnected structures always accumulate more activation than partially interconnected structures. Therefore, it cannot be expected that the pattern of results, as shown in Table 8.3, will change for partially interconnected structures. For this reason we forego a discussion of partially interconnected structures.

8.5 DELIMITING THE SPREAD OF ACTIVATION IN MEMORY

Any memory theory is faced with a fundamental problem: Which assumptions should be used to explain why spreading activation remains limited to the relevant parts of the network and does not ultimately continue to spread to the entire memory structure? The connectivity model attempts to solve this problem on the basis of those assumptions guaranteeing that a search process terminates as soon as indirect activation spreads back to one of the source nodes.

We show in the following that even in a case in which the nodes of an interconnected code are connected to other interconnected codes, the activation process may be terminated as quickly as with isolated codes, that is, codes not connected to any other codes. In order to prove this, consider the different ways in which two or more codes can be connected to each other.

Keep in mind that any interconnected code must have only one source node. Furthermore, the feature nodes must be connected in a way that results in closed structures (section 8.3 and Fig. 8.2). When considering these restrictions, there are only two possibilities of connecting a code X with a code Z. They can be connected either by common components (Case 1 of Fig. 8.6) or by additional links (Case 2 in Fig. 8.6).

8.5.1 Case 1: Codes X and Z Share a Common Node xz

Independently of whether or not the search process proceeds from X or Z, a common node xz can only be activated by the end of the first activation stage, that is, after $1/a$ time units. Assume that the search process proceeds from x. Then, the first activation stage in code Z begins with a delay of $1/a$ time units. In other words, activation in code Z lags behind that of code X by exactly one activation stage. Even before the second activation stage ends in code Z, code X has already completed the third stage and the search

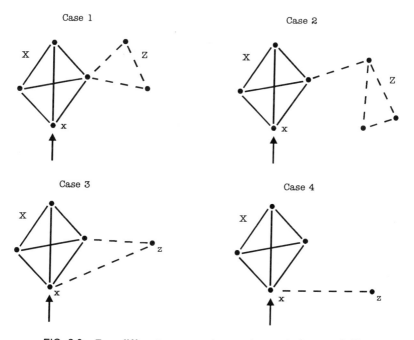

FIG. 8.6.   Four different ways a node z can be attached to a code X.

process is terminated. This must always be the case because the third activation stage is always faster than the second. Furthermore, we have to consider the fact that it is only the third activation stage that leads to a decrease in activation time (cf. the expressions $1/[a + b(n - 2)]$ and $1/[a + bf(n - 2)]$ in Equations 8.4 and 8.5). Therefore, it is not possible for the spreading activation process in code Z to interfere with that of code X.

8.5.2 Case 2: Codes X and Y Are Connected By an Additional Link

If any node of X is linked to a node of Z and if the search process starts from x (Case 2 in Fig. 8.6), then activation can only pass on to the link connecting X and Z after time $1/a$ has elapsed. If we assume then that the link leading to Z is activated in the amount c (where c may be smaller or equal to b), then Z is activated after $1/a + 1/c$ time units. In the meantime, however, after time $1/a + 1/b$, the second activation stage ends in X and the third and fastest stage is triggered. In other words, in code Z the first activation stage begins during the initiation of the third and fastest activation stage in code X. Because the third activation stage is always the fastest, the search process is terminated, before Stage 2 in Z can be completed.

   The same considerations also apply in those cases in which more than one common component or link connect codes X and Z. Even in such cases, the termination criterion is not affected. The only requirement is that additional links or common components must not change the geometric properties in a way that the definition of interconnected codes is contradicted. Because two codes may never have the same source node, in the second code spreading activation does not begin until the completion of Stage 1 in the first code. It is therefore not possible for spreading activation in the second code to interfere with that in the first code.

   Finally, consider those cases in which code X is linked to another node and not, as has been the case in previous examples, with another code. Here, we may distinguish between two possibilities. A node z can either be interconnected to code X, as in Case 3, or just linked with any given node of X, as in Case 4.

8.5.3 Case 3: Node z Is Connected with Source Node x and At Least One of the $n - 1$ Nodes of X

According to the definition of interconnected structures, it follows that in this case node z is itself part of code X (Fig. 8.6, Case 3).

8.5.4 Case 4: Node z Is Connected with Any
Given Node of Code X

Because the connectivity model does not admit the assumption of reverberating activity, an isolated node has no effect on the spread of indirect activation (Fig. 8.6, Case 4).

These considerations have led to an important discovery. For now it can be seen that the connectivity model does not require a dampening function in order to guide the activation process toward the relevant parts of the network. In contrast to this, all network models (J. R. Anderson, 1976, 1983a, 1983b, 1983c; Collins & E. F. Loftus, 1975; Dell, 1986) assume that the amount of activation decreases as the number of activated links increases. According to ACT and ACT*, spreading activation decreases as an exponential function (cf. the review in J. R. Anderson & Pirolli, 1984).

As a result of the assumption of a dampened spreading activation, information relevant to the search process must be located very near the source node. If, however, the respective network parts are located far away from the source node, there is a danger of not finding the relevant sought-after information.

8.5.5 Delimiting Spreading Activation By Inhibition
and Preactivation

In all previous considerations we proceeded from the fact that at the beginning of the search process all the nodes and links of a network are in a neutral state of "zero" activation (Assumption 7). If, however, we assume that certain network parts are inhibited or preactivated, then the activation process would comprise entirely different parts of a network.

The activation state of a network at the beginning of a search process can be either *neutral, inhibiting,* or *activating.* It is neutral if the nodes and/or links are activated with zero; it is inhibiting if these show negative values; and it is activating if they already show positive values. This latter case is known as *preactivation.* Inhibited network parts decelerate or stop the process of spreading activation. In contrast to this, spreading activation is attracted to those network parts that are preactivated.

Network theories are unfairly criticized for the way in which information is stored. It is said to be too rigidly determined by geometric properties. Furthermore, these properties can only be changed by learning processes and, as a result of this, only relatively slowly. However, this objection completely ignores the fact that inhibition and preactivation processes can, in a functional sense, cause an abrupt change in the geometric properties of the network.

A dampening function has a decisively negative effect on inhibition and preactivation: The sooner spreading activation is diminished, the less it can be influenced by inhibition and preactivation processes. The application of these concepts is therefore only appropriate within the confines of those network theories that do not proceed from a dampened spreading activation. The concepts of inhibition and preactivation therefore increase the applicability of the connectivity model, though they only have a small effect on the explanatory power of ACT and ACT*.

8.6 THE DETECTION OF COMMON PATHWAYS BETWEEN DIFFERENT NETWORK PARTS

Almost all network theories assume that the search process emanates from at least two source nodes and aims at the detection of convergent activation meeting on common pathways. Up to now, we have only discussed the simple case of activating a single code. But the connectivity model can just as easily explain how a common pathway can be found between two or more codes. Depending on whether or not the sought-after codes share common components, we have to distinguish between two different cases, which are discussed in the following sections.

8.6.1 Case 1: Two Codes X and Y Share Common Components

If two codes X and Y have common components and if the search process begins simultaneously at both source nodes x and y, then — because of Assumption 7 (section 8.3.3) — the two activation processes will meet simultaneously at the common node(s). Let the activation emanating from x be $a(x)$ and that coming from y be $a(y)$. According to Assumption 3, $a(x)$ and $a(y)$ sum up at the common node(s), yielding a value of $2a$.

The following discussion refers to the example depicted in Fig. 8.7, which shows two codes X and Y sharing a common node xy.

In the first activation stage (section 8.3.4.1) all nodes, with the exception of the common node xy, are activated by an amount equal to a. The common node receives twice that activation, which equals $2a$. Activation processes originating at different source nodes meet at the common node xy and sum up. This is known as preactivation (section 8.2.2; Assumption B, last paragraph) as opposed to indirect activation.

The term preactivation refers to additional activation stemming from another activation process. It does not necessarily imply that one of the activation processes arrives earlier. If they meet at the same time, as is the case in our example, the resulting effect is the same as in the case in which preactivation arrived earlier but within a critical time span $t(k)$ (Assumption

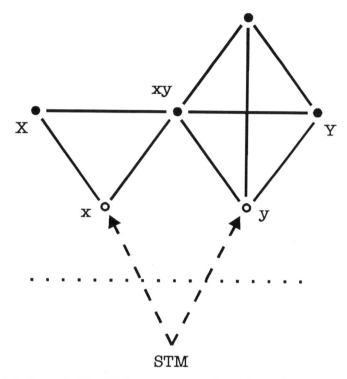

FIG. 8.7.   Two codes X and Y share a common node xy. The search process starts in
STM and simultaneously activates the two source nodes x and y. The dotted line
symbolizes the transition between STM and LTM.

2 in section 8.3.3). Thus, within this critical time span the exact time of
arrival of preactivation is irrelevant. For this reason — and in the interest of
simplifying the terminology — we also call a simultaneous convergence of
activations "preactivation," providing they originated at different source
nodes.

At the beginning of the second activation stage, no activation can flow
back to either of the two source nodes (Assumption 5). That is why
activation — as in the examples discussed in section 8.3.1 — flows on to other
corresponding nodes in networks X and Y. Thus, the rejection of reverberating activation (Assumption 5) prevents activation from flowing along the
geometrically shortest pathway between the two codes X and Y (i.e.,
directly along the links from xy to x and y). It is not until the beginning of
the third stage that indirect activation flowing back to one of the source
nodes triggers the termination of the search process.

During the second activation stage the common node is not only
indirectly activated by the $n - 2$ nodes of code X, but also by those of code
Y. Let $n(x)$ be the number of nodes of X and $n(y)$ be the number of nodes

of Y. Then, at the end of the second stage, the amount of indirect activation of the common and already preactivated node xy is:

$$Ip(xy) = 2a + b[n(x) - 2] + b[n(y) - 2]. \tag{8.15}$$

Ip denotes indirect activation *I*, strengthened by preactivation *p*. Equation 8.15 holds for completely interconnected codes, but by substituting $f(n - 2)$ it can easily be modified for partially interconnected codes.

In the third stage, *Ip*(xy) flows back to the source nodes of X as well as Y and there is added to that activation arriving from the remaining nodes of the network. It should be noted that at the beginning of the third stage the nodes of X and Y are—due to the preactivation of common node xy—activated to different extents. Because node xy, in comparison to all other nodes, exhibits by far the highest amount of activation, its activation will be the first to arrive at the source nodes. According to Assumption C, the search process would terminate before the activation of all of the other nodes arrives at the source nodes. Thus, the activation of weaker nodes arriving later would no longer be of any importance.

Assumption D, however, draws explicit attention to the fact that the entire amount of indirect activation is not only an important indicator of the amount of positive evidence the search process yields, but also the only factor determining the speed of further processing the search result. Consequently, there is little point in retaining Assumption C in its original form. Assumption C must thus be modified to the extent that it no longer contradicts Assumption D.

In trying to solve this problem, we must first consider the question of how a common pathway can be detected between X and Y. Thereby we determine a criterion that enables not only a termination of the search process, but also a clear evaluation of its results. Assume that the search process continues to the point where indirect activation *I*, flowing back to one of the source nodes, exceeds the amount that would be expected in the "standard case" *s*, in which no common pathway and, therefore, no preactivation exists. This amount of indirect activation flowing back to source nodes x and y is denoted by *Is*(x) and *Is*(y), respectively. In contrast to this, indirect activation *I*, strengthened by preactivation *p* and accumulating at the end of stage three at source nodes x and y, is denoted by *Ip*(x) and *Ip*(y), respectively. The termination criterion now refers to the comparison of the amount of indirect activation *I* of a current search process with the standard case *Is*.

Assume that the standard values *Is*(x) and *Is*(y) are stored at the source nodes. The result of the search process can then be checked at any source node by comparing *I* with *Is*. If *I* exceeds the standard case *Is*, the result is positive. If, however, this value is not exceeded, then the result of the search process is negative. We can determine a positive result according to Equation 8.16:

$$I = Ip > Is. \qquad (8.16)$$

We arrive at a negative result, on the other hand, if the amount of indirect activation equals the standard case:

$$I = Is. \qquad (8.17)$$

The termination criterion becomes effective as soon as it is met by one of the two source nodes.

Ip is in any case larger than Is and, therefore, operates to speed up the third activation stage (Equations 8.4 and 8.5). It thus follows that two codes with one or more common nodes not only cause more indirect activation but can be searched faster than a similar, but isolated, code. For the same reasons, a negative search result causes less indirect activation and lasts longer than a positive one.

The two basic predictions of the connectivity model — I increases with the number of nodes and $t(I)$ decreases with the number of nodes — are entirely supported in this case: The greater the number of nodes that codes X and Y comprise, the more indirect activation flows back to the source node and the faster a search process is terminated.

The explanation offered this far is not only based on Assumptions 1–7 of section 8.3, but also on two new assumptions that can be regarded as an extension of Assumption C. The first new assumption refers to the beginning of the search process, the second to the type of termination criterion. These assumptions explain how common pathways between different codes are detected.

Assumption C1: If two or more codes are being searched, then the search process begins at the corresponding source nodes at the same time and with the same activation strength.

Assumption C2: The termination criterion depends on the goal of the search process. If common pathways are to be found, then the search process will be terminated with a positive result, if activation I, flowing back to the source node, exceeds indirect activation Is, which would have originated in a standard case, that is, in the absence of preactivation. If I does not exceed Is (Equations 8.16 and 8.17), the search process terminates with a negative result. The termination criterion becomes effective as soon as it is reached by one of the source nodes.

In summarizing our findings, we have determined four factors that influence the amount of indirect activation and the speed of the search process. Three of these factors refer to search processes with a positive result. The more components (a) code X and (b) code Y comprise, and (c) the more common components they share, the more indirect activation will accumulate at the source nodes and the faster the search process will take place. For a search process with a negative result, on the other hand, only the number of nodes of that code that is first to reach the termination criterion is of importance. Thus, search processes with a negative result are only influenced by one single factor, namely, (d) the number of components of the code that comprises the most components.

If we compare search processes with positive and those with negative results, the following additional prediction can be considered: (e) Because preactivation is absent in a search process with a negative result, the search time will be longer than one with a positive result.

8.6.2 Case 2: Two Codes X and Y Do Not Share Common Components but Are Connected Via Other Codes

In the following discussion we refer to the example illustrated in Fig. 8.8. Here we see two different codes (code X and code Y) with source nodes x and y, which are connected to each other by two other codes (code W and Z). It is the goal of the search process to determine whether or not codes X and Y are connected to each other by a common pathway.

According to Assumption C1, the search processes start out simultaneously from x and y. Because of Assumption 7 the two activation processes meet on the link between nodes w(2) and z(2). It should be noted that the search process coming from x finds node z(2) already preactivated. Similarly, the activation process coming from y finds node w(2) preactivated. Depending on the speed of the search process and on the length of $t(k)$, up from this point other nodes lying in the path of the search process may be preactivated. Thus, preactivation not only helps to speed up but also to guide the search process along the common path.

Let $ap(xi)$ be that amount of activation a, which stems from y and at time i arrives in the form of preactivated activation ap at source node x. That activation coming from x and arriving at node y at time j is denoted $ap(yj)$. Nodes x and y are not only activated by Is, but in addition also receive activation ap from the source node of the opposite side of the common path. The sum of both activations Is and ap is denoted by Ip. Therefore: $Ip(x) = Is(x) + ap(xi)$ and $Ip(y) = Is(y) + ap(yj)$. Of those activations $ap(xi)$ and $ap(yj)$ the one with the highest amount will be the first to reach the corresponding source node. According to Equation 8.16: The faster of the two activations is responsible for terminating the search process.

The most important difference between Case 1 and Case 2 concerns the fact that activation ap, which is crucial in the evaluation of the termination

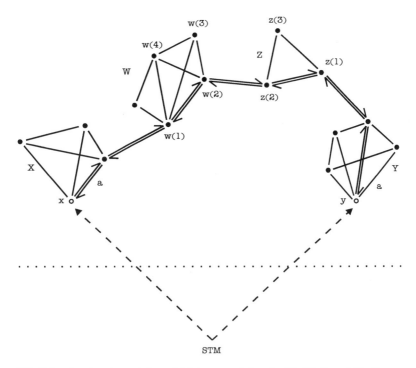

FIG. 8.8.   A network consisting of 4 interconnected codes (X, W, Z, and Y). Due to processing Assumption 7, the activations spreading from x and y meet at the middle of the link w(2), z(2).

criterion, can arrive later than *Is*. This shows that in Case 2, search times will be longer than those in Case 1 — independently of whether or not there is a positive result. Let us take a closer look at the process of spreading activation in order to better understand the consequences of this result.

At the end of the first activation stage all X and Y nodes are activated. At the beginning of the second stage, activation not only flows to all $n(x) - 2$ and $n(y) - 2$ nodes, but likewise to nodes w(1) and z(1). In other words, in the second stage the activation process already goes beyond codes X and Y. Here we can observe another important difference between Cases 1 and 2: In contrast to Case 1, Assumption 5 does not prevent activation from flowing along the geometrically shortest route (see the double links in Fig. 8.8) between the two source nodes x and y.

In the third stage, indirect activation $Is(x)$ and $Is(y)$ flows back to source nodes x and y. In networks belonging to Case 2 the two codes X and Y must be connected by at least one other code. Thus, the shortest pathway between x and y is at least three links long. If the common pathway is more than three links long, the third activation stage of code x and y will have always been finished before activation *ap* arrives at the corresponding source node.

This shows that reaching the termination criterion (according to Equation 8.16) in structures belonging to Case 2 will usually require more time than in structures belonging to Case 1. The additional time needed here depends not only on the length of the common pathway, but among other factors, also on the effectiveness of preactivation. Generally we should expect that the longer the common pathway, the more time it will take to reach the termination criterion. However, depending on how intensively interconnected the common pathway is, preactivation will be an important factor speeding up the search process flowing on the common pathway.

The delayed arrival of preactivation raises the question of how to differentiate between a negative search result belonging to Case 1 and a positive one belonging to Case 2. Which criterion should be used in order to avoid mistakingly terminating the search process before a positive result (belonging to Case 2) can come about? In attempting to answer this question, we must first determine the extent to which a search process can be accelerated. In doing so, we notice that, apart from the length of the common path and the amount of preactivation, there are other powerful factors that contribute to an acceleration of the search process. The geometry of codes W and Z lying on the common pathway, as well as the second activation stage of codes X and Y make a considerable contribution to the quicker activation of the common pathway.

8.6.2.1 Preactivation: The Mutual Strengthening of Both Search Processes. In the network of Fig. 8.8 both activation processes meet in the middle of the link connecting nodes $w(2)$ and $z(2)$. If, in order to simplify matters, we assume that no dampening function is effective, then the strength of each of the two activation processes proceeding on the common pathway and meeting in the middle of the link between $w(2)$ and $z(2)$ is equal to a. Beyond that point, each activation process finds node $w(2)$ and $z(2)$ already activated with amount a. Here, activation sums up to an amount equal to $2a$. Thus far, we have only considered activation of the first activation stage. However, as is demonstrated later, the value of $2a$ arrived at here will increase by a factor of 5, if we consider the second activation stage of code X and Y, which will reach nodes $w(2)$ and $z(2)$ even earlier than the the first stage.

If the subsequent nodes lying in the same direction have not yet lost their activation (Assumption 2), there will be an additional strengthening of the search processes at nodes $w(1)$ and $z(1)$, respectively. Any further strengthening depends not only on the length of the critical time interval $t(k)$ (Assumption 2), but above all on the way indirect activation spreads within codes W and Z.

8.6.2.2 The Effect of Codes W and Z Lying on the Common Pathway. In our example, indirect activation spreading within codes Z and W (see the paths going via w(3) and w(4)) leads to an additional strengthening of preactivation. By the time the activation process coming from x reaches z(2) it has passed through four links. The activation process coming from y but leading over z(3) has passed through just as many links. That is why both activation processes meet at node z(2), with the result of further strengthening the activation process coming from x. The same happens to that activation process coming from y, which at node w(2) is further strengthened by activation coming from x and leading over nodes w(3) and w(4). Thus activation equal to $4a$ accumulates at node w(2), which is activated by x, y, w(3), and w(4), each with amount a. In contrast to this, only activation equal to $3a$ accumulates at node z(2). Code W, which is richer in components, therefore contributes more to the acceleration of the search process than code Z, which contains fewer components.

Here too, we have to emphasize that only the effects of the first activation stage were taken into account. The strengthening effect of W and Z, however, continues to increase if the second activation stage is considered.

As a rule, we see that those codes lying on the common pathway can significantly increase the speed of spreading activation. The extent of this acceleration effect is all the greater, the more components are exhibited by the codes lying on the common pathway. This effect is quite plausible if one considers that codes rich in information (i.e., codes with many components) increase the importance of a common pathway: The more information a common pathway represents, the more activation flows back to at least one of the source nodes and the higher the amount of preactivated indirect activation $Ip(x)$ and $Ip(y)$. The strengthening effect of these codes lying in between also enables very long pathways to be searched very quickly.

8.6.2.3 The Effect of the Second Activation Stage of Codes X and Y. The amount of $Ip(x)$ and $Ip(y)$ is positively influenced not only by the complexity of codes lying between them, but also by the complexity of codes X and Y. In considering the second activation stage of X and Y, this effect becomes even more important. The reason being that in the second activation stage the common pathway receives considerably more activation than in the first stage. Now, instead of a — as in the first stage — activation equals $a + b(n - 2)$ or $a + bf(n - 2)$ (Equations 8.2 and 8.3). One can therefore expect that activity of the second stage can catch up with that of the first stage. In our example this applies to both activation processes coming from x and y. Activation of the first stage reaches node w(2) or z(2) after $1/a + 1/a + 1/a = 3/a$ time units. That of the second stage reaches nodes w(2) and z(2) after $1/a + 1/b + 2[1/(a + 2b)]$ time units. Assume that a equals b. Then for the second stage we arrive at: $2/a + 2/3a = 8/3a = 2.67/a$. As this amount is smaller than $3/a$, we can see that the second activation coming from X and Y has already caught up with the first at nodes w(2) and z(2). If nodes w(1) and z(1) are still activated by amount a from the first stage (Assumption 2), then activation of Stage 2 reaches nodes w(2) and z(2) even sooner, after $2/a + 1/3a + 1/4a = 2.58$ time units.

When arriving at nodes w(1) and z(1), activation of the second stage shows an amount of $3a$. By this time, activation of the first stage 1 has not yet reached node w(2) or z(2). It can thus be assumed that nodes w(1) and z(1) are still activated by amount a, which adds up with the second stage, resulting in a total of $4a$. In the first stage, nodes w(2) and z(2) are activated almost simultaneously with amount a, and in the second stage with amount $4a$. The activations of w(2) and z(2) therefore amount to $5a$ after a total of $3/a$ time units. Because both activation processes meet and cross on the link between w(2) and z(2), the amount of activation of w(2) and z(2) increases still further — due to preactivation — to a value of 10a. In addition, one must consider the strengthening effect of that activation that travels over w(2), w(3), and z(3) and arrives at node w(2) and z(2).

These considerations confirm the predictions of the connectivity model. Because the number of components of X and Y increase the strength of activation in the second stage, the speed of the search process will increase, the more components the two codes X and Y comprise.

Here, in contrast to all of the previously discussed examples, it is impossible to give a generally valid quantitative prediction about the arrival time of preactivation $ap(xi)$ and $ap(yj)$. We have been able to show, however, that the arrival time of preactivation is not only dependent on the length of the common pathway. The three factors of spreading activation described earlier — the mutual strengthening of both search processes, the influence of codes lying in between, and the influence of the second activation stage of X and Y — all lead to a massive acceleration of the activation of the common pathway. However, it is the exact geometry of the network that determines the exact time of arrival of $ap(xi)$ and $ap(yj)$.

As we have been unable to find a general rule governing the time of arrival of $ap(xi)$ and $ap(yj)$, the question concerning the differentiation between a positive result belonging to Case 2 and a negative result belonging to Case 1 has remained unanswered. In what follows, we attempt to solve this problem, which we call "Problem 1."

8.6.2.4 Problem 1: On Differentiating Between a Positive Result of Case 2 and a Negative Result of Case 1. If we could know in advance how difficult a memory search will be, we would easily be able to distuingish between Case 1 and Case 2. However, there would be little point in looking for an exact criterion with which to estimate the level of difficulty. For this, one would in advance need that information about the common pathway that the search process aims to determine. But instead of an exact criterion, it is possible to define a rough criterion that allows us to distinguish between a simple and a complex search process. Although even this rough criterion will not be available at the very beginning, it will reveal itself during the course of the search process.

We now want to show that, as soon as the third activation stage in the most complex code X and Y is finished, a rough estimate is at hand. In order to make this idea plausible, reconsider the results of Case 1: There we found that $Ip(x)$ and $Ip(y)$ accumulate faster at the respective source node than $Is(x)$ and $Is(y)$. If two codes are not connected by common components, then it is clear that at the time of arrival of $Is(x)$ and $Is(y)$ a positive answer will never be obtained. If, however, common nodes exist, then—because of the strengthening effect of preactivation—indirect activation will arrive much faster. At the moment when Is of the code richest in components arrives at the corresponding source node, it is clear that code X and Y do not share common components. If, in spite of this negative result, a common pathway should be found, a complex search process must be initiated. It is crucial here to remember that whether or not the termination criterion for a negative result is accepted depends on the goal of the search process (Assumption C2). If the goal consisted in finding common components, then the search process must be terminated as soon as Is accumulates at a source node (no response to Case 1). If, however, the search goal was defined in a relatively vague manner, then from the moment Is accumulates at a source node, a critical waiting period $t(wI)$ must be fixed to allow for the arrival of $ap(xi)$ and $ap(yj)$. In estimating $t(wI)$, the definition of the search goal is used. The more vague the search goal, the longer $t(wI)$ will be and conversely: The more exact the search goal, the shorter $t(wI)$ will be. As Fig. 8.9 shows, by the time Is arrives it is clear whether or not a complex search must be initiated.

There is, however, another and easier way of defining a criterion with which to distinguish between simple and complex search processes. This criterion is only applicable if we replace Assumption 1 with the assumption of partially limited capacity (section 8.4.1). Here we can make use of the fact that with the number v of links leading from a node activation $o(j)$ of each link decreases (cf. Equation 8.10 and Table 8.1). This characteristic now enables us to state whether or not a code is isolated, that is, not connected with other components. If a code is isolated, then at point $t(Is)$ indirect activation Is arrives at the source node. This is to be expected in a standard case, and is evidence for a negative answer in Case 1. But if at least one pathway is leading from this code, then—because of this additional branching—less activation I flows back to the source node in the third activation stage. If I falls short of the value of Is, then it is clear that we are involved in a complex search process.

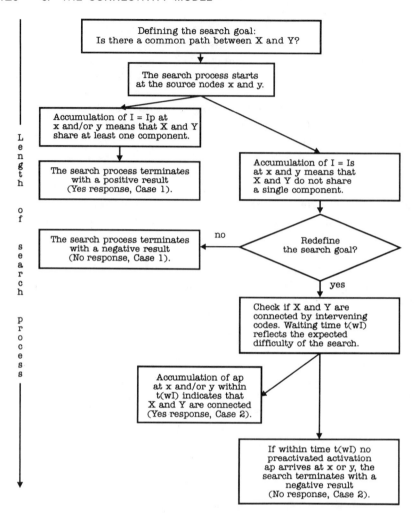

FIG. 8.9.   On the distinction between a simple and a complex search.

This criterion is only mentioned in passing because we would have unneccessarily complicated all of our previous examples had we proceeded from the assumption of partially limited capacity. However, all of the conclusions considered thus far would have held true, if instead of Assumption 1 we had proceeded from the assumption of partially limited capacity.

But let us return to the discussion of a complex search process. The attentive reader will not have failed to notice that we must also confront another problem, which deals with the limitations of spreading activation.

8.6.2.5 Problem 2: How Can It Be Guaranteed That the Search Process Is Not Terminated By Indirect or Preactivation Stemming from Irrelevant Codes? In illustrating this problem, we assume that code X is not only connected with code Y lying on a common pathway, but also with another code V, which does not lie on the common pathway between X and Y (Fig. 8.10). Indirect activation flowing back from code V is irrelevant for the discovery of the common pathway, but in spite of this it is capable of terminating the search process with a positive result. A similar consideration also applies to code U, which likewise does not lie on the common pathway and would mistakenly lead to an overvaluation of the relationship between X and Y.

As complicated as Problem 2 may appear, solving it is rather easy. In doing so, we proceed from the fact that there are always three activation stages in interconnected codes. In taking advantage of this fact, we assume that from the moment *Is* arrives at source node x or y, spreading activation of all other codes is terminated by the end of the second activation stage. This new assumption (Assumption C3) can thus be stated as follows:

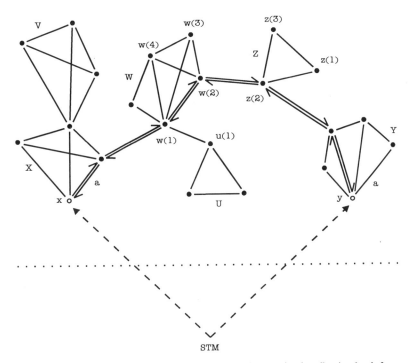

FIG. 8.10.   An example illustrating Problem 2: Indirect activation flowing back from code V to x terminates the search process between x and y before a common pathway can be found.

Assumption C3: The criterion needed for the beginning of a complex search process belonging to Case 2 is the arrival of *Is* at one of the two source nodes x or y. *Is* is the larger of the two activations *Is*(x) and *Is*(y), and therefore the one that arrives soonest. From time *t*(*Is*) onward, spreading activation within all other codes is terminated at the end of the second activation stage. The effectiveness of Assumption C ends as soon as the search process has been terminated according to Equations 8.16 and 8.17.

Assumption C3 prevents indirect activation from flowing back to that node of a code that was the first to be activated. Codes X and Y are not affected by Assumption C3, because they contain the source nodes from which the search process originated. As a result, the irrelevant effects of codes not lying on the common pathway are excluded (codes U and V in Fig. 8.10).

In those codes lying on a common pathway one must distinguish between two types of connections: With the common pathway a code may share links (e.g., code W) or nodes (e.g., code Z in Fig. 8.10). It is an important consequence of Assumption C3 that codes sharing only one single node with the common pathway cannot influence the search process. For example, take code Z (in Fig. 8.10) and look at the activation process proceeding from y. Once activation has reached node z(2), the second activation stage of code X and Y has already been concluded, and the third and fastest stage begins. Indirect activation *Is* therefore arrives at source nodes x and y, before nodes z(1) and z(3) can be reached. Assumption C3 becomes effective at this point. As a result, while the second activation stage in code Z can be terminated, the third activation stage does not occur. Thus no indirect activation flows from node z(1) and z(3) to either the common pathway or to node z(2).

In spite of Assumption C3, those codes sharing a link with the common pathway, however, do influence the search process and contribute to a strengthening of activation. Consider the following pathways within code W: Although activation flowing over nodes w(3) and w(4) is terminated at nodes w(1) and w(2), it contributes to a strengthening of the common pathway.

Codes sharing a link (i.e., two nodes) with the common pathway contribute more to its importance than codes sharing only one node. It is therefore quite plausible that only those codes having at least two nodes lying on the common pathway contribute to a strengthening and therefore to a higher evaluation of the common pathway.

Finally, it should be noted that Assumption C3 does not change any of the conclusions discussed in previous examples. Let us now turn to another problem. It arises out of Assumption 5, but plays only a subordinate role in its importance.

8.6.2.6 Problem 3: Assumption 5 May Briefly Interrupt the Search Process.   If activation coming from source nodes x and y meets at one and the same node (node w(2) in Fig. 8.10; not to be confused with Fig. 8.8), then — because of Assumption 5 — activation can only spread in the opposite direction after time $1/sh$ has elapsed. Because we had originally assumed that h equals 1, a delay of $1/s$ becomes effective. If we were to choose a value for h that is larger than 1 (e.g., 2), there no longer would be any delay if both activations met in the middle of the link (see the example in Fig. 8.8). In addition, it must be remembered that — in contrast to source activation — we have arrived at very high values for the activation of a common pathway. The more activation is transported along one link, the shorter will be the blockage time $1/sh$. It can therefore be seen that Assumption 5 does not lead to any significant delay of the search process.

But Assumption 5 can also lead to a situation in which subsequent and faster activation will catch up with a slower activation flowing ahead on the common pathway. But it is just as likely that activations flowing equally fast will only meet if Assumption 5 delays that activation flowing ahead. Thus, Assumption 5 may also contribute to an accelerated activation of the common pathway.

In summarizing our findings, we see that the predictions of the connectivity model also are supported by complex networks belonging to Case 2. The evaluation of the termination criterion for search processes with positive and negative outcomes is basically the same as in Case 1. Therefore, the predictions described for Case 1 are also applicable here. As we have seen, the number of components of X and Y is an important factor, which helps to speed up the search process. However, it may also be the case that a strongly interconnected common pathway can increase the amount of indirect activation to such an extent that the quantitative effect of X and Y is pushed into the background.

If we compare the length of the search process of Case 1 and 2, then, in addition to Predictions (a)-(e), the following prediction can be stated:

(f) Search times in Case 2 are, as a rule, longer than those in Case 1. This applies to search processes with a positive as well as with a negative result.

8.6.3 Control Processes Monitoring the Spread of Activation: On the Validity of Assumption C3

Traditional memory theories proceed from structural and processing assumptions. The connectivity model not only is based on these two types (Assumptions A and B 1-7), but also requires a third class of assumptions (see all assumptions belonging to C) concerning the way activation processes are monitored.

In answering the question of how Assumption C can be physically materialized or "implemented," consider a simulation program or a neuronal network. Here we encounter explicitly and for the first time the notion that those memory structures that serve to store information are not capable—at least not without additional assumptions—to explain control or monitor processes. It is a consequence of Assumption C3 that some type of monitoring authority must exist for each code to hold information about the three stages of spreading activation. Because it is connected to all the components of a code, the source node is well suited to take over this task. In fulfilling this task, it is necessary for each of the $n - 1$ links that connect the source node with the remaining nodes to transport also the information that is relevant for the status of spreading activation. This information may be coded by another impulse series as that information referring to the activation process. But we may also assume that there are separate "control links" running parallel to the network links.

With the help of the latter assumption, it is easy to explain the control of spreading activation that is monitored at the source node. At the time of its activation, each of the $n - 1$ nodes of a code sends a feedback signal via the control link back to the source node. When and how often each of the $n - 1$ nodes was activated is registered at the source node. The effectiveness of Assumption C3 can then be explained as follows: As soon as one of the $n - 1$ nodes has sent a feedback signal for a second time, spreading activation in this code is interrupted. It is important to note that even if the source node itself is not activated first, but another of the $n - 1$ nodes, it can still fulfill its monitoring and control function.

Our considerations so far have centered on the "local" representation of Assumption C3. This indeed suffices to explain why the spread of activation can be kept on the relevant points on the network: Any code that did not receive source activation stops the activation process after the second stage. But there are other tasks not yet considered. After the search process has terminated with a positive result, information must be available, with which intensity each of the codes was activated. This information will guide the retrieval process to access relevant parts of the common path. In order to guarantee this function, we must assume that the source nodes of all the codes are connected to a separate "control network." As this network only connects all the source nodes, but not the nodes of a code, it will be much smaller than the memory network.

We wish to emphasize the fact that the assumption of a control network should in no way be regarded as a special feature of the connectivity model. Each memory theory must confront the neglected question of how control processes are represented. For example, consider ACT and the experiments discussed in section 6.1. In sentence verification tasks, the search goal consists in finding common nodes that are activated by at least two pathways. In the framework of our discussion, it is important to find out how this information is retrieved, and not just how it is sought after. No details regarding this are given in the representational assumptions underlying ACT and ACT*. However, if we assume control networks that deliver a feedback concerning the amount of activation each code has received, then it is possible to directly access those parts of a network that have been activated rather intensively by a search process.

In other words, the information discovered or activated by a search process must also be capable of being retrieved. For this to happen, however, the relevant place in a network must be able to be directly accessed. We return to this question in section 8.7.1, where we distinguish between general and specific search processes.

8.7 THE TRANSITION BETWEEN STM AND LTM: LIMITED VERSUS UNLIMITED SPREADING ACTIVATION CAPACITY

Search processes are conducted with a specific goal in mind and under conscious control. It may therefore be assumed that they originate in STM (Assumption C1 and the comparison of consciousness and memory processes in Klimesch, 1989). This, however, does not imply that all the information activated during the course of a search process is at the disposal of or is communicated to STM or consciousness. It is much more plausible to assume that a search process in LTM, though initiated in STM, takes place largely automatically and independently of STM (A. Baddeley, Lewis, Eldridge, & Thomson, 1984). Because of the large amount of information that is activated during the course of a search process in LTM, the capacity of STM would simply not suffice to transfer all of that information to STM. Thus, the amount of information a search process yields must correspond to the capacitative limits of STM. As a result, only an extremely small part of the information activated by the search process in LTM can be communicated to STM.

Assume that the empirically well-supported concept of a limited STM capacity does not only apply to the amount of information stored in STM but also to the strength of activation processes. According to this idea, we have to assume that search processes starting out from STM are subject to capacity limitations. In section 8.4.1 we showed that the issue of limited capacity of spreading activation refers to the relation between input and output activation (Fig. 8.5). We emphasized that the processing assumptions of ACT and ACT* correspond to the assumption of a limited capacity of search processes. It thus seems appropriate to apply the assumptions of

ACT or ACT* to STM, and that of the connectivity model to LTM (section 8.4.1).

It appears plausible to assume that there is a limited amount of activation A that is at the disposal of STM in order to start a search process in LTM. Depending on the number of source nodes to be accessed in LTM, the amount of activation each of the source nodes receives, decreases according to Equations 6.1 and 6.3. The example shown in Fig. 8.11 illustrates this transition from STM to LTM.

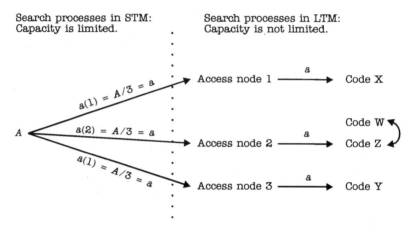

FIG. 8.11.   The amount of activation, A, to initiate a search is limited in STM. If the search starts at more than one access node in LTM, equal activation amounts, a, are allocated to each access node. In LTM, however, there are no capacity limitations which would further weaken the activation process.

The assumption of a limited spreading activation capacity results in the prediction that the speed of a search process in STM decreases, the more source nodes need to be accessed. Because not only spreading activation but also storage capacity is limited in STM, it must be assumed that the number of access points to LTM is also limited. This idea relates to Assumption C, which states that the amount of indirect activation flowing back to each access point reveals the result of a search process. The more access points used, the more information is delivered in the result of the search process, and the more strain there will be on the capacity of STM.

8.7.1 The Search Goal and the Limited Capacity of STM: General and Specific Search Processes

We have emphasized that only part of that information activated during the course of a search process can be made available to STM. But which criteria allow a selection of the relevant information? In answering this question we show that the extent to which the capacity of STM is strained depends on the type of search goal.

All of our previous considerations have assumed that the result of a search process only gives information on whether or not the sought-after information is available. This information is reflected by the amount of indirect activation I. The aim of this kind of a "general" search process, therefore, does not consist in recalling the content of one or more codes, but only in establishing whether or not the sought-after information is stored and how quickly it can be recalled. General search processes pursue the goal of establishing whether the sought-after information is available in memory. Specific search processes, on the other hand, pursue the goal of retrieving the contents of the sought-after information.

8.7.1.1 General Search Processes. A good example by which to explain the difference between general and specific search processes are semantic judgment tasks of the type "Is concept X (e.g., "eagle") a Y (e.g., "bird")?" In tasks of this kind it must be established whether a certain semantic relationship holds true for both concepts. This is a typical example of a general search process. Here, the extent of indirect activation suffices (section 8.6 and Equations 8.16 and 8.17) in order to judge the search goal, that is, the validity of the superordinate relation between "eagle" and "bird." The extent of indirect activation not only yields information on the validity of this relation, but also on the extent to which it is correct or incorrect. The question "Is an eagle a bird?" can be answered immediately, compared to the question "Is a penguin a bird?" Although, in a zoological sense, a penguin is also a bird, and the superordinate concept is correct in this case, "penguin" as opposed to "eagle" is an untypical example, and the superordinate relation is therefore not as relevant as it is for "eagle." Although the amount of indirect activation suffices in order to give a positive evaluation of the sought-after relation (i.e., $I = Ip > Is$), it is much less pronounced in comparison to "eagle."

General search processes show two important characteristics. First, the search goal always consists of recalling a relation (semantic relation, similarity relation, location relation, time relation, etc.) assumed to exist between two or more codes. Second, the result of a search process can be judged with "yes" or "no." Further examples of a general search process are: "Is a tree a living being?", "Do persons X and Y resemble each other?", "Is place X in state Y?", "Did fact X take place within time Y?", and so forth.

8.7.1.2 Specific Search Processes.   A completely different kind of search process is used to determine why, for example, an eagle is a bird. Here the search goal consists not only in the discovery of common pathways, but also in the retrieval of that information represented by these common pathways or characteristics. According to the connectivity model, it can be assumed that the search goal is reached in two stages. The first stage, which is equivalent to a general search process, is used to test whether or not the sought-after information is available in memory. The amount of indirect activation will give information on this. In the second stage, which is the specific search process, relevant information is retrieved. Only then can it be established whether or not a certain fact is correct.

How and according to which criteria is relevant information selected? The connectivity model assumes that those codes of the common pathway that have received the highest amount of activation represent the relevant information for that specific search process. Here, the crucial importance of a control network becomes evident. Direct access to relevant parts of the network requires a separate control network.

Consider the question "Why is an eagle a bird?" Furthermore, assume that both concepts share common features or code components in memory (section 9.1). In doing so, we are concerned with a network belonging to Case 1 (section 8.6.1). During the first stage, that is, the general search process, all code components of both codes are activated. Because of their high degree of integration common nodes receive the highest amount of activation (Equation 8.15). The specific search process now accesses those components that have been most strongly activated. These are the common nodes for both codes. If we assume that "eagle" and "bird" share the two common components "has feathers" and "can fly," then we have found the solution to the problem posed in our example. The specific search process directly accesses the most activated nodes, which are the common components, and the answer reads: "An eagle is a bird because it has feathers and can fly."

The explanation of specific and general search processes show that they both enable a very economical burden on the capacity of STM. In each case only an insignificantly small amount of information activated in LTM is transferred to STM. General search processes are even more economical than specific ones. Their search result consists only of one single measurement, and that is the amount of indirect activation. It is therefore to be expected that general search processes can be conducted and evaluated much faster than specific ones. This assumption is undoubtedly correct, as the examples discussed show. The question of whether or not an eagle is a bird can certainly be answered more quickly than the question of why an eagle is a bird.

8.8 THE IMPORTANCE OF PARAMETERS I AND $t(I)$
FOR THE PREDICTION OF REACTION TIMES IN
MEMORY EXPERIMENTS

Before turning our attention to the predictions of the connectivity model in the next chapter, we must point to the following important facts: Ratcliff and McKoon's (1981) results suggest that activation and search processes are conducted with such a high speed that they can hardly be used to predict reaction times in memory experiments. This result was also decisive in the revision of ACT and in the adoption of new assumptions by ACT*. It was assumed that the activation time per network link is so small as to be insignificant.

The assumption of an extremely fast activation and search time, which is empirically well grounded, does not present a problem for the predictions of the connectivity model. Both parameters I (the amount of indirect activation) and $t(I)$ (the spreading speed of I) are highly correlated: The larger I is, the smaller the value of $t(I)$. The extent of indirect activation I corresponds to the extent of positive evidence, which was discovered in a search process. The more positive evidence was found, the faster the result of the search process can be processed and the shorter reaction time (Assumption D). The amount of indirect activation can therefore be regarded as a primary factor in the prediction of reaction times.

Despite the outstanding importance of I and the close correlation between I and $t(I)$, there are cases in which the values of $t(I)$ alone can be decisive in the prediction of reaction times. The importance of $t(I)$ becomes apparent, above all, if the termination criterion for a search process is the critical factor. A good example of this is Prediction d (section 8.6.1): A search process with a negative result will only be influenced by the number of components of the code richest in characteristics, because it exhibits the shorter search time $t(Is)$ than the competing code, which comprises less components. Only an insignificant – and in the prediction of reaction times completely irrelevant – time difference between both values of $t(Is)$ will decide on which of the source nodes, x or y, the search process will terminate and which amount of indirect activation – that of X or Y – should be used in predicting the reaction time. It is thus the search time $t(Is)$ that is the critical factor in predicting reaction times.

As this example shows, the explicit consideration of activation and search times is necessary in order to make exact predictions. Had assumptions on $t(I)$ been lacking, we would not have been in a position to distinguish between the amounts of indirect activation stemming from codes X and Y.

Even if we are convinced that search times in memory are so short that they can have no influence on the prediction of reaction time, we should not make the mistake of omitting them from theoretical considerations. Memory theories that do so, for example ACT*, run the danger of not being able to distinguish between important determinants of reaction time.

9 A Connectivity Model for Semantic Processing

The central issue confronting semantic memory research is the investigation of word meaning. As demonstrated in chap. 7, most models of word meaning proceed from two basic hypotheses: the decomposition hypothesis and the hypothesis of a hierarchical structure of semantic features. The first hypothesis assumes that the meaning of a word is not represented as a holistic unit but instead by semantic features. The second hypothesis specifies that the structure connecting the features of a concept is hierarchical (McNamara & Sternberg, 1983). This view, described by Gentner (1981) as the complexity hypothesis, leads to the prediction that concepts with many features are processed more slowly than concepts with fewer features. However, when it turned out that the prediction of the complexity hypothesis could not be confirmed (Kintsch, 1974; Gentner, 1981; E. E. Smith & Medin, 1981), Kintsch (1980) was inclined to conclude that words are represented not by features but by holistic "supraword units" (Fodor et al., 1980). Thus, this controversy essentially refers to the question of whether or not concepts are represented by holistic or component codes.

Kintsch (1980) argued that the failure of the complexity hypothesis contradicts the decomposition hypothesis. Though widely accepted (E. E. Smith & Medin, 1981, p. 43), this conclusion is by no means conclusive. The failure of the complexity hypothesis may just as easily speak for the invalidity of the assumption of a hierarchical semantic structure.

Chapters 3 and 4 emphasize that the assumption of a holistic coding format results in a variety of contradictions. For this reason it would be wrong to abandon the decomposition hypothesis from the outset in favor of the assumption of holistic supraword units. All the results of our previous discussion indicate that the assumption of a hierarchical coding format is not only incorrect, but can also be regarded as the most important cause for the contradictions cited earlier.

Whereas the previous chapter dealt exclusively with the theoretical basis of the connectivity model, the aim of this chapter is to test its predictions. We want to show that the connectivity model enables a consistent interpretation of the results of semantic memory experiments. Semantic memory experiments are used because the representational assumptions (Assumption A and Assumption 1, section 8.3.3) of the connectivity model refer exclusively to the structure of LTM. The development of intensive interconnections between different coding components (features) requires time. Thus, it can hardly be assumed that the representational assumptions of the connectivity model can also be applied to STM or nonpermanent memory systems (cf. the experimental paradigms on fact retrieval and the discussion in sections 8.4.1 and 8.7). As emphasized in chap. 5 and 7, pure LTM demands exist only in semantic memory experiments, but not in experiments on fact retrieval. It therefore seems obvious to use semantic memory experiments when examining the connectivity model.

9.1 EVIDENCE FOR INTERCONNECTIONS BETWEEN SEMANTIC FEATURES

The connectivity model for semantic processing assumes that the features of a concept form an interconnected structure that represents the meaning of a concept. From chap. 8 we know that the maximum possible number of interconnections between n nodes increases exponentially with increasing n. However, in considering this tremendous increase in interconnections one might be tempted to object that the strength of the interconnections decreases as the number of semantic features increases. If this was true, the degree of interconnectedness would not be positively correlated with the number of features, and the complexity of a code could not be considered a meaningful predictor of reaction time. This possible conjecture was tested in Experiment 1 of Kroll and Klimesch (1992). We measured the strength of individual interconnections by asking subjects to rate the strength of each of the connections between a concept and its features (reflecting the connections between a concept node and its components) as well as the connections between all possible pairs of features. For a set of concepts, previous subjects had listed the features they felt were most characteristic and important (Klimesch, 1987). For this set of concepts, the actual number of features (variable: number of features, NOF) and the rated number of attributes (variable: number of attributes, NOA, from Toglia & Battig, 1978) were available. The most important measures obtained from Experiment 1 were the average rating values for the strength of connection between each concept and its features (variable: rated strength of concept--feature connections, RCF) and the average ratings for the strength of connection between the features (variable: rated strength of feature–feature connections, RFF) of each concept.

The results show that neither NOF nor NOA is significantly correlated with RCF. This indicates that the connection strength of a concept feature link does not vary with the complexity of a code. Most importantly, however, a highly significant and positive relationship was found between RFF and NOA ($r = .50$; $n = 48$) as well as RFF and NOF ($r = .65$; $n = 48$). Thus, the strength of the interconnections between the features of a concept *increases* as the complexity of a code increases. When interpreting this result, we have to keep in mind that, according to the connectivity model, any feature node must be linked to the concept node and, therefore, the degree of interconnectedness is solely reflected by the network interconnecting the features of a code. Thus, the strong positive correlation between the complexity of a concept and the strength of connections between the features provide good evidence for the assumption that features are indeed interconnected.

9.2 THE REPRESENTATION OF WORD MEANING ON THE BASIS OF INTERCONNECTED STRUCTURES

Apart from the question of how semantic information is represented in memory (cf. the review in Johnson-Laird, 1987), there appears to be general agreement regarding the following two assumptions of word coding (cf. the reviews in D. L. Nelson, 1979, and Klimesch, 1982a):

- The semantic and graphemic-phonemic information of a word is represented in different memory systems that are functionally independent. Graphemic-phonemic information refers to the perceptual characteristics of a word in its function as a sign or symbol and will hereinafter be referred to as *perceptual word code*.
- The semantic information of a word can be retrieved only after the perceptual word code has been accessed.

These basic assumptions are derived from the simple fact that the perceptual word code does not reveal the meaning of the word. Consequently, the graphemic-phonemic information of a word represented in isolation must be completely encoded before the word meaning becomes accessible. This, however, holds true only if we control for processes of expectancy and priming, which result from the linguistic context in which a word is usually embedded. The important conclusion, however, is that the semantic code of a word must reveal a specific access point in semantic memory. This specific access point is termed *concept node*.

The meaning of a word is not represented by the concept node itself, but by the structure of semantic features to which the concept node gives access. The type, number, and structure of semantic features are therefore the crucial variables in the encoding of word meaning. Figure 9.1 illustrates the assumptions discussed thus far. It now becomes clear that concept nodes serve to access the meaning of a word in semantic memory and vice versa, *word nodes* serve as access nodes in the movement from semantic memory to the graphemic-phonemic network (see Adams, 1979, and G. D. Brown, 1987, for a review of the different word coding models). When applying the connectivity model to the encoding of semantic information, the term *source node* becomes synonymous with concept node.

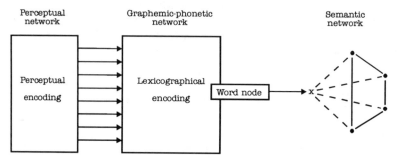

FIG. 9.1.   The meaning of a word becomes available only after a word is perceptually and lexicographically encoded. Word nodes and concept nodes (x) serve as access points in the transition from the graphemic-phonetic to the semantic network.

9.2.1 In the Transition from One Memory System to Another, Component Codes Can Be Used as Holistic Units

In contrasting holistic codes with component codes in chap. 3, we explicitly pointed out that only holistic, but not component codes, require specific access points or addresses. Are we then contradicting ourselves if we proceed from the assumption of specific access points? The answer is no, because we use the assumption of specific access points in order to explain the transition between two functionally different networks: the graphemic-phonemic and the semantic network. Activation spreading within semantic memory can activate any subset of components of a semantic code. There is no need to activate the concept node in order to get access to the components of that code. Consequently, the same also applies to the graphemic-phonemic network. Only the transition from one network to the other is guided by specific access points. In other words, Assumption A of the connectivity model (section 8.3) applies only within the semantic or graphemic-phonemic network and specifically to the codes stored in these networks, but not to the connections between both networks.

These considerations allow us to make the following interesting conclusion: A component code can be functionally holistic if it is accessed from another storage network. If the semantic component code of a word is retrieved by the graphemic-phonemic network or by the perceptual word code, then the semantic code will exhibit functionally holistic characteristics, and the all-or-nothing principle described in section 3.4 will govern retrieval attempts. A good example of this are word-finding disturbances (such as in aphatic syndromes) or the related "tip-of-the-tongue" phenomenon: A word cannot be recalled from memory at a particular point in time, even though its semantic information is available. At a later date, however, the sought-after word may suddenly and unexpectedly be available. But the findings of R. Brown and McNeill (1966) and other researchers (see A. S. Brown, 1991, for a more recent review) have also shown that in the event of a word-finding disturbance the first and final letter of the sought-after word may in all probability be guessed. The availability of single letters thus supports the assumption of component codes (see the argument in section 3.5) but refers to the graphemic-phonemic code and not to the transition between the graphic-phonemic and the semantic network. Therefore, with respect to this transition we may apply the all-or-nothing principle that is characteristic for holistic codes: A sought-after word becomes available in an abrupt as opposed to a gradual manner.

9.2.2 Semantic Features and Word Meaning

When applying the connectivity model to semantic processing we assume that word meaning is not only represented by semantic features but also by the links and relations between them. The structure of the features is just as important as the features themselves.

Those semantic features, on which the meaning of a word is based, are not seen as information components that are independent of each other. On the contrary, they refer to each other and form interconnected codes. This assumption is closely related to the notion that semantic features of natural concepts are co-related or will, in all probability, appear together (Malt & E. E. Smith, 1984; Medin & E. E. Smith, 1984; Rosch, 1978). Thus, for example, an animal that has feathers is in all probability capable of flying and will thus exhibit features like "wings," "beak," "feet," "claws," and so forth. The links of an interconnected code represent the relations between features. Therefore, a link between the features "wing" and "feather" means that the wings of a bird, but not those of an airplane or insect, have feathers.

What are semantic features? A variety of answers to this question have been put forward elsewhere (chap. 7). But whatever semantic features are, whether they consist of visual characteristics or abstract semantic primitives, they are definitely not verbal units.

In order to demonstrate the significance of this conclusion, consider again the concept *bird* and the features "fly," "feathers," and "wings." These so-called features are themselves concepts with a word node, a concept node, and a structure of features. If we were to assume that the concept nodes of "fly," "feathers," and "wings" are feature nodes of the concept *bird*, then we will inevitably have to accept that the features of a concept are verbal units. In this case the meaning of a word would no longer be represented by object-related features, but instead by other words (see the critique of traditional network theories by Johnson-Laird, Herrmann, & Chaffin, 1984).

Likewise, the connectivity model prevents us—albeit for different reasons—from proceeding from this assumption. Section 8.5 demonstrates that different interconnected codes may in no way exhibit common source nodes. Consequently, the feature nodes of a code may not at the same time be concept nodes for other codes.

An obvious solution to this problem is the assumption of an overlapping feature representation (Assumption I in section 9.2.4). For example, consider the hypothetical encoding structure in Fig. 9.2 for the concept "bird" and the features "fly," "feathers," and "wings."

The crucial idea here is that in the context of a certain concept every feature has a very special and specific meaning. Within the concept "bird," "wing" has a very specific meaning that can best be represented by its special form and function. It now becomes clear that the feature "form of a wing" [f(wing)] cannot be equated with the concept "wing." Furthermore and most importantly, f(wing) is a feature for both concepts "bird" and "wing." Similar considerations apply to the feature "fly," which likewise has a very specific meaning in this context and can in no way be equated with the concept "flight."

The notion of an overlapping feature representation is also consistent with the idea that features are not verbal units. The specific form of a wing, just as the specific type of flight of, for example, a bird, an airplane, or a helicopter, may be circumscribed verbally. However, they lack a verbal concept with which to describe the subject in a single word. We thus see that semantic features can only be circumscribed linguistically, whereas a concept can be expressed in one word.

The assumption of an overlapping feature network, in which one or more concepts share the same feature, is in agreement with the connectivity

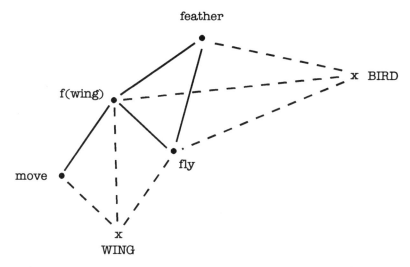

FIG. 9.2.   Semantic features are neither words nor concepts (shown in capital letters). Wing in the context of BIRD denotes a very specific form of a wing [f(wing)] which also is a feature of the concept WING. Although not shown here, the same holds true for the other features of BIRD, fly and feather.

model. In section 8.6, for example, we made explicit reference to cases in which codes share common components.

9.2.3 Word Meaning and Context

The meaning of a word cannot be known without reference to its defined context (Fodor et al., 1980). Feature theories are therefore confronted with the following problem: How is it possible to define the meaning of a word while using a particular set of semantic features, if their number and structure varies as a result of different contexts?

On the basis of the connectivity model, this question can be answered quite easily. Preactivation and inhibition (section 8.5.5) are processes capable of changing the meaning of a word without changing the geometry of the network. "Wings" in the context of "bird" has a different meaning when placed in the context of "airplane" or "insect." The specific meaning of a word is a result of the context that triggers the activation of relevant and/or the inhibition of irrelevant features. If, for example, in a priming experiment, first "bird" and then "wing" is represented, it may be assumed that the features of the preactivated concept "wing" refer to the typical wing form of a bird, while at the same time the feature of the typical form of an airplane is being inhibited. Preactivation and inhibition guarantee the selection of a specific meaning at the expense of other possible meanings and, therefore, prevent all aspects of meaning from entering consciousness at the same time.

In good agreement with these suggestions, the results of priming experiments have shown that relevant features (relevant "primes") generally lead to shorter reaction times than irrelevant ones (Tabossi & Johnson-Laird, 1980; Tanenhaus & Lucas, 1987). The findings by Kroll and Klimesch (1992), outlined in section 9.7, also provide evidence for the specific effectiveness of preactivation.

Johnson-Laird (1987) differentiated between three different context effects. The context allows:

- the selection of ambiguous concepts with different meanings,
- the specification of the meaning of a concept, and
- the emphasis of particular aspects at the expense of other aspects.

All three context effects may be explained within the framework of the connectivity model through preactivation and inhibition processes. This applies to the selection, specification, and rejection of irrelevant aspects of word meaning.

9.2.4 Conceptual Hierarchies, Typicality, and Interconnected Structures

The assumption of a hierarchical arrangement of concepts is empirically well supported (chap. 7). This not only holds true for verbal-semantic, but also for visual-semantic information processing (Hoffman & Zießler, 1986; Palmer, 1977). But how can a hierarchical structure be represented by interconnected codes? Is this a contradiction in itself? Is it necessary to assume that hierarchically structured information must also be represented hierarchically? In the following we show that this objection would be misleading and that interconnected codes are well capable of representing hierarchically structured information.

The point of interest here is the way in which concepts of the same category but with a differring hierarchical status are connected to each other. Here *category* means a set of concepts subordinate to the superordinate concept denoting that category. When applying the connectivity model to conceptual hierarchies we proceed from the following assumptions, which are based on the idea of an overlapping feature structure:

Assumption I: The features typical for a category are those that the superordinate concept shares with its subordinate concepts.

Assumption II: Each feature of a category is represented at only one particular place in the network.

The purpose of Assumption II is simply to avoid a redundant storage of semantic features. It is consistent with the general principle of the economical use of storage capacity and is thus in no way specific to the connectivity model. The conclusions that can be derived from Assumption I are discussed in greater detail later. Prior to this, however, it may be helpful to take a closer look at the concept of typicality.

9.2.4.1 Typicality, Basic Level Concepts, and Typical Features. The research on typicality is closely related to the research of Eleanor Rosch. In her view (e.g., the review in Rosch, 1978), typicality is a relation that is only valid within one and the same category. It refers to the degree with which a subordinate concept is a more or less characteristic example of the corresponding superordinate concept.

In a broader sense, the typicality relation may be applied to all different types of categories as well as all different types of sub- and superordinate relations. In a narrower sense, however, typicality applies to a very specific level in the conceptual hierarchy, which was termed "basic concept level" (Rosch, et al., 1976) or "primary concept level" (Hoffmann, 1986). Basic level concepts and primary concepts (e.g., "car" or "bird" in contrast to "vehicle" or "living being") are complex (i.e., have many semantic features) and comprise many subordinate concepts. They are located on the highest level in the conceptual hierarchy, that can still be described by sensory prototypes or schemas. For example, consider the typical shape of a car or a bird that can be used to summarize a great number of differing but similar objects (Rosch et al., 1976). The more a concept resembles its prototype, the more typical that concept is.

Typical features represent the most important characteristics of a category, but they do not allow one to arrive at a strictly logical definition, stating whether or not a concept belongs to a certain category (see McCloskey & Glucksberg, 1978; Medin, Altom, & Murphy, 1984; as well as the reviews in Medin & E. E. Smith, 1984, and E. E. Smith & Medin, 1981). One of the most comprehensive definitions of typicality was given by Rosch and Mervis (1975). They demonstrated that the extent of typicality can be indicated by the number and frequency of those semantic features that occur in most concepts of that category. If in a feature-listing experiment the frequency with which each feature occurs in all other concepts of the same category is determined, and the sum of these frequencies is calculated for all of the features of a concept, the result is a good indicator of typicality. This measure will increase the more common and frequent features a concept contains.

For example, take a hypothetical category consisting of four concepts and six different features (F1, F2 . . . F6). Furthermore, assume that one of the four concepts (Concept 4) comprises only two features (F1 and F6); one feature (F1) occurs in all other concepts, but the other feature (F6) is only confined to this concept and does not occur in any of the other concepts (Table 9.1). Thus, F1 occurs four times whereas F6 occurs only once. The frequency sum for Concept 4 therefore amounts to 5. Using this measure— the frequency sum of the features of a concept—Rosch and Mervis (1975) coined the term *family resemblance*. They found a significant relationship between family resemblance and typicality (as measured by a rating scale). This result thus suggests that typicality is not a holistic prototype but may ultimately be described by a particular structure of semantic features. Those features that occur most frequently in the entire category determine the extent to which a concept may be regarded as typical. We can, therefore, denote those features that occur frequently in a category as typical features.

The linear-additive structure underlying the measurement of family resemblance could mistakenly create the impression that typical features exist independently of each other (Armstrong, L. R. Gleitman, & H. Gleitman, 1983). Because the independence of features implies a hierarchical structure, we would end up contradicting the representational assumptions of the connectivity model. (See the distinction made between independent cue and relational encoding models in section 9.2.5). However, in a series totaling seven experiments, Medin, Wattenmaker, and Hampson (1987) demonstrated that the measurement of family resemblance yields adequate results only if the relevant features are correlated. The authors therefore assume that typicality may be described by a structure of related features (Murphy & Medin, 1985).

9.2.4.2 Typical Features and the Conceptual Hierarchy. Although Assumption I agrees in all essential aspects with the findings of Rosch, there is an important difference to be pointed out. Rosch's approach only concerns that distribution of features assumed to exist between the subordinate concepts of a category. The conclusion to be derived from Assumption I, however, refers to the structure of superordinate concepts: The typical features of a category are at the same time the features of the superordinate concept denoting this category.

TABLE 9.1
The Measurement of Family Resemblance

Concepts	Feature Weights			Family Resemblance
Concept 1	F1(4)	F2(2)	F3(2)	8
Concept 2	F1(4)	F3(2)	F4(1)	7
Concept 3	F1(4)	F2(2)	F5(1)	7
Concept 4	F1(4)	F6(1)	----	5

Note: The numbers in parentheses refer to the frequency a feature occurs in the set of concepts; the sum of these frequencies gives the degree of family resemblance.

What do Rosch's findings mean in the light of Assumptions I and II? Because typical features are those occuring most frequently in a category, and because each feature may only be represented in one place in the network, typical features must be intensively interconnected with many other features. Typical features therefore lead to an essentially stronger interconnection within the category than less typical features. Thus, typical features take on a special status, not only because they generally lead to a higher degree of interconnectedness but also because they serve as the most important connection between sub- and superordinate concepts.

The way in which a conceptual hierarchy can be represented by an interconnected structure is shown in Fig. 9.3. Here there are three interconnected codes, each belonging to one of three different conceptual levels that, according to Hoffmann (1986), can be denoted as sub-, middle-, and superordinate concept levels. The code for "animal" comprises two, the

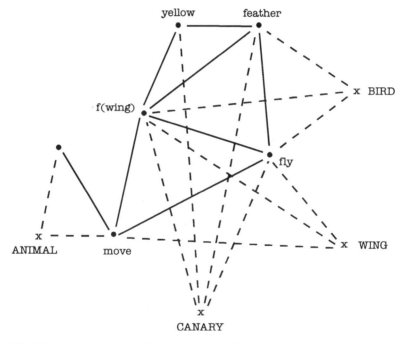

FIG. 9.3. An interconnected structure is capable of representing a conceptual hierarchy. The example shows four codes, a subordinate concept (canary), a middle level concept (bird) and a superordinate level concept (animal). Concept "wing" illustrates the difference between a feature [f(wing)] and a concept. The middle level concept which in our example is a basic level concept shares its features with the subordinate concept (Case 1 in section 8.6.1). The superordinate concept "animal," however, is linked only by common pathways (Case 2 in section 8.6.2) with other concepts of the same category.

code for "bird" three, and the code for "canary" four components. Thus, the lower the hierarchical level of a concept, the more features it comprises. It should also be noted that common features exist only between "canary" and "bird" but not between "canary" and "animal" and not between "bird" and "animal," because the features "feathers," "wings," and "fly" may be regarded as typical for the majority of concepts belonging to the middle-level concept "bird."

Because of Assumptions I and II, a subordinate concept like "canary" must, in our example, share the typical features of the middle-level concept. In contrast to subordinate concepts, however, the middle-level concept shows no specific features such as "yellow" for "canary." The middle-level concept is defined exclusively by typical features. Because subordinate and middle-level concepts share common features in our example, the network structure assumed here corresponds to Case 1 in section 8.6.1, and the predictions outlined there are also applicable here.

The importance of the basic concept level for typicality can also be demonstrated here. It becomes obvious if we consider the degree of abstraction and specificity of the features. "Wings," "feathers," and "fly" are highly specific features because they can be visualized easily. Although more abstract than the subordinate concept "canary," the middle-level concept "bird" can still be visualized, but in a more abstract way and in the form of a prototype only. On the other hand, unlike in the case of "bird," no common visual prototype exists for "animal," which would agree in the same way with all other breeds of animal. When compared to those of subordinate concepts, the features of "animal" are abstract and nonspecific. This is a consequence of the conceptual hierarchy requiring that a superordinate concept must apply to a very large and heterogeneous number of subordinated concepts. Consider the superordinate concept feature "move." It is abstract and unspecific, because it may denote many different forms of "movement" such as "creep," "crawl," "go," and so forth, and not only "fly," which is typical and specific for birds. It would, therefore, be wrong to assign "fly" to the superordinate concept "animal."

As can be seen in the example outlined in Fig. 9.3, the superordinate concept does not share a single feature with the subordinate and middle-level concepts "canary" and "bird." There is only one common pathway between the superordinate and subordinate concept level. This network, therefore, corresponds to Case 2 in section 8.6.2. Although similar predictions apply to Cases 1 and 2, it must be remembered that search times in Case 2 generally tend to be longer than those in Case 1 (Prediction f).

Asumption I is only valid for Case 1 but not for Case 2. Whether or not typical features exist between the superordinate and subordinate concept level depends on the heterogeneity of the concepts of the category. In the case of very heterogeneous categories (e.g., animals), which comprise very different middle-level concepts, it is necessary to proceed from relatively abstract superordinate concept features such as "move." Thus, in this case of very heterogeneous categories the concept of typicality is meaningless.

According to the connectivity model, the hierarchical status of a concept can therefore be indicated by three criteria: the number, structure, and type of its features. Apart from the special hierarchical status of basic concepts, the following general relationship can be suggested: The more abstract a concept is, the fewer features it will comprise and the more heterogeneous and therefore less interconnected its features will be. The level of the conceptual hierarchy not only determines the number of features but also the type of features: The higher the hierarchical status of a concept, the more abstract it will be and the fewer features it will comprise.

Within the framework of the connectivity model, typicality can be explained by the structure of features that exists between sub- and superordinate concepts. Thus, typicality may not be considered as an additional characteristic of concepts, but instead as a result of its feature structure: Many common, that is, overlapping, features of a category lead to an intensely interconnected structure, which determines the "typical meaning" of this category.

Basic concepts and typicality are thus closely related concepts. Previously we have emphasized that basic concepts share many features with their subordinate concepts. These overlapping features form an interconnected network that at the same time determines the meaning and the typical structure of basic concepts. Typicality and the structure of basic concepts both refer to the different aspects of the central tendency of a category's meaning (Rosch et al. 1976; Whitney & Kellas, 1984; and albeit with certain reservations also Barsalou, 1985; Chumbley 1986; Medin et al., 1984). Whereas basic concept refers to a superordinate concept with a high number of intensely interconnected features, typicality refers to the structure of overlapping features that connects a superordinate concept with its subordinate concepts. The greater the degree of overlap, the more typical the subordinate concept is in relation to its superordinate concept.

Consequently, typicality is best applied to those categories that actually show a high degree of feature overlap. It therefore makes sense to speak of an "eagle" as a typical "bird." But it hardly makes any sense to denote an eagle as a typical animal or a typical living being. Is there anything like a "typical animal" or even a "typical living being?" The more abstract a category is, the less sense it makes to speak of typical concepts.

The result of our discussion can be summarized as follows: The interconnected structure of overlapping features is the central concept used in explaining typicality, conceptual hierarchy, and the structure of basic concepts.

9.2.5 The Connectivity Model and Other Categorization Models

The connectivity model explains semantic relatedness in terms of overlapping features. Previous sections have shown that Rosch's prototype corresponds also to this structure of overlapping features. According to the connectivity model, categorization processes can be described as search processes emanating from two codes (chap. 8): If common features exist, then a concept may be quickly recognized as belonging to a specific category. All the predictions made for Case 1 in section 8.6 (i.e., two codes share common features) and Case 2 (i.e., two codes are only connected by a common pathway) can be applied to categorization processes. Sections 9.6 and 9.7 deal with these predictions in greater detail.

Many other categorization models focus on the way features can be used in classifying concepts. Thus the question arises as to how the connectivity model differs with respect to conventional theories. When answering this question, we should keep in mind that the connectivity model was conceived with the goal of explaining how the coding format determines the speed of search processes in LTM. Because it was designed for that purpose, it comes as no surprise that the representational assumptions of other categorization models are not nearly as explicit as those of the connectivity model. This makes it difficult to compare our model with others. The literature distinguishes between probabilistic, prototype, and exemplar models (cf. the review in Medin & E. E. Smith, 1984). More recently, connectionist approaches such as the distributed memory model (Knapp & J. A. Anderson, 1984), as well as independent cue and relational encoding models (Medin et al., 1984), have received widespread attention.

In the foregoing sections, we saw that prototype models agree to a great extent with the assumptions of the connectivity model. The same also holds true for probabilistic models. Whether features are regarded as variables and their relative importance is indicated by probabilities, or whether they are defined within the framework of a network theory, is primarily a matter of the accuracy with which representational assumptions are defined. Both approaches, although different, can nevertheless be compatible. Thus, for example, activation values of individual features in a network can easily be interpreted in terms of probabilities.

Similarly, exemplar models are also compatible with the basic assumptions of the connectivity model. One or more typical examples of a category can serve to describe their central characteristic, as outlined in the foregoing section. Typical examples establish the intensely interconnected structure of overlapping features and therefore define the essential aspects of what is characteristic and typical of a category. So the exemplar model refers to some of those assumptions that also underlie the connectivity model. The question of how the similarity between the concepts of a category may be described, whether by a probabilistic approach, by typical examples (Hintzman, 1986; Hintzman & Ludlum, 1980), or by set theoretical approaches (Sattath & Tversky, 1987), is once again a matter of the accuracy of the representational assumptions.

The models described previously, however, are only compatible with the connectivity model if they accept the assumption of correlating features. Independent cue models are, in contrast to relational coding models, not compatible with the connectivity model because they are based on the assumption that independent dimensions can be used to represent the meaning of concepts. However, a series of experiments (Medin et al., 1984, 1987; Murphy & Medin, 1985) support the validity of relational encoding models and thus also an important assumption of the connectivity model.

Distributed memory models proceed from the basic idea that similar codes overlap and are thus not stored independently of each other (Knapp & J. A. Anderson, 1984; McClelland & Rumelhart, 1985). These models are therefore not only compatible with the assumption of a correlated and interconnected feature structure, but also with Assumptions I and II (section 9.2.4) of the connectivity model.

The most important distinction between the connectivity model and other theories refers to the question of how the complexity of a code can be a factor that either speeds up or slows down processing speed. The models addressed earlier do not give an answer to this question (chap. 12).

9.3 THE CONNECTIVITY MODEL AND EMPIRICAL FINDINGS ON THE HIERARCHY EFFECT

Collins and Quillian (1969) discovered that reaction time decreases in semantic decision tasks of the type "Is X a Y?" the further apart both concepts X and Y are in their hierarchical status. A number of experiments (Hoffman, 1986; Hoffman & Klimesch, 1984) repeated these findings. However, there are some important exceptions to this rule. But is the connectivity model capable of explaining these findings?

The simplest explanation of the semantic hierarchy effect is based on the assumption that subordinate concepts comprise more features than middle-level concepts and these, in turn, have more features than superordinate concepts. This assumption appears to be plausible, as superordinate concepts are more abstract than the more concrete and specific ones. As shown in chap. 8, codes with many features can be processed faster than codes with only a few features. Consequently, in a semantic decision task, subordinate concepts will be judged faster than middle-level concepts and these, in turn, faster than superordinate concepts.

In a feature listing experiment, Hoffman and Zießler (1982) were actually able to demonstrate that the number of features decreases as the hierarchical status of a concept increases (Hoffman, 1986, p. 68). This result thus provides a simple and straightforward explanation of the hierarchy effect: The more features a concept comprises, the quicker it can be processed.

There are, however, exceptions to the hierarchy effect. Most interestingly, the hierarchy effect fails to appear in those cases in which the superordinate concept does not coincide with the basic concept level (Hoffman, 1982; Hoffman, Zießler, & Grosser, 1984; Jolicoeur, Gluck, & Kosslyn, 1984; Murphy & Smith, 1982; Rosch et al., 1976; E. E. Smith, Balzano, & Walker, 1978). Consider the following concept hierarchy as an example: "oak" — "deciduous tree" — "tree." Here the superordinate concept "tree" is the basic concept because it is the highest ranking concept that can still be represented by a common sensory prototype. In the conceptual hierarchy "jeep" — "car" — "vehicle," the middle-level concept "car" is the basic concept. However, it is also possible that the basic concept lies on the level of the subordinate concept, as is illustrated in the example "banana" — "fruit" — "nourishment." Here the middle-level concept "fruit" shows no common sensory characteristics that would apply to all or at least the majority of the various types of fruit. Using concept hierarchies of that type, Hoffman (1986, p. 89) and Hoffman and Klimesch (1984, p. 17) demonstrated that in a semantic decision task of the type "Is X a Y?" the basic concepts "tree," "car," and "banana," reveal the shortest decision times, and their rank in the concept hierarchy does not play any role (Fig. 9.4).

These results clearly indicate that the hierarchical rank of a concept can in no way be the only factor influencing reaction times in semantic decision experiments. Simple hierarchical coding models (e.g. Collins & Quillian, 1969) are, therefore, not in a position to explain the findings discussed here.

The most conclusive evidence supporting the connectivity model is an additional finding that was discovered in the aforementioned feature-listing experiment by Hoffman and Zießler (1982). Here it was demonstrated that subordinate concepts comprise the highest number of features only if they are at the same time basic concepts, and that basic concepts generally have more features than other concepts of the same hierarchical level. Similar findings were also reported by Tversky and Hemenway (1984). They found that subjects list many features (here understood more specifically as "parts of objects") for basic concepts, but only a few for those concepts ranking higher in the conceptual hierarchy.

These important findings provide additional support for the hypothesis that it is the number of features, and not the hierarchical status per se, which determines the length of semantic decision times. The more features

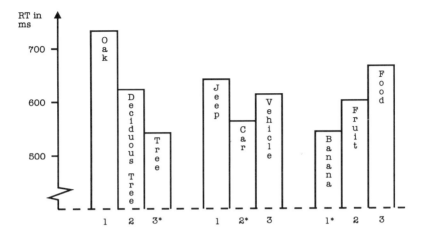

FIG. 9.4.   In a semantic decision task, basic level concepts (marked with "*") show the fastest RTs, regardless of their hierarchical rank (1 = subordinate level; 2 = middle level; 3 = superordinate level). Data from *Die Welt der Begriffe* (p. 89) by Hoffmann, 1986. © 1986 by VEB. Reprinted with permission.

a concept comprises, the faster it can be processed. Because basic concepts possess the most features, they show the shortest decision times.

Section 8.6.1 emphasized that the number of overlapping (i.e., common) features is an additional factor that speeds up processing time. Basic concepts are defined by virtue of the fact that they have many sensory features that they usually share with a variety of subordinate concepts. We have assumed that common features are at one and the same time typical (Assumptions I and II). Consequently, basic concepts are also processed faster because they show many typical (i.e., common or overlapping) features. (See the example in Fig. 9.3 in which "bird" is the basic concept.)

The large number of overlapping features that exist between basic and subordinate concepts leads one to expect that reaction time differences between typical and less typical concepts are not very pronounced. For example, take the superordinate concept "tree," which is at the same time the basic concept. The typical oak should not be recognized any sooner than the untypical acacia. This assumption arises because, in this example, the degree of family resemblance will be generally very high for all of the concepts in that category. Consequently, the lack of a few common features will only have a small effect. If, however, we consider the typicality relation between the superordinate concept "nourishment," which is not a basic concept, and subordinate concepts (like "bread," "banana," and "pumpkin," etc.), then it becomes evident that there are only a small number of overlapping features. Consequently, the degree of family resemblance will be very low. It is precisely for this reason that the differences between typical and untypical concepts in more heterogenous categories should be more pronounced. Hoffman's (1986, p. 90) findings support this assumption and demonstrate that typicality differences are much more pronounced if the superordinate concept is not a basic concept.

9.4 THE CONNECTIVITY MODEL AND EMPIRICAL FINDINGS ON THE TYPICALITY EFFECT: EVALUATING ASSUMPTION I

The findings described thus far have shown that the connectivity model is capable of explaining those effects that refer to the hierarchical structure of concepts. This section focuses on Assumption I, which states that the typical features of a category are the features of the superordinate concept denoting this category. This crucial assumption was tested in an experiment designed especially for this purpose (Experiment 1, Klimesch, 1987).

In this study, subjects were asked to list features for a series of 72 subordinate concepts and 6 middle-level concepts ("bird, "fruit," "vegetable," "article of clothing," "vehicle," "weapon"). The sample of 72 subordinate concepts comprises 6 groups of 12 concepts, each group belonging to one of the 6 middle-level concepts. For each of the 72 words, the following word norms (taken from Toglia & Battig, 1978) were available: imagery, categorizability, meaningfulness, familiarity, and the estimated number of features as well as the typicality scores collected by Rosch (1975, p.229). Subjects were instructed to associate each word with those properties that determine important features, parts, or functions of the object denoted by the respective word (see the instructions in Klimesch, 1987, p. 56). For data analysis, only those features listed by at least two subjects were considered. After this first selection, which yielded a total of 397 different features, the frequency with which each feature occurred was determined. Then a split-half reliability coefficient was calculated: The sample of subjects was devided into two halves, and within each half the frequency with which a feature occurs was calculated. Thus, two frequency values were collected for each of the 397 features. Correlating the frequencies within the selected sample of features yielded a coefficient of $r = .71$ ($p < .001$, $N = 397$).

Before Assumption I can be tested, we have to make sure that super- and subordinate concepts do indeed share common features.

9.4.1 Do Super- and Subordinate Concepts Share Common Features?

In analyzing the features of middle-level concepts together with those of their subordinate concepts, we find that in 62 of the 72 cases common features do exist. Thus, in about 90% of all examined cases a subordinate concept shares at least one feature with its corresponding superordinate concept. The results for the categories "vehicles" and "birds" are listed in Table 9.2. Keeping in mind that the collected features are just verbal correlates of inferred features, and that the way of associating the respective verbal label may vary considerably from subject to subject, the extent of feature overlap found in this experiment is undoubtedly large enough to validate Assumption I.

9.4.2 Are Common Features Also Typical Features?

In examining this question we proceeded from the notion that features frequently listed (e.g., "fly" for bird in Table 9.2) are more important for a concept than those indicated less frequently (e.g., "lays eggs"). Accordingly, frequencies may be interpreted as weights. For common features, two different types of weights or frequencies must be considered. One of the two frequencies indicates how important a feature is for the superordinate concept (see the column entries in Table 9.2), whereas the other frequency reveals how important this same feature is for the subordinate concept (see the unbracketed numbers in the rows of Tables 9.2, Part A, B).

According to the connectivity model, typicality is a function of the number of common features. The extent of a concept's typicality may thus be expressed by the weighted sum of common features (variable WSC; see the bracketed numbers in the rows of Table 9.2). Variable WSC can be interpreted as a measure for the typicality of a subordinate concept (see the values in the last column of Table 9.2). It indicates to what extent a subordinate concept shares important features with its superordinate concept. The higher the WSC, the more typical is the respective concept.

The procedure described here is similar to that used by Rosch and Mervis (1975) in determining family resemblance. The essential difference between both methods lies in the way common features are defined. According to Rosch and Mervis, common features are those that occur in many subordinate concepts of a category. In contrast, we proceed from the hypothesis that common features are those that a superordinate concept shares with its subordinate concepts. However, we also have to keep in mind that features occurring frequently in a category are most likely to be at the same time the features of the respective superordinate concept. It can therefore be assumed that both definitions will lead to similar conclusions.

In verifying this hypothesis, the following procedure was used. In Step 1 those features were determined for each of the six categories which occurred in at least 4 of the 12 subordinate concepts. In Step 2 these features were compared with those of the corresponding superordinate concept. As

TABLE 9.2
Distribution of Features for the Concepts "Vehicle" and "Bird"

A. Concept "Vehicle"

Concept	Transportation 14	Wheels 13	Fast 7	Motor 7	Driving 4	WSC
Car	10(140)	17(221)	5(35)	11(77)	2(8)	481
Truck	6(84)	18(234)	0	9(63)	0	381
Scooter	4(56)	15(195)	3(21)	9(63)	0	335
Jeep	2(28)	14(182)	3(21)	2(14)	2(8)	253
Jet	3(42)	0	16(112)	6(42)	0	196
Tractor	0	14(182)	0	2(14)	0	196
Trailer	0	14(182)	0	0	0	182
Train	4(56)	2(26)	3(21)	10(70)	0	173
Trolley	4(56)	6(78)	0	0	0	134
Boat	0	0	3(21)	9(63)	0	84
Ship	0	0	0	2(14)	0	14
Yacht	0	0	0	0	0	0
Sum	33	100	33	60	4	
Mean WSC						202
SD						143

B. Concept "Bird"

	Fly 20	Feather 14	Wing 13	Beak 12	Sing 7	Makes a Nest 6	Lays Eggs 5	WSC
Sparrow	12(240)	10(140)	10(130)	7(84)	4(28)	6(36)	3(15)	673
Robin	11(220)	11(154)	10(130)	4(48)	9(63)	2(12)	2(10)	637
Eagle	12(240)	13(182)	9(117)	7(84)	0	0	2(10)	633
Duck	7(140)	18(252)	5(65)	9(108)	0	0	2(10)	575
Lark	12(240)	7(98)	6(78)	4(48)	13(91)	0	0	555
Pigeon	9(180)	10(140)	11(143)	7(84)	0	0	0	547
Hawk	11(220)	10(140)	7(91)	8(96)	0	0	0	547
Cardinal	10(200)	10(140)	8(104)	7(84)	0	0	0	528
Owl	10(200)	14(196)	5(65)	3(36)	0	0	0	497
Bluejay	8(160)	11(154)	8(104)	2(24)	3(21)	3(18)	2(10)	491
Swallow	10(200)	7(98)	7(91)	6(72)	2(14)	0	0	475
Crow	8(160)	8(112)	9(117)	7(84)	0	0	0	473
Sum	120	129	95	71	31	11	11	
Mean WSC								554
SD								67

Note: The number in each column represents the frequency with which a feature was listed by a sample of 28 subjects; numbers in parenthesis represent weights and are obtained by multiplying the features in each row and column; WSC stands for Weighted Sum of Common Features, which is the sum of weights in each row.

a result it was found that 70% of the features determined in the first stage were features of the superordinate concept. This high degree of overlap confirms the assumption that WSC and the measure of "family resemblance" yield similar results.

Is WSC in fact a suitable variable with which to define typicality? In trying to answer this question, variable WSC was correlated with the typicality scores (variable typicality TYP) collected by Rosch (1975). The result shows the highly significant correlation between WSC and TYP of $r = -.39$ ($p < .001$; $n = 72$). The fact that the correlation is negative is due to the way variable TYP is scaled: A low rating score indicates high typicality, whereas a high WSC score indicates low typicality. In order to avoid any misinterpretation, it should be emphasized that variable TYP used here was determined by ratings and not on the basis of family resemblance measurements.

9.4.3 Overlapping Features, Degree of Interconnectedness, and Basic Concepts

Assumption I and the arguments outlined in section 9.3 suggest that subordinate concepts belonging to a basic concept show a greater number of features than subordinate concepts not belonging to a basic concept. As we have pointed out, variable WSC reflects the weighted sum of features a superordinate concept shares with the subordinate concepts. It can thus be expected that basic concept categories will, on average, show higher WSC values than those categories that do not belong to a basic concept. Only one of the six superordinate concepts used in the following experiment, namely "bird," is a basic concept. The average WSC values and standard deviations of the 12 subordinate concepts of each category are listed in Table 9.3.

As the results in Table 9.3 show, the basic concept "bird" comprises more than twice as many common features than the remaining categories. According to the connectivity model, this result means that basic categories show an especially high number of intensely interconnected features that can therefore be processed very quickly. This particular prediction of the connectivity model (discussed in more detail in section 9.6) is also supported

TABLE 9.3
Weighted Sum of Common Features (WSC) for Six Different Categories

	Bird	Fruit	Vegetable	Weapon	Vehicle	Clothes
Mean	554	162	136	103	202	80
SD	67	69	159	86	143	80

Note: Bird is the only basic category concept; it has the lowest standard deviation and the highest mean.

by Hoffman's findings, as depicted in Fig. 9.4: Independently of their status in the concept hierarchy, basic concepts show by far the shortest processing times in semantic decision experiments.

The connectivity model also enables a better understanding of those findings indicating that typicality effects in basic concept categories are much weaker than in nonbasic concept categories (Hoffman, 1986, p. 90). This result is to be expected when considering the fact that for the basic concept "bird," variable WSC has the smallest standard variation while at the same time showing the largest mean. The large number of common features and the small variance between different subordinate concepts indicate a consistently high degree of overlapping features in that category. Consequently, average typicality will be high, but differences in typicality will be small.

9.5 THE CONNECTIVITY MODEL AND EMPIRICAL FINDINGS ON TRADITIONAL WORD NORMS

It is well known that word norms such as Typicality (TYP), Concreteness (CON), Imagery (IMG), Familiarity (FAM), Meaningfulness (MNG), Categorizability (CAT), Pleasantness (PLS), and the Number of Attributes or Features (NOA/NOF) have a strong influence not only on reaction time but on memory performance as well. The definition and empirical investigation of these variables has been described in detail by Rosch (1975), Toglia and Battig (1978), and Rubin (1980). In this section we want to show that the connectivity model is capable of explaining a variety of effects that word norms exert on reaction time and memory performance. The way in which the typicality of concepts is represented has already been explained.

Let us first examine variables CON and IMG. It seems plausible to assume that concrete and imaginable concepts are represented by a variety of sensory features. Presumably, the more concrete and imaginable a concept is, the more sensory features it will comprise. The representation of CON and IMG can therefore be explained by the number and type of features a concept comprises. Because an increase in the number of sensory features is related to an increase in CON and IMG, it is to be assumed that concrete and imaginable concepts are not only processed faster, but are also better remembered than less concrete and imaginable concepts.

A similar argument also applies to variables FAM and MNG. We may assume that the frequent use of a concept will lead to an increasing differentiation in its meaning. This results in an increase in the number of features and their interconnections. Most likely, similar factors also apply to MNG: The more meaningful a concept is, the larger the number of features is and the more intensely interconnected they are. As we already know, these factors operate to speed up processing time and to increase memory performance.

Variable CAT may be explained in a similar way as typicality. Here we are concerned with the number of common features. Many common features will facilitate the ease with which a concept can be categorized. However, in contrast to processing speed in semantic tasks, an increase in the number of common features may not necessarily lead to an improved memory performance.

The representation of PLS is, in comparison with all other variables, more difficult to explain, because here the positive or negative valency of emotionally important features must be considered. This issue, as well as the question of whether or not pleasant concepts are represented by a larger number of emotional features than less pleasant concepts, cannot be decided on the basis of theoretical considerations. The lack of experimental results on the representation of emotional features adds to the difficulty of explaining the effects of PLS within the framework of the connectivity model.

9.5.1 The Relationship Between the Number of Features and Traditional Word Norms

The correlations reported later are based on the sample of 72 concepts used by Klimesch (1987, Experiment 1). As outlined earlier in this chapter, three different variables are available to estimate a concept's complexity: number of attributes (NOA) as determined by Toglia and Battig in a rating experiment, number of features (NOF), and weighted sum of features (WSF). Because it was determined by a rating procedure, variable NOA can be considered a more indirect measure of the number of features. In contrast to this, variable NOF indicates the average number of features subjects actually have listed for a concept. Variable WSF not only reflects the number, but also the frequency with which individual features were listed. Let $f(i, j)$ be the frequency with which a certain feature j was listed as belonging to concept i. In summing up the frequencies of all the features j gives the corresponding value of variable WSF for concept i.

Our sample of 72 concepts is heterogenous because it was drawn from six different categories. Thus, we are not only concerned with the variance within each category but also with the variance between the categories. If both variances vary in the same direction, the correlation coefficient will increase, otherwise it will decrease. In order to prevent a distortion of the correlation coefficient by this effect, we have transformed the data in such a way as to completely eliminate the differences between the category means.

In Table 9.4 the results of the transformed as well as the nontransformed

TABLE 9.4
Intercorrelations Between Concept Variables

A. Data Transformed

	1 TYP	2 CON	3 IMG	4 CAT	5 MNG	6 FAM	7 NOA	8 PLS	9 WSC	10 NOF	11 WSF
1 TYP	*										
2 CON	− .05	*									
3 IMG	− .13	.49	*								
4 CAT	− .17	.51	.71	*							
5 MNG	− .17	.49	.46	.41	*						
6 FAM	− .21	.24	.39	.32	.69	*					
7 NOA	− .19	.29	.25	.43	.58	.43	*				
8 PLS	− .08	.22	.25	.20	.24	.06	.20	*			
9 WSC	− .39	.08	.10	.09	.06	.16	.19	− .08	*		
10 NOF	− .33	.04	.30	.32	.36	.36	.40	− .04	.38	*	
11 WSF	− .40	.08	.35	.45	.34	.37	.37	− .03	.42	.84	*
Mean	2.1	6.0	5.8	5.9	4.5	6.1	3.8	4.3	206	5.5	53.8
SD	.82	.29	.31	.38	.44	.32	.40	.49	103	1.7	17.6

B. Data Not Transformed

	1 TYP	2 CON	3 IMG	4 CAT	5 MNG	6 FAM	7 NOA	8 PLS	9 WSC	10 NOF	11 WSF
1 TYP	*										
2 CON	− .08	*									
3 IMG	− .15	.49	*								
4 CAT	− .26	.55	.68	*							
5 MNG	− .12	.38	.41	.20	*						
6 FAM	− .19	.28	.37	.26	.69	*					
7 NOA	.07	.02	.17	.00	.50	.22	*				
8 PLS	− .19	.27	.35	.47	.15	.16	− .03	*			
9 WSC	− .28	− .04	.08	.24	− .14	− .17	.07	.22	*		
10 NOF	− .30	− .09	.28	.18	.34	.21	.41	.10	.44	*	
11 WSF	− .44	.03	.36	.43	.25	.24	.19	.13	.43	.81	*
Mean	2.1	6.0	5.8	5.9	4.5	6.1	3.8	4.3	206	5.5	53.8
SD	.88	.32	.33	.46	.48	.36	.57	.76	190	2.0	19.6

data are shown. In interpreting the results, however, we rely on the transformed data.

Inspection of Table 9.4 reveals that the hypotheses derived from the connectivity model are confirmed (see the correlations of variable NOA in row 7 with variables CON, IMG, CAT, MNF, FAM). The more features a concept comprises, the more concrete, pictorial, easy to categorize, meaningful, and familiar these concepts are. Variables NOF and WSF, as determined by Klimesch (1987), show a similar result (refer to rows 10 and 11): IMG, CAT, MNG, and FAM are positively and significantly correlated with NOF as well as WSF.

The correlations reported by Toglia and Battig (1978), which are based on a very large sample of more than 2,000 words, yield further support for the connectivity model (Table 9.5). Here too, variable NOA shows significant correlations with CON, IMG, CAT, MNG, and FAM.

PLS is the only variable that is not significantly correlated with any of those variables reflecting the number of features. However, variable PLS is only weakly correlated with other variables. There are only two correlations with PLS that slightly exceed the 5% level of significance. A similar pattern of results can be found in Toglia and Battig (Table 9.5). Here too, variable PLS shows the weakest intercorrelations in comparison to all other variables. This result supports the assumption mentioned earlier stating that emotionally important information may not be represented by semantic features. Without considering the emotional valency it would be difficult to grasp the encoding structure of emotionally important concepts.

Toglia and Battig's results are in accordance with those correlations that were found for the transformed variables. This is at first surprising, because Toglia and Battig did not undertake any data transformation. However, in considering that the number of natural categories is limited, it is plausible to assume that the distorting influence of different categories decreases as the number of concepts increases. A comparison of sample size ($N = 2,854$ in Toglia & Battig; $N = 72$ in Klimesch) supports this assumption and shows that large samples with nontransformed data apparently yield results similar to small samples with transformed data.

Section 9.4 pointed out that typicality can be explained by the number of common features that a superordinate concept shares with its subordinate concepts. According to this hypothesis, it seems obvious to assume that a concept's number of common features increases as the number of features in the entire category increases. Consequently, significant correlations are to be expected between typicality and those variables reflecting the number

TABLE 9.5
Intercorrelations Between Word Norms

	CON	IMG	CAT	MNG	FAM	NOA	PLS
CON	*						
IMG	.883	*					
CAT	.887	.905	*				
MNG	.425	.675	.589	*			
FAM	.319	.557	.488	.820	*		
NOA	.386	.543	.524	.749	.554	*	
PLS	.215	.267	.278	.309	.267	.390	*
Mean	4.40	4.55	4.33	4.03	5.59	3.56	4.01
SD	1.23	1.14	1.19	0.89	1.13	0.73	0.84

Note: Data from *Handbook of Semantic Word Norms* (p. 47) by Toglia and Battig, 1978. © 1978 by Lawrence Erlbaum Associates. Adapted with permission.

of common features. However, no systematic relationship can be expected with respect to the remaining variables. The results of Table 9.4. confirm this conjecture and show that variable typicality (TYP), as defined by Rosch, takes on a special status: It fails to correlate with any of the traditional variables such as CON, IMG, CAT, MNG, FAM, and PLS. But highly significant correlations do exist with variables WSC and WSF. The high correlation between TYP and the weighted sum of common features (WSC) has already been discussed and corresponds nicely with the predictions of the connectivity model. The highly significant correlation between the number of features (NOF) and WSC was to be expected. As indicated by the results in Table 9.1, categories with many features also tend to have more common features. The negative correlations with typicality are due to the way in which typicality is measured: A low typicality value characterizes a highly typical concept.

The results discussed here may be summarized as follows:

1. In confirming the predictions of the connectivity model, the number of features (measured by NOA, NOF, and WSF) correlates significantly and positively with the traditional variables IMG, CAT, MNG, FAM, and partly with CON.

2. These findings support the assumption that variables CON, IMG, CAT, MNG, and FAM can be explained by the number of semantic features a concept comprises. Therefore, it is to be expected that these five variables are also highly correlated among each other. The results confirm this assumption (see the respective correlations in Tables 9.4 Part A and 9.5).

3. In contrast to CON, IMG, CAT, MNG, and FAM, variable PLS constitutes an exception: It does not correlate with the number of features (neither with NOA nor with NOF or WSF) and shows no systematic correlations with other variables.

4. Rosch's typicality is also exceptional: It is the only variable that can be explained exclusively by the number of common features. Variable TYP is not significantly correlated with any of the traditional variables, which confirms this explanation.

9.5.2 The Relationship Between the Number of Features and Memory Performance

The predictions of the connectivity model refer not only to processing speed but also to memory performance. The more components a code has, the better it is integrated in long-term memory and the easier it is to remember (refer to the component-decay model of section 4.3). It can therefore be expected that concepts with many features can be remembered better than concepts with only a few features. The results of an extensive study from Rubin (1980), in which 51 different word norms were correlated and factors analyzed in a sample of 125 words, allow us to examine our hypothesis. The most important variables in Rubin's study are free recall and recognition scores that were determined in an experiment designed especially for that purpose. Those findings relevant here are listed in Table 9.6.

Rubin's results show a highly significant and positive relationship between memory performance and the number of features (as measured by variable NOA) and thus confirm an important prediction of the connectivity model. The more features a concept comprises, the better it can be remembered. This holds true not only for free recall (see variable FRE in Table 9.6), but also for recognition performance (see variable REC).

It is surprising, however, that NOA is only weakly and unsystematically correlated with CON, IMG, CAT, MNG, and FAM. This contradicts the findings of Klimesch (1987) and Toglia and Battig (1978), as depicted in Tables 9.4 Part A and 9.5. Possibly Rubin (1980), though using a comparatively small sample, did not make an attempt to transform his data in order to eliminate the distorting influence of intercategory variance. This view is confirmed by comparing his results with those of the nontransformed data in Table 9.4 Part B. In accordance with Rubin's findings, the corresponding correlation coefficients in Table 9.4 Part B are also only weakly pronounced.

The fact that free recall performance increases with the number of semantic components is also demonstrated by Johnson-Laird, Gibbs, and de Mowbray (1978). In the first part of the experiment, subjects were asked to decide whether or not a series of words shows one or both of the two features "solid" and "consumable" (e.g., "apple" shows both, "cream" and "hammer" only one, "gasoline" shows neither of the two features). Fol-

TABLE 9.6
Intercorrelations Between Word Norms

	41 FRE	51 REC	13 CON	12 IMG	16 CAT	17 MNG	24 FAM	19 NOA	31 PLS
41 FRE	*								
51 REC	.42	*							
13 CON	.19	.02	*						
12 IMG	.31	.23	.88	*					
16 CAT	.20	.12	.91	.89	*				
17 MNG	.18	.12	.67	.73	.67	*			
24 FAM	.20	.25	.15	.26	.22	.22	*		
19 NOA	.28	.32	− .19	− .05	− .16	.01	.33	*	
31 PLS	.29	.29	.24	.32	.25	.28	.38	.31	*

Note: Data from Rubin, 1980, *Journal of Verbal Learning and Verbal Behavior*, 19, p. 746. © 1980 by Academic Press. Adapted with permission.

lowing this simple categorization task, subjects performed a memory task in which all words — not just those judged positive — were to be recalled. The results showed that memory performance is a function of the number of features: Words that showed both features were remembered more easily than those with only one feature and these, in turn, were remembered more easily than words that showed neither of the two characteristics.

Free recall and recognition tasks consist of a mixture of episodic and semantic demands (see Tulving, 1983, and the detailed discussion in Klimesch et al., 1988). Although up to now we have considered only purely semantic tasks, Rubin's results point to the fact that the predictions of the connectivity model are also applicable to episodic tasks. The findings reported by Klimesch et al. (1988) support this assumption.

9.6 THE CONNECTIVITY MODEL AND EMPIRICAL FINDINGS ON CASE 1: SEARCHING TWO CODES THAT SHARE COMMON FEATURES

The previous sections have dealt with the general predictions of the connectivity model. It was shown that not only processing speed but also memory performance increases with an increasing number of semantic features. The connectivity model, however, also enables far more sophisticated predictions, if the relationship between two codes X and Y (to be judged, for example, in a semantic decision experiment) is taken into consideration. As we know from section 8.6.1, two different cases must be distinguished: Either both codes are connected by common features (Case 1 in section 8.6.1) or by a common pathway (Case 2 in section 8.6.2). Detailed predictions for Case 2 depend on the exact geometric characteristics of the common pathway, which can hardly be determined empirically. In testing Case 1, on the other hand, it must only be guaranteed that two codes share common features. In this case, which we have discussed in detail in section 8.6.1, precise predictions can be made.

In section 9.4 we were able to demonstrate that a subordinate concept X (e.g., "eagle") does indeed share common features with its natural superordinate concept Y (e.g., "bird"). Thus, the data collected in the feature listing experiment by Klimesch (1987, Experiment 1) can now be used to design a semantic decision task of the type "Is X a Y?", in which the reaction times for yes and for no responses are measured as dependent variables. It is crucial in deriving predictions for Case 1 that a yes response can only be carried out if common features exist between the two concepts X and Y. As we know from section 8.6, more indirect activation flows back to the source nodes if common features exist. This strengthening effect of preactivation provides positive evidence for a yes response (refer to the detailed explanations in section 8.6.1). The speed with which a yes response can be carried out depends on three factors: the number of features of X, the number of features of Y, and the number of common features (cf. Equation 8.15 in section 8.6.1). Thus, we can proceed from the following three predictions:

Prediction 1: The speed with which a yes response can be carried out increases with the number of features subordinate concept X comprises,

Prediction 2: With the number of features superordinate concept Y comprises, and

Prediction 3: With the number of features X and Y share.

If two concepts do not share common features, then the accelerating influence of preactivation is lacking, and the search process terminates as soon as indirect activation *Is* flows back to the source nodes. Because indirect activation *Ip* is always greater than *Is* and will thus always spread more quickly, the arrival of *Is* at one of the two concept nodes provides clear evidence for a no response. Therefore, the only factor influencing a negative decision is the number of features of that code comprising the most features. We have shown that—with the exception of basic categories— subordinate concepts always tend to have more features than superordinate concepts. It can therefore be expected that it is only the feature number of the subordinate concepts X that determine the reaction times for no responses. When comparing yes and no responses, we see that for negative decisions the accelerating effect of the feature number is less pronounced than for positive decisions. This is due to the following reasons:

1. In all of those instances in which superordinate concepts are basic concepts and as a result comprise more features than the subordinate concept, the degree of correlation between the number of features of X (variable NOF) and decision time for no responses will be lowered.
2. The extent of preactivation in yes responses is not only a function of the total number of features, but also a function of the number of features X and Y share. In negative decisions this additional and multiplicative influence of the number of common features is missing (see equation 8.15 in section 8.6.1).

In summary, the following predictions are valid for no responses:

Prediction 4: Reaction time decreases with an increasing number of features, subordinate concept X comprises.

Prediction 5: The number of common features does not affect reaction time.

If one considers that Is is smaller than Ip, then it can also be shown that the reaction time for no responses must be longer than that for yes responses.

Prediction 6: Reaction times for no responses are generally longer than those for yes responses.

Prediction 7: As compared to yes responses, the number of features of X has a smaller effect on reaction time.

Whereas Predictions 4, 6, and 7 are obvious and straightforward, Prediction 5 may require some explanation. A negative trial in a task of the type "Is X a Y?" consists of a subordinate concept X not belonging to Y. Concept X, however, will share features with another superordinate concept Z. Prediction 5 simply states that, in this case, the number of common features between X and Z will not have any effect on the decision "Is X a Y?"

Semantic decision experiments (Experiments 2 and 3 by Klimesch, 1987) of the type "Is X a Y?" were used to test the predictions listed earlier. For the calculation of analyses of variances, the 12 subordinate concepts in each of the six categories were divided into two groups. Group NOF + represents those six concepts of each category that are rich in features (i.e., that fall above the respective mean), whereas group NOF − represents those that show fewer features (i.e., those that fall below the respective mean). The same procedure was applied to variable WSC.

For yes responses, the results of Experiment 2 support Prediction 1 and show a highly significant effect of the number of features: Concepts with many features can, on average, be processed 42 ms faster than those with fewer features. A similar result was found for Prediction 3: Subordinate concepts with many common features are, on average, processed 28 ms faster than subordinate concepts sharing only a few features.

In accordance with Prediction 5, variable WSC did not yield any significant effects for no responses. Similarly, no significant effects were found for variable NOF. Prediction 4 was also supported. Even for no responses, more complex concepts can be processed slightly faster than less complex concepts. However, the respective reaction time difference is only 13 ms and is therefore three times smaller than for yes responses. This latter result lends support to Prediction 7. Comparing RT differences between yes and no responses reveals a highly significant result that agrees with Prediction 6: Reaction times for yes responses are on average 67 ms shorter than those for no responses.

Experiment 3 was designed to test Prediction 2 and to replicate the results of Experiment 2. Here the same set of 72 subordinate concepts was used. But in Experiment 3 the superordinate concepts were replaced by the two abstract concepts "living" (birds, fruits, and vegetables) and "nonliving" (vehicles, weapons, and articles of clothing). Subjects no longer had to judge whether or not an eagle is a bird, but whether or not an eagle is a "living being." Compared to the 12 superordinate concepts of Experiment 2, the superordinate concepts "living" and "nonliving" are on a higher level of abstraction. Thus, according to the arguments outlined in section 9.3, it must be assumed that they show fewer features than the superordinate concepts of Experiment 2. Their comparatively small number of features, which are presumably too abstract in nature to allow for an intense interconnection with subordinate concepts, leads to the hypothesis that the reaction times of Experiment 3 must be generally longer than those of Experiment 2. Variable WSC was only determined for the superordinate concepts of Experiment 2. Thus, we do not expect WSC to exhibit any effects in Experiment 3. With regard to variable NOF, on the other hand, all of the predictions are equally applicable.

The results of Experiment 3 confirm Prediction 2 and show that abstract superordinate concepts require longer processing times (Table 9.7). As expected, variable WSC shows no significant effects, neither for yes responses or no responses. On the other hand, variable NOF yields highly significant results that match those of Experiment 2. Furthermore, an examination of the respective reaction times shows once again that complex concepts can be processed faster than less complex ones. The average difference in reaction time for yes responses is 44 ms (42 ms in Experiment 2) and 18 ms for no responses (13 ms in Experiment 2). These results, therefore, confirm Predictions 1, 4, and 7. In addition, the average reaction time difference between yes and no responses lies in the same direction (Prediction 6) and on a similar scale to Experiment 2 (57 ms in Experiment 3 and 67 ms in Experiment 2).

The correlations outlined in Table 9.7 accord with the variance analytical findings. As the highly significant correlation coefficient between NOF and

TABLE 9.7
Intercorrelations Between Reaction Times, NOF, and WSC

	No3	Yes3	No2	Yes2	NOF	WSC
No3	*					
Yes3	.56	*				
No2	.19	.12	*			
Yes2	.45	.43	.16	*		
NOF	− .21	− .38	− .05	− .51	*	
WSC	− .00	− .26	− .13	− .27	.38	*
Mean	821	764	764	697	5.5	206
SD	63	62	79	53	1.7	103

Note: No3, Yes3, No2, and Yes2 refer to No and Yes responses in Experiments 3 and 2. Data from Klimesch, 1987, *Psychological Research*, 49, p. 60. © 1987 by Springer. Reprinted with permission.

reaction times for yes responses in Experiment 2 demonstrates, the number of features accounts for more than 25% of the reaction time variance.

This clear and convincing confirmation of the connectivity model should not prevent us from testing whether or not competing models would also be in a position to explain the previous results. The accelerating effect of common features is consistent with all of the other models of semantic memory (Medin et al., 1987; Rosch & Mervis, 1975; and the reviews in Johnson-Laird, 1987; E. E. Smith, 1978; E. E. Smith & Medin, 1981). However, the fact that an increasing number of semantic features operates to speed up processing time cannot be explained by any other model. But we have to be careful in evaluating this hypothesis. If it turns out that the number of features (NOF) is so highly correlated with the number of common features (WSC) that NOF cannot be considered as an independent predictor for reaction time, then the validity of a crucial hypothesis of the connectivity model would be seriously threatened.

In order to test a possible confounding of NOF by WSC, partial correlations were calculated. If the influence of WSC on the correlation between NOF and Yes2 (reaction times of yes responses in Experiment 2) is eliminated, then the original value of $r = -.51$ decreases slightly to $r = -.46$. A similar result was found for the correlation between NOF and Yes3. Here too, the elimination of WSC causes only a small decrease from the original $r = -.38$ to $r = -.31$. These results demonstrate that NOF can be considered an independent and significant predictor for reaction time.

9.7 THE CONNECTIVITY MODEL AND EMPIRICAL FINDINGS ON THE PREACTIVATION OF SEMANTIC FEATURES

The predictions of the connectivity model are not only applicable to the relationship between sub- and superordinate concepts, but also to the relationship between a concept and its features. Priming experiments are particularly well-suited in examining this question. If a subject is asked to make congruency judgments for serially presented word pairs (e.g., one denoting a concept such as "bird," the other a feature such as "flies"), it can be demonstrated that congruent words are judged much faster than incongruent words. These positive priming effects have long been known and have been described in detail elsewhere (Collins & E. F. Loftus, 1975).

The connectivity model is also suited to explain priming effects. For example, consider the congruent word pair "flies"—"bird," and the incongruent word pair "swims"—"bird." In the following we show that the extent of preactivation in priming experiments essentially depends on the number of features and the degree of feature overlap.

In priming experiments, semantic features such as "swims" or "flies" are presented as words. However, in section 9.2.2 we emphasized that semantic features are not verbal units. It is therefore necessary to introduce a notation that reflects this distinction between features and their verbal label representing a concept. Let us first look at the features "flies" or "swims." In their general meaning they are concepts that again have features. In this sense we refer to them as "feature concepts" and denote them with Z. The features of the feature concept "fly" refer to the different and specific forms of "fly" (e.g., to the specific way an airplane, an insect, a bird, a rocket, or a thrown stone is flying). We use the notation $F(z)$ when denoting the features of Z. The semantic code of concepts like "bird," "fish," and so forth, will be termed X, its features $F(x)$. Finally, features shared by concepts X and Z are denoted by $F(x,z)$. In using this notation it will be easy to outline the hypothetical encoding structure for priming experiments:

- Feature words such as "fly" and "swim" serve to access the meaning of certain features $F(z)$.
- A congruent word pair is defined by the fact that codes Z and X share at least one feature $F(x,z)$ (see Case 1 in section 8.6.1).
- An incongruent word pair is characterized by the fact that the two codes Z and X do not share any common feature. They, however, may be connected via a common pathway (see Case 2 in section 8.6.2).

In illustrating these assumptions, first consider the way the congruent word pair "fly"—"bird" is represented. As a feature concept Z, "fly" comprises a variety of features $F(z)$ denoting different forms of flying. One of these features refers to the typical form a bird is flying. Consequently, the two codes Z ("fly") and X ("bird") share a common feature $F(x,z)$. Now consider the order of presentation. If "fly" is presented first, then activation spreads to all of the features $F(z)$. But because Z and X share a common feature, this feature $F(x,z)$ will have already been preactivated by the time concept X ("bird") is encoded. Due to the strengthening effect of preactivation, a congruent pair can be judged faster than an incongruent pair, such as "swim"—"bird." Though a potential feature of some birds, "swim" is a typical feature of "fish." Accordingly, "swim" and "bird" will not share any features but instead may be connected via a common path, as shown in Fig.9.5. The smaller the degree of interconnectedness between X and Z, the smaller will be the effect of preactivation. As a result, incongruent (or less congruent) pairs will always require more processing time than congruent pairs.

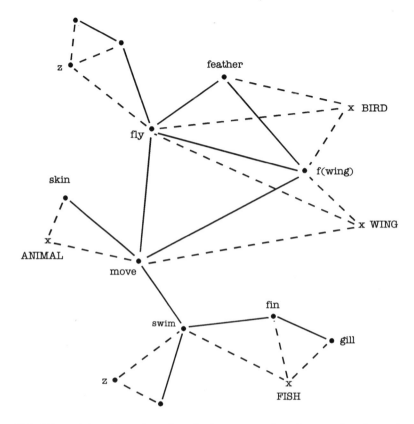

FIG. 9.5. Priming effects depend on the interconnectedness between the prime and the primed item. In contrast to "fly," "swim" is an inefficient prime for "bird." Although some birds can swim, this is not a typical feature for bird. "Swim" is closely connected with fish but not with bird.

Positive priming effects for congruent pairs can be easily explained by considering Assumption C in section 8.2. It postulates that the search process for a code terminates as soon as indirect activation flows back to the source node. In priming experiments the two concepts X and Z are typically presented in succession.

Accordingly, subjects do not know whether or not the second word is congruent. We therefore have to assume that the search process terminates after the prime (i.e., the first word of a pair) is presented and continues as soon as the second word appears. Thus, it is clear that the accelerating effect of preactivation can be effective only if the prime and the primed concept share common features (see Case 1 in section 8.6.1). The more features they share, the more features will be preactivated by the time the second concept is encoded and the stronger the priming effect will be. In an incongruent pair such as "swim" and "bird" the goal of the search process is to find a common pathway between X and Z. However, the detection of a common pathway (see Case 2 in section 8.6.2) will in any case last longer than it takes to detect common features.

9.7.1 Complex Concepts Exert Stronger Priming Effects

Up to now we have shown that the connectivity model is capable of explaining priming effects. However, more specific predictions can be arrived at if we consider the number of features that the prime and the primed item comprise. If the presentation order is X-Z, then concept X is the prime and (feature) concept Z is the primed item. If presentation order is reversed, then X is the primed concept and Z functions as the prime.

The extent to which a common feature $F(x,z)$ is preactivated depends on how many features the prime comprises. As an example, consider the item pair "fly"—"bird," where feature Z is the prime and X is the primed item. Because Z will have been already encoded when X is presented, the extent of preactivation of $F(x,z)$ is a function of $n(Z)$. If, however, the presentation sequence is reversed, then the amount of preactivation $F(x,z)$ receives depends on $n(X)$.

The reason behind this conjecture is obvious, if we consider Equations 8.2 and 8.3 in section 8.3. There we have shown that, by the end of the second activation stage, indirect activation equal to $a + b(n - 2)$ or $a + bf(n - 2)$ gathers at the feature nodes of an interconnected code. This means that n and interconnection density f determine the amount of activation a feature node receives. It is for this reason that the number of features the prime comprises is crucial for the extent of preactivation. These considerations clearly show that the effectiveness of a prime depends on its number of features: The more features a prime comprises, the faster the congruency between the prime and the primed concept can be judged and the shorter reaction time will be.

When predicting reaction times in priming experiments, the extent of preactivation (as determined by the number of features of the prime) is not the only decisive factor. What influences reaction time is also the number of features of the primed concept itself. The more features the primed item has, the faster indirect activation (strengthened by preactivation) will flow back to its concept node and the shorter reaction time will be (see Equation 8.15).

Now consider the way in which presentation sequence affects reaction time and assume that code X has more features than code Z. Is reaction time in the presentation sequence X-Z shorter than that in the case of Z-X? The following two facts are important in answering this question: First, the extent of preactivation depends on the number of features the prime comprises. Second, as the prime is being encoded, activation already spreads to the concept node of the concept to be primed, provided common features F(x,z) exist, because the activation process within the semantic code of the prime does not terminate until the third stage. In the meantime, however, activation has spread over the common node(s) F(x,y) to the concept node as well as to some features of the concept to be primed. It is important to keep in mind that the amount of this activation flowing to the primed concept is already a function of the number of features the prime comprises. As a result, the concept node of the second code (i.e., the primed concept) receives activation already weighted with the number of features of the first code (i.e., the prime). When the primed concept is presented, preactivation stemming from the prime adds to and multiplies with that activation spreading within the semantic code of the primed concept. Due to the fact that the concept node is already preactivated and the amount of preactivation reflects the number of features of the prime, this quantity affects all three activation stages of the second code. Unlike the first code, the number of features of the second code does not play a role until the second stage of activation. Consequently, the number of features of the first code must play a greater role than those of the second. Thus it follows that the presentation sequence X-Z (if X is the code comprising more features) will generally lead to shorter reaction times than the sequence Z-X.

In summarizing, the following three hypotheses can be put forward:

1. The more features the prime comprises, the more effective it is and the shorter the duration of reaction time.
2. The number of features of the primed concept operates to speed up reaction time.
3. Presentation sequence is important. It is the number of features of the prime that will have a comparatively stronger effect on reaction time.

The relative importance of these hypotheses depends primarily on the quantitative relationship between $n(X)$, $n(Z)$, and the number of common features $n(X,Z)$. If, for example, in the presentation sequence Z-X, $n(Z)$ and $n(X,Z)$ are small and $n(X)$ is comparatively large, the enhancing effect of $n(X)$ may outweigh the effects of $n(Z)$ and $n(X,Z)$.

These hypotheses hold true both for congruent and incongruent pairs. The only difference is that the coding structure of congruent pairs corresponds to Case 1 (described in section 8.6.1), whereas that of incongruent pairs corresponds to Case 2 (section 8.6.2). As we saw in section 8.6, the predictions derived from Case 1 also apply to Case 2. However, there is little chance of empirically describing the complex coding structure of Case 2. As a result, it would be extremely difficult to indicate to what degree the common pathway between the two codes Z and X is preactivated. The uncertainty resulting from the unknown geometry of the common pathway may lead to a strong weakening of the predicted effects.

Using the sample of concepts described in section 9.4, the hypotheses outlined here were tested in an experiment by Kroll and Klimesch (1992). In testing our hypotheses, one important precondition required that the semantic codes of congruent pairs share common features. Accordingly, for congruent pairs such as "lark" — "sings" only those features were selected that indeed were components of the respective concepts.

The features of incongruent pairs stem from other concepts of the same sample of data. Incongruent pairs do not share common features but in all probability are connected by common pathways. Variable frequency of attributes (FOA; Experiment 1 in Klimesch, 1987), which represents the percentage of times a feature was listed in response to its corresponding concept, was used in an attempt to separate the effects of feature frequency from the effects of NOA.

The results of the priming experiment (Experiment 2a in Kroll & Klimesch, 1992) are summarized in Table 9.8. In supporting Hypothesis 1, the data indicate that concepts X with many features generally lead to stronger priming effects. As could be expected in accordance with Hypothesis 2, the number of features of X speed up reaction time even in the case concept X has been presented after feature Z (see condition Z-X in Table 9.8). The results of an analysis of variances support this interpretation and show the highly significant influence of NOA and the significant influence of presentation sequence.

It should be noted that variable NOA refers to concepts X, but not to the feature concepts Z. Because there were no estimates of NOA for concepts Z, Hypothesis 3 can only be tested indirectly. In doing so, we assume that

TABLE 9.8
Mean Reaction Times in the Semantic Congruency Task of Experiment 2

Congruent Pairs		Sequence of Presentation	
		Concept-Feature	Feature-Concept
NOA	FOA	X-Z	Z-X
low (3.42)	low (32)	1002	1115
low (3.23)	high (60)	907	1118
high (4.41)	low (30)	904	1012
high (4.14)	high (61)	904	993

Note: NOA, number of attributes; the values in parentheses give the mean rating values; FOA, frequency of association; the numbers in parentheses show the mean percentage with which a feature was listed in response to the respective concept. Data from Kroll and Klimesch, 1992, *Memory and Cognition, 20*, p. 197. Copyright © 1992 by Psychonomic Society. Reprinted with permission.

feature concepts Z are, in comparison to concepts X, either more hetero-geneous and therefore less interconnected (e.g. "fly" and its different meanings), or have fewer features. For example, the feature concept "yellow" obviously has fewer features than the concept "canary." Given this interpretation, the longer reaction times in presentation condition Z-X (as compared to X-Z) are in accordance with Hypothesis 3.

9.8 THE CONNECTIVITY MODEL AND THE ENCODING OF PICTURES

Early experimental psychologist (Kirkpatrick, 1894) understood that pictures are remembered more readily than words, as do cognitive psychologists (Paivio, 1971, 1976; Shepard, 1967; Standing, 1973; see also the extensive review in Yuille, 1983). The question, as to how this basic finding (generally described as "picture effect" or "picture superiority effect"; cf. Madigan, 1983; D. L. Nelson, Reed, & Walling, 1976) may be explained, has led to a variety of different theoretical approaches. The most important approaches are the *dual coding theory*, the *discrimination hypothesis*, the concept of *encoding depth*, and *representational approaches* (cf. see the review in Madigan, 1983).

9.8.1 Traditional Approaches Explaining the Picture Effect

Within the framework of his dual coding theory, Paivio (1971, 1976; Paivio & Csapo, 1973) assumed that pictures—like concrete words but in contrast to abstract words—are represented by a pictorial as well as a verbal code. Thus, according to Paivio, the picture effect is due to the double encoding of pictures in the visual and verbal system.

The discrimination hypothesis proceeds from the assumption that it is the ability to discriminate more easily between pictures that makes them superior in memory performance. Comprising much more information than words, pictures offer not only more retrieval cues in a free recall task, but also more clues with which to differentiate between targets and distractors in a recognition task (R. E. Anderson, 1976).

According to the concept of encoding depth (Craik & Lockhart, 1972), it is assumed that pictures are more deeply encoded and access semantic information more quickly and easily than words (D. L. Nelson, 1979; D. L. Nelson, Reed, & McEvoy, 1977). We deal with this notion more closely within the framework of visual-semantic memory models (refer to section 9.8.3).

Representational hypotheses attempt to explain the picture effect by the specific characteristics of the encoding format for pictures. They ultimately lead to the well-known dispute of whether pictures are represented by analagous codes and whether verbal linguistic information is encoded in the form of propositional codes (cf. the review in Anderson, 1978; Kosslyn, 1981; Pylyshyn, 1981).

9.8.2 The Connectivity Model and the Picture Effect

The connectivity model gives a very simple explanation of the picture superiority effect. Pictures are essentially much richer in information than words and it therefore must be assumed that picture codes are much more complex and comprise more coding components than word codes (Mandler & N. S. Johnson, 1976). According to the connectivity model, the high complexity of visual codes is the very reason that they are not only processed faster but also retained better in memory. As we already know from chaps. 8 and 9, complex codes are remembered more easily, forgotten more slowly, and processed more rapidly. Thus, in assuming that pictures are represented by codes richer in information than those of words, the connectivity model leads to the following three predictions:

1. Pictures are remembered more easily than words (picture superiority effect).
2. Pictures are less likely to be forgotten than words.
3. Pictures are processed faster than words.

The superiority of pictures over words is a general principle that holds true for free recall as well as for recognition tasks (review in Madigan, 1983). Priming experiments (Kroll & Ramskoff, 1984) also support the notion of the superiority of visual encoding. In addition to these classic findings, Paivio (1976) was able to show that concrete words are remembered more easily than abstract words, and that visualized (concrete) words are more easily remembered than nonvisualized words. The imagery instruction requires the subject to imagine the object denoted by a particular word. According to Paivio (1971), imagery effects can be ranked on a hypothetical scale. On this scale, pictures are ranked highest, concrete words are second, then nonvisualized concrete words, and finally abstract words. According to the connectivity model, imagery effects can be explained by the complexity of the visualized code. If we follow Paivio's idea that visualized words are represented by a more complex (because dual) code than nonvisualized words, and if we furthermore proceed from the assumption that concrete words comprise more features than abstract ones (see the results reported in Toglia & Battig, 1978, and Experiment 1 by Klimesch, 1987), then the results arrived at by Paivio are entirely consistent with the predictions of the connectivity model.

Section 4.3 argued that "forgetting" can be best understood by a gradual loss of individual code components. The effect of this gradual loss depends on the number of features (or components) a code has. As compared to a code with only a few features, the loss of some features will have only a small effect if the degrading code comprises many features. Consequently, a picture code will be more resistant to forgetting than a word code. This interpretation is confirmed in an experiment by T. O. Nelson, Metzler, and Reed (1974) in which recognition performance for pictures and verbal descriptions was tested immediately after presentation and following a retention interval of 7 weeks. T. O. Nelson et al. (1974) found that after 7 weeks only 10% of the pictures but more than 20% of the verbal descriptions were forgotten. Similar results had already been discovered by Kirkpatrick (1894) and Calkins (1898) in free recall tasks using words and real objects as stimuli.

The results of semantic decision experiments in which concepts (such as "eagle," "trout," etc.) are presented as words and pictures (or line drawings) have shown repeatedly and consistently that pictures can be judged much faster than words (Guenther & Klatzky, 1977; Hoffmann & Klimesch, 1984; Klatzky & Stoy, 1978; Klimesch, 1981, 1982a; Pellegrino, Rosinski, Chiesi & Siegel, 1977). As the results depicted in Fig. 9.6 show, pictures are, on average, processed at about 170 ms faster than words.

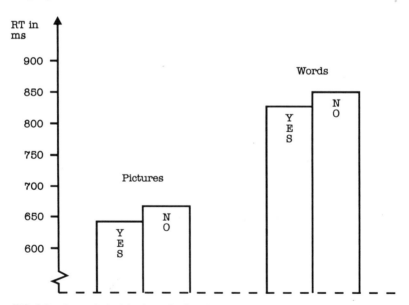

FIG. 9.6.   Semantic decision latencies for pictures and words. On average, pictures are processed about 170 ms faster than words. For pictures and words, the difference between positive and negative decision latencies is about 35 ms. Data from Klimesch, 1981, *Zeitschrift für Experimentelle und Angewandte Psychologie, 28,* 609–636. © 1981 by Hogrefe. Reprinted with permission.

The hypotheses derived from the connectivity model are thus reliably confirmed. Though other theories (such as the dual coding theory, the discrimination hypothesis, the concept of encoding depth and representational approaches) accord with Predictions 1 and 2, none of these traditional theories is capable of simultaneously explaining all of the aforementioned three predictions. This underlines the special status of Hypothesis 3 and points to the crucial importance of the general notion that complex information may be processed faster than less complex information.

9.8.3 The Connectivity Model and the Semantic Encoding of Pictures and Words

In discussing the validity of the dual coding theory, one must distinguish between trivial and nontrivial aspects. The trivial aspects refer to the fact that pictures and acoustically presented words are encoded in different perceptual systems. Inspite of this, however, we can easily name pictures and imagine the objects described by words. It is this fact that brings us to the nontrivial aspect of the dual coding theory, namely, what are the processes and structures that form the bridge between the visual and the verbal system?

The dual coding theory assumes that both systems, though operating independently, enable a mutual activation of visual and verbal information. The independence of both systems not only applies to the perceptual but also to the semantic level of encoding: Visual and verbal semantic information is represented in two distinctive and independent memory structures (Bleasdale, 1983, p. 205).

An alternative theory was suggested by Potter (Potter & Faulconer, 1975; Potter, So, von Eckardt, & Feldman, 1984), Nelson (D. L. Nelson, 1979; D.L. Nelson, Reed, & McEvoy, 1977), Klimesch (1982a, 1982b, 1982c), Hoffman and Klimesch (1984), Jolicoeur, Gluck, and Kosslyn (1984), and Snodgrass (1984). In their view, pictures and words use different routes to access a common semantic network. Empirical results supporting this view are discussed in detail elsewhere (for an extensive review see Te Linde, 1982). We do not intend to give another review of these results, but instead focus on an argument of special importance to the way in which words are accessed in semantic memory.

Section 9.2 emphasized that the perceptual word code gives no insight into its meaning per se. This, in turn, leads to the assumption of the presence of specific access points in semantic memory, which we have termed concept nodes. In sharp contrast to a word, the perceptual code of a picture does provide insight into the meaning of a picture. For pictures, but not for words, there is a gradual transition between the perceptual and the semantic code. For example, consider a semantic judgment task of the "Is X a Y?" in which pictures of animals and tools are presented, and in which subjects are asked to give a yes response whenever a picture represents an animal (Klimesch, 1981, 1982a, 1982c). The recognition of a single visual feature such as an eye, a feather, or a leg provides evidence that the presented picture is an animal. Thus, perceptual features of a picture provide direct access to semantic information (Flores d'Arcais & Schreuder, 1987; Zießler & Hoffman, 1985). Consequently, it is impossible to make a clear distinction between visual and semantic information (Klatzky & Stoy, 1978). As depicted in Fig. 9.7, pictures, in contrast to words, do not depend on specific access points or concept nodes in order to activate semantic information.

Figure 9.7 shows that, in contrast to words, the perceptual code of pictures has direct access to the features of a common semantic network. On the one hand, this assumption explains that pictures are processed semantically faster than words and, on the other hand, that it generally takes longer to name a picture than a word (Potter & Faulconer, 1975; but see also Jolicoeur et al., 1984, Experiment 1).

If we assume that a visual code (e.g., consider the code for "eagle")

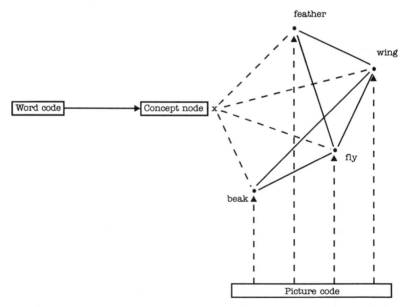

FIG. 9.7. Visual and verbal semantic information is stored in a single common network. However, the access routes differ for pictures and words. Pictures have direct access to semantic features whereas words have direct access only to the concept node.

consists of a structure of interconnected subcodes that represent individual picture components (e.g., eyes, feathers, wings, etc.), then we find an explanation not only for the gradual transition between visual and semantic information, but also for the effortless visualization of concepts and their semantic features.

It is a consequence of the assumptions discussed earlier that concept nodes serve primarily as access nodes for the verbal system (cf. the discussion on functional holistic codes in section 9.2.1). In considering the enormous complexity of semantic knowledge in comparison to the limited number of words contained in a language, it becomes evident that semantic memory holds far more codes having no link to a word code than codes that actually do possess a direct link. Thus, semantic memory stores far more concepts not directly related to the verbal system.

The model outlined in Fig. 9.7 may also be used to explain multilingualism (Snodgrass, 1984). Here, the decisive notion is that the meaning of corresponding words in different languages (e.g., "animal" and the German word *Tier*) is in most cases similar, but by no means identical. For example, in contrast to *Tier*, "animal" stands primarily for "mammal." Therefore, we assume that the semantic codes for *Tier* and "animal" share many common features but have two different concepts nodes. One concept node is linked with *Tier*, the other with "animal." Thus, according to the connectivity model, learning a new language, on the one hand, means establishing new concept nodes and, on the other hand, elaborating new semantic features that cover the special meaning of the foreign concept in relation to the native concept. Thus, the meaning of words in different languages is represented by a common semantic network to which each language has a different and distinctive access.

10 The Simulation Program CONN1

This chapter and the next are concerned with the implementation of the connectivity model. In this chapter a simulation program (CONN1) is described that was developed in colaboration by Winkler (1991). The next chapter discusses the possible neurophysiological basis for the connectivity model.

The simulation of the connectivity model provides insight into the way in which the model deals with rather complex networks. Furthermore, in implementing the model we encounter new problems that will show whether or not the assumptions described thus far must be modified in order to support the predictions of the connectivity model. In all cases requiring modifications, additional assumptions were adopted that do not contradict but supplement the assumptions already described in chaps. 8 and 9.

10.1 ARGUMENTS FOR MODIFYING ASSUMPTIONS

Winkler drew attention to three problems: the delta problem, the problem of preventing echoes between codes, and the halt problem. These problems are discussed in the next sections. The way in which CONN1 deals with these problems is described in section 10.2.

10.1.1 The Delta Problem: Asynchronous Activation Stages

General zero activity in the network is considered a theoretical neutral status at the beginning of a search process (Assumption 7). However, priming and inhibiting processes will occur during the spreading activation process. Preactivated and inhibited nodes exert a strong effect on spreading activation. Due to different activation values, Stage 3 or Stage 2 may propagate asynchronously. Because the nodes do not "know" when a stage is finished, they will send out activation back to the source node and to other codes. These asynchronous activation stages may trigger additional processes. It is thus necessary to define a procedure that allows to coordinate different activation processes within a certain activation stage. In trying to overcome this problem, one may define a critical waiting time *delta*. Within that interval the activation of asynchronous processes is allowed to accumulate. Activation is passed on only after delta is exceeded.

However, depending on the choice of delta, *n* activations received by a particular node may trigger up to *n* different activation processes. Activation speed might vary considerably between different processes, so this problem of unforeseeable reproduction of search processes can hardly be overcome by a "right" choice of delta, because this choice does not exist.

It should be emphasized that the delta problem is not only due to preactivation and inhibition. Even within a single code, Stage 3 activations may spread asynchronously if the degree of interconnections varies. Depending on the exact geometry of overlapping codes, Stage 1 activation may also propagate with different speeds into neighboring codes.

In considering code X in Fig. 10.1, assume that node x2 is preactivated with strength 1, whereas the remaining nodes x1, x3, and x4 are not activated (i.e., are activated with zero). If a search process starts at time 0 at the source node x with strength 1, Stage 1 will be received by x1, x2, x3, and x4 at time 1. The activation value of x2 will be 2, whereas x1, x3, and

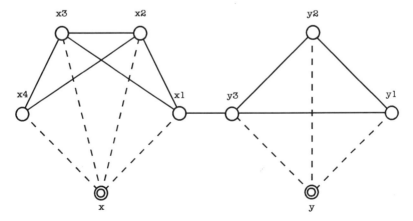

FIG. 10.1.   The delta problem refers to the fact that asynchronous activation stages may be triggered if nodes are already preactivated. In this example we assume that x2 is preactivated when activation starts to spread from x.

x4 will be activated by only half of that amount. Thus, Stage 2 will proceed from x2 twice as fast as from the remaining nodes. As a consequence, x1, x3, and x4 receive Stage 2 from x2 at time 1.5 and send out activation back to x and at the same time to connected or overlapping codes with strength 3. In our example a search process is triggered from x1 to y3 at time 1.5. It should be noted that already at time 1 activation was sent to y3 as a result of Stage 1 activation spreading from x. Later, at time 2, all the other Stage 2 activations will be received and new activation processes will be initiated that spread back to node x and to the environment (x1 sends out a second search process to code Y!).

10.1.2 The Problem of Preventing Echoes Between Codes

Assumption C3 was suggested in an attempt to prevent echoes between codes. However, when considering more complex cases such as overlapping codes sharing more than one node (Fig. 10.2), it can be seen that Assumption C3 is not capable of preventing echoes stemming from Stage 2. As an example, assume that node x2 in Fig. 10.2 is preactivated. In this case, a search process initiated in x and entering code Y via Stage 1 from x1 to y2 will return to code X (from y2 to x2) as Stage 2 activation and will trigger a new search process.

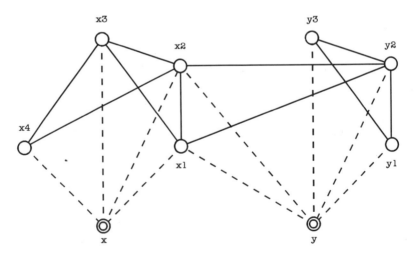

FIG. 10.2. Echoes between codes may occur if a common node such as x2 is preactivated and if cyclic pathways exist between the common node and code Y. Activation is assumed to spread from x.

10.1.3 The Halt Problem

Consider the symmetric example in Fig. 10.3. Here, search processes starting simultaneously in A and B will meet in c2. Because at this time both connections a2-c2 and b2-c2 are inhibited, the search processes may only propagate into code C. Assumption C3 prevents Stage 3 activation, and as a result the search process comes to a complete standstill. In this example the path between A and B will never be found. If node c2 would be a hierarchical node, not connected to code C, activation would also stop at c2. But this latter case is in accordance with the basic assumptions of the connectivity model (see section 8.3 and Fig. 8.3).

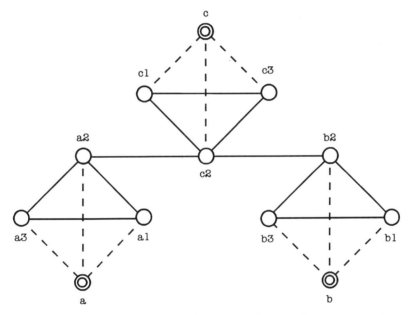

FIG. 10.3.   The halt problem occurs in the rare case of two search processes spreading in completely symmetric structures. Search processes starting at a and b meet at c2 and, according to Assumption C3, terminate without sending an echo back to a or b.

10.2 THE SPREAD OF ACTIVATION IN CONN1

Winkler proceeded from the idea that a node — as an intelligent processing unit — waits to send out other stages of activation subsequent to a distributed stage until it has received all of the activations necessary to complete this stage. *Distributed* means that the activations of a certain stage are initiated in more than one node. A good example for this is the spread of activation in Stage 2. A more specific case refers to Stage 1 activation processes spreading into an overlapping code sharing two or more nodes (Fig. 10.2).

This approach renders the delta problem meaningless, because there is no need to define a critical waiting time. Any node is provided with all information necessary to determine which activations have to be awaited before sending out activation. Neglecting the possibility of cyclic structures for the moment, CONN1 prevents the multiplication of search processes.

The echo problem is also eliminated. Every node of a certain code can check to see to which code(s) connected nodes belong. No activation is sent back to those nodes that belong to codes where activation originates.

Any node knows which type of activation stage is to be sent to which other node(s) in a given situation, so the halt problem also becomes meaningless within this approach. Consequently, Assumption 5, which is responsible for the halt problem and states that links are inhibited after carrying activation, is no longer necessary.

10.2.1 Sending and Receiving Information

Any node is capable of sending and receiving activation. Accordingly, we distinguish between the two functions SEND ACTIVATION and RECEIVE ACTIVATION:

SEND ACTIVATION (stage,   /* activation stage
              send time,   /* time of sending activation
              act node,   /* sender
              to node,   /* address
              primary set, /* nodes which in a given situation
                                  received activation from outside
                                  the code
              strength)   /* activation strength

RECEIVE ACTIVATION (stage,
                      receive time, /* time of receiving
                                      activation
                      from node,   /* act node from function
                                      SEND ACTIVATION
                      act node,   /* node receiving activation
                      primary set,
                      strength)

As the first argument of each function shows, the information about the stage of activation must be enclosed, whenever activation is processed (i.e, sent or received). We distinguish between four different stages of activation:

Stage 0: A code either receives source activation (i.e., is activated from STM) or is activated by a connected code.

Stage 1: A node activated by Stage 0 — which thereby becomes the primary node of its code — sends activation to the remaining nodes of that code. In case of overlapping codes Stage 1 is triggered by Stage 2.

Stage 2: A node $x(i)$ activated by Stage 1 sends activation to and receives activation from the neighboring nodes $x(j)$. Stage 2 waiting period is finished for node $x(i)$ when all activations from these neighboring nodes have been received.

Stage 3: Activation flows back to the primary node(s).

Any activation defined by SEND ACTIVATION arrives after $t = 1/\text{strength}$ at the address and is received by function RECEIVE ACTIVATION. Activation strength always equals the sending node's activation value ACT (See Assumption B1).

Within a given code, the primary set parameter holds that set of nodes first activated and that have to send Stage 1. This set contains more than one node only if overlapping codes share two or more nodes.

10.2.2 Information Accessible to a Node

In the following we describe the information stored in a node and that is available to a node. Every node holds static structural information defining the geometry of the network:

1. The name of the node.
2. Whether or not the node is a source node.
3. Whether or not the node is a hierarchical node.
   (A feature node is assumed if the node is neither a source nor a hierarchical node.)
4. A linklist defining all those nodes that are linked with a particular node:
   links (node) = <n1,n2,n3 . . .>

Dynamic information changes with every activation received. It refers to the state of the node, as defined by

1. act, holding the node's activation value,
2. activation list = <order 1, order 2. . . .>
   order k = (waiting list, order list)

waiting list = <wait item 1, wait item 2. . . .>
wait item k = (node, stage)
    order list = <order item 1, order item 2 . . .>
        order item k = (node, stage)

The algorithm working on activation list is relevant only in the case of distributed stages. At the beginning of a search process the activation lists of all nodes are empty. Instead of a detailed description of the complex activation logic we refer to Fig. 10.1 and discuss an example in section 10.2.3.

10.2.3 Functions Accessible to All Nodes

Determining the node from which activation is to be expected and to which activation is to be sent requires a series of functions that dynamically check the local geometry of the network.

CONNECTED (nl, n2): Checks whether two nodes nl, n2 are connected to each other. It yields a positive result if nl is in the link list of node n2 (and, of course, if n2 is in the link list of nl).

COMMON CODES (n1, n2): Checks whether two nodes belong to one or more common codes. It yields a positive result if there is at least one source node connected to nl and n2.

CONNECTED TO SET (n1, N): Checks whether node nl is connected to a node of set N.

COMMON CODES TO SET (n1, N): Checks whether node nl has a common code with a node of set N.

It is important to note that the idea of local processing is not violated by these functions. Each node may call them only with parameters available to it by RECEIVE ACTIVATION or by its own static informations. As an example we refer to Fig. 10.1. Again assume that node x was activated from STM. Function RECEIVE ACTIVATION will have the following parameters:

RECEIVE ACTIVATION (type = stage 0
                    receive time = 0
                    from node = STM
                    act node = x
                    primary set = {} / not used for stage 0
                    strength = 1)

As the act node, node x determines the processing steps to be carried out: Sending Stage 1 to all the members of a set N containing the nodes in the same code.

N = { n(i) | CONNECTED (act node, n(i)) and
              COMMON CODES (act node, n(i)) }

Note, that act node = x and N = {x1, x2, x3, x4}.

As a result, Stage 1 is sent to nodes x1, x2, x3, and x4. Thus, function SEND ACTIVATION takes the following form:

SEND ACTIVATION (type = stage 1
                  send time = 0
                   act node = x
                   to node = x1; [Function SEND ACTIVATION
                                  also is carried out for x2, x3, x4]
                primary set = {x}
                   strength = 1)

Now consider node x1, which receives Stage 1 at time 1. Function RECEIVE ACTIVATION shows the following form:

RECEIVE ACTIVATION (type = stage 1
                         time = 1
                    from node = x
                     act node = x1
                  primary set = {x}
                     strength = 1)

Now, two different types of operations must be carried out by node x1. On the one hand, stage 2 activations are sent to the neighboring nodes of the same code:

N = { n(i) | CONNECTED (act node, n(i)) and
              COMMON CODES (act node, n(i)) and
              COMMON CODES (from node, n(i)) }

Note, that act node = x1, from node = x and N = {x2, x3}

SEND ACTIVATION (type = stage 2
                  send time = 1
                   act node = x1
                   to node = x2 (Function SEND ACTIVATION
                                 also is carried out for x3)
                primary set = {x}
                   strength = 1)

On the other hand, Stage 2 activations from the remaining nodes of set N are expected and activations are planned for to be carried out for that time when the last of the expected activations will arrive:

waiting list = $<$(x2, Stage 2), (x3, Stage 2)$>$

order list = $<$(x, Stage 3), (y3, Stage 0)$>$

Note, that x is the from node and y3 is the only node for which

CONNECTED (act node, n(i)) and

not COMMON CODES (act node, n(i))

yields a positive result.

Waiting list and order list are inserted as order 1 into state of x1.

order 1 = (waiting list, order list)

activation list = $<$order 1$>$

Considering the fact that two or more search processes can be active at the same time and may meet at an individual node makes clear why an activation list may contain more than one order k entry. Matching Stage 2 activations arriving from x2 and x3 cancel corresponding waiting items. Whenever a waiting list is deployed by this kind of operation, the order items are executed. In our example the activations from x2 and x3 will be received simultaneously at time 2, but due to preactivations they may arrive at different times. In this case, node x1 waits until the slowest activation arrives.

As a final example, consider Fig. 10.2, which shows two codes X and Y sharing two nodes x1 and x2. As before, we assume that a search process was initiated at node x. Here, another timing problem is given by the asynchronous Stage 1 activations from code X to code Y. As compared to x1, node x2 is connected to more nodes in code X. Consequently, x2 will send stronger and faster Stage 1 activations to y and y2 than x1 does. In order to prevent the multiplication of the search process in y and y2, CONN1 again uses the waiting mechanism. We do not want to go into details here and therefore mention only some of the problems that can be easily handled on the basis of the assumptions described so far.

Determining the nodes from which additional Stage 1 activation is to be expected is nontrivial. This is the reason why the parameter "primary set" exists. Node y2 plans to send Stage 0 and Stage 1 to other codes — provided there are any — and Stage 3 back to those nodes Stage 1 came from (from nodes). Additionally y2 plans Stage 2 activations. Stage 2 is not sent to all connected nodes within code Y, the from nodes being excluded. We deal with sets of nodes rather than with single nodes here, and therefore some checks require the functions CONNECTED TO SET and COMMON CODES TO SET instead of CONNECTED and COMMON CODES.

10.3 CONN1 AND SPREADING ACTIVATION IN A SIMPLE SEMANTIC NETWORK

The examples described thus far allow us to understand the basic structure of CONN1. A more detailed description can be found in Winkler (1991). Here, CONN1 is discussed on the basis of a simple semantic network, shown in Figs. 10.4–10.8. It consists of the two superordinate categories *animals* and *vehicles*.

Within each category, different concepts are represented by overlapping and interconnected codes (chap. 9). Numbers in the white square of each node reflect the activation state at that time when a search process terminates. A black circle denotes a feature node and an additional white ring denotes a concept node. Interconnections between feature nodes are shown as solid lines, whereas interconnections between a source node and its features are shown as dashed lines.

Between the two categories, the two networks are linked only by hierarchical nodes. Hierarchical nodes represent very heterogenous concepts such as "move" and "wing," which have different meanings when placed in the context of category *animal* as opposed to *vehicle*. As an example, consider that the meaning of concept "wing" should be retrieved. In this case, WING (which represents the source node of the semantic code for wing) is used as an access node, and activation spreads to the different meanings of wing. In our example, two different meanings are represented. WING1 stands for "wings of birds" and comprises the two features "typical form of a wing" [f(wing1)] and "feathers." WING2, on the other hand, refers to "wings of an airplane" and consists of the two features "typical form of a wing" [f(wing2)] and "aluminum." According to the connectivity model, the meaning of "wing" is retrieved if at least the standard echo *Is* is received at WING1 or WING2. This situation is shown in Fig. 10.4.

Due to the passive processing properties of hierarchical nodes, activation never spreads from the *animal* network to the *vehicle* network or vice versa. Fig. 10.5 gives an example of a search process starting at BIRD and terminating at time 2.25 after the standard echo has been received. The source node of the highly overlapping code Canary carries strong activation, code MOVE1 is activated with Stage 1, but none of the concepts in category *vehicle* has received activation. When comparing Figs. 10.4 and 10.5 we see that the highly interconnected code "BIRD" can be searched much faster than "MOVE".

In order to demonstrate how strong and fast a search process spreads in a more complex network, we assume that a search process starts simultaneously at "CANARY" and "BIRD." This case corresponds to a semantic decision task in which a subject has to judge whether or not a canary is a

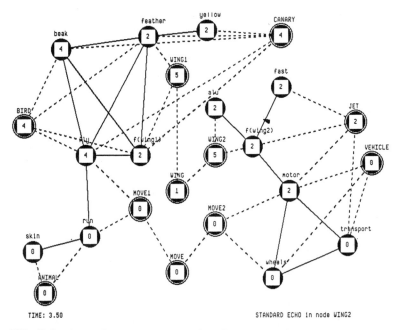

TIME: 3.50   STANDARD ECHO in node WING2

FIG. 10.4.   A search process was started at the source node WING. The numbers reflect the activation pattern after the standard echo was received by WING.

bird. As Fig. 10.6 shows, the search process terminates with a positive result already at time 1.63 when the source node BIRD receives activation from CANARY.

The codes representing canary and bird share four features. In contrast to this, the codes for bird and animal do not share a single feature. Consequently, judging the question "Is a bird an animal?" will require more processing time than in the case of "Is a canary a bird?" This is indeed the case, as Fig. 10.7 shows.

As a final example, consider a subject starting a general search process (refer back to section 8.7.1 for the distinction between general and specific search processes) in order to judge the question "Is a jet a bird?" In this case, which is shown in Fig. 10.8, no activation flows from the *animal* network to the *vehicle* network or vice versa, and the search process terminates with a negative result after all of the activation processes are carried out. Nonetheless, activation accumulates at the common nodes "MOVE" and "WING." This information could be used, for example, in evaluating the outcome of a specific search process that was initiated in response to the question "Are there any similarities between a jet and a bird?" The answer would be, "Yes, both move and have wings."

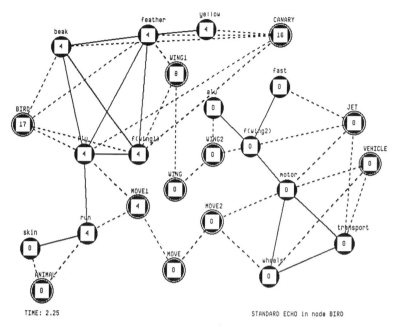

FIG. 10.5. A search process was started at the source node BIRD. The numbers reflect the activation pattern after the standard echo was received by BIRD.

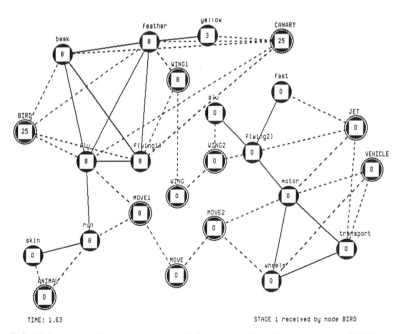

FIG. 10.6. A search process was started simultaneously at the source nodes BIRD and CANARY. The numbers reflect the activation pattern after activation from CANARY was received by BIRD.

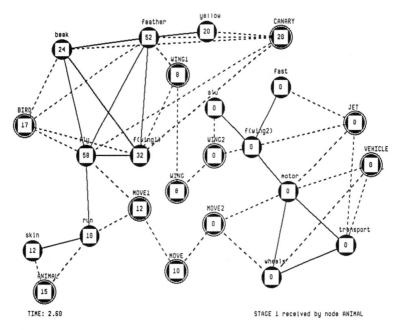

FIG. 10.7. A search process was started simultaneously at the source nodes BIRD and ANIMAL. The numbers reflect the activation pattern after activation was received by ANIMAL.

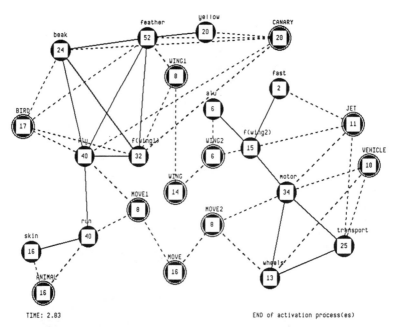

FIG. 10.8. A search process was started simultaneously at the source nodes BIRD and JET. The numbers reflect the activation pattern after all of the activation processes were carried out.

11 Representational Assumptions and their Possible Neural Bases

The ideas presented in this chapter are based on two arguments: First — as emphasized repeatedly — a comprehensive memory theory requires explicit and specific representational assumptions. Second, the physical bases of memory are physiological processes in the neural network of our brains. Thus, when pursuing the representational problem, we finally confront the question of how information is represented or coded in the brain. This interdisciplinary approach which is rather vaguely described under *neurosciences*, is the connecting link between memory psychology, cognitive psychology, artificial intelligence, and neurophysiology.

In illustrating the crucial problems inherent to this approach, hypothetically consider an "ideal situation" that would provide us with all of the necessary neurophysiological knowledge to evaluate the assumptions of memory theories. Needless to say, we are far from achieving this goal. But even in the case where this ideal situation could be realized, a neurophysiological testing of memory theories would be extremely difficult.

Such an attempt would encounter the problem of (neural) implementation, that is the question of whether or not the properties of neural information processing pose restrictions on cognitive processes. In order to explain this issue, first consider the problems that arise when a cognitive model is implemented by a simulation program. By *implementation* we mean the level of physical technical realization of a model described on an abstract level. The implementation converts relevant assumptions and algorithms into a concrete computer architecture and programming language. By that procedure of implementation, the theory to be modeled is enriched with additional representational assumptions, which result from the concrete technical features of the computer architecture and programming language.

The decisive dispute now is whether or not the level of implementation has any effect on the abstract model level. In other words: Is the type of implementation indifferent to the simulation of a cognitive model? According to the traditional view in cognitive psychology, the issue of implementation is not only beyond its scope, but does not even affect cognitive modeling (e.g., J. R. Anderson, 1987, and the confrontation between Broadbent, 1985, and Rumelhart & McClelland, 1985). This view may be correct as long as time-critical processes are not of crucial interest. As an example, it is possible to simulate a particular semantic network theory by using different programming languages with comparable results. If, however, time-critical processes (e.g., search processes in the semantic network) and their modeling under real time demands are of interest, then the type of implementation (i.e., the type of computer architecture and programming language) will play a decisive role. In order to solve a mathematical task, one may use paper and pencil, a calculator, or a personal computer. Solving this task may in itself be independent of the technical aid or implementation. But the time we need to perform this task is of course affected by the type of technical aid we use. If we consider that in psychology and especially in cognitive psychophysiology time-critical variables such as reaction times and the variety of different EEG parameters play an important role, then one easily arrives at the conclusion that the issue of implementation must not be excluded from our field of research.

In an analogous sense, the problem of *neural implementation* refers to the question of whether or not the properties of neural information processing pose restrictions on the abstract level of cognitive information processes. The problems underlying the two types of implementations are very similar to each other. Thus, it is a logical consequence when those researchers who regard implementation as an irrelevant technical detail are also sceptical about the relevance of neurophysiologically based representational assumptions. On the other hand, those researchers who believe that implementation is an essential part of cognitive modeling will readily accept the importance of the neural implementation problem. This latter view, which is also inherent to a variety of different connectionist and neural network models, will serve as a guideline for the following sections of this chapter.

The status of neurophysiologically based representational assumptions, however, is linked not only to the problem of implementation but also to the question of whether or not neural network models are capable of representing symbolic (such as semantic) information. As the example of connectionist theories demonstrates, most models focus on the level of non symbolic (such as elementary sensory) information processing. In contrast to traditional symbol-processing models (e.g., ACT or ACT*), connectionist models (refer to the series of articles in *Cognition*, 1988, Vol. 28, or the overviews in J. A. Anderson & Rosenfeld, 1988, or Hinton & J. A. Anderson, 1989) proceed from networks whose nodes are interpreted as "formal neurons" (McCulloch & Pitts, 1943). Formal neurons are interconnected according to Sherrington's well-known divergence/convergence principle, and the connections between them can be modified according to the Hebb rule (Hebb, 1949). Although connectionist architectures are not based on the most recent neurophysiological findings, they were designed according to important principles governing neural networks. Therefore, these models also became known under the name "neural networks." The extent to which these models—and, hence, also the neurophysiologically based representational assumptions, which were adopted—are also capable of representing symbolic structures, is still a matter of debate (Fodor & Pylyshyn, 1988).

In summarizing the arguments presented thus far, both types of implementation problems are to be considered whenever time-critical processes and/or subsymbolic structures play an important role. Because the central assumptions of the connectivity model refer to time-critical processes, it is clear that the issue of neural implementation is of crucial importance. The following section, therefore, focuses on the question of whether or not the assumptions of the connectivity model appear plausible when compared with basic neurophysiological findings.

11.1 BASIC PRINCIPLES OF NEURAL INFORMATION PROCESSING

The discussion of network models distinguishes between structural and processing assumptions. In order to enable a clear comparison between neural processing principles and the assumptions of the connectivity model, we keep up with this distinction. Thus, we focus first on structural and then on processing principles of neural networks.

11.1.1 Cortical Modules and Interconnection Principles

An interesting fact to start with is the enormous complexity of the cortex, which is the region of the brain that probably holds long-term memory representations and semantic memory in particular. The number of nerve cells in the human cortex is estimated at some 10,000 million (10^{10}), the number for the entire brain at some 100,000 million (between 10^{11} and 10^{12}). The number of synapses (sites of information transfer between nerve cells) varies between 1,000 and 10,000 per nerve cell (for a comprehensive review see Braitenberg & Schüz, 1991). For the cortex alone a conservative estimate identifies at least 10^{13} different synaptic connections or interconnection sites.

Each of the 10^{10} cortical neurons has "only" between 10^3 and 10^4 synapses, so it follows that an individual cortical neuron is not connected to all of the remaining neurons of the cortex. This fact is not in accordance with connectionist or neural network models, which assume that in a given layer every formal neuron is connected to each of the remaining neurons, and demonstrates the necessity to assume functionally important subunits or a "modular" architecture of the cortex.

It should be noted that the term *module* is used in at least two different ways. It may be used to denote a purely theoretical concept (Fodor's "psychological modules," e.g., 1983, 1985) or an anatomical substructure of the cortical network. In this latter sense, used here, module is synonymous with "cortical column."

Based on the pioneering research of Hubel and Wiesel (1959; see the review in Hubel, 1988), the modular organization and interconnection principles of the visual cortex were described in great detail. Although most of the principles discussed here were found for the visual cortex, it is generally held that they apply also to other areas of the cortex.

The neocortex and thus each module (cortical column) is organized in six horizontal layers. Exceptions are the allo-cortex or archi-cortex (of the hippocampus) and the paleocortex (located in medial parts of the temporal lobe), which comprise only three layers. Modules appear as vertical columns with a height of some millimeters and a radius of a few tenths of a millimeter. In the primary visual cortex there are highly specialized modules or columns of neurons, which encode the angle of line segments of complex visual contours (Hubel, 1988).

These horizontal and vertical structuring principles give insight into important processing characteristics of the cortex (Martin, 1985). The neurons in layer IV are the target of afferent fibers, which originate in specific nuclei of the lateral thalamus. From layer IV, (sensory) information is transmitted to neurons in other layers of the same cortical column. Neurons in layers II and III receive their information from other regions of the brain. Layers V and VI are specialized for transmitting output information to other columns as well as to other parts of the brain. Layer I consists primarily of closely interconnected dendrites (apical dendrites), which typically originate in lowerlying pyramidal cells. It is generally assumed that the EEG (as an extracellular recording method with macroelectrodes attached to the scalp) primarily — but not exclusively — records postsynaptic potential changes at the apical dendrites in layer I (see the review in Martin, 1985).

Two large groups of nerve cells can be distinguished in each cortical column: pyramidal cells and stellate cells. Pyramidal cells are excitatory and have a pyramid-shaped cell body (hence the name), long axons (which transmit information to other regions of the brain), and a very complex apical dendritic tree with a "trunk" that is always oriented at a right angle toward the surface of the cortex. The amino acids (glutamate or aspartate) serve as transmitters. Especially important for their function is the fact that cortical pyramidal cells feature "booster zones" at certain points in their dendritic tree. These zones serve to strengthen excitatory signals arriving from distant regions of the brain by amplifying excitatory postsynaptic potentials (EPSPs). One can easily imagine that a certain geometric arrangement of booster zones in the dendritic tree will lead to a selective strengthening of signals from certain other regions of the brain.

Stellate cells form a very heterogeneous group of interneurons. There is some evidence that stellate cells with vertically oriented axons work excitatorily, whereas those with horizontally oriented axons are inhibitory and use GABA as a transmitter (Martin, 1985). It is generally assumed that stellate cells are especially suited to "local" information processing within a cortical column as well as between adjacent cortical columns. With respect to this assumption, it is worth mentioning that excitatory stellate cells with vertical axons are primarily interconnected with cells of the same cortical column, whereas inhibitory cells with horizontal axons are primarily connected with cells of neighboring columns. These facts support the assumption that GABAergic stellate cells are at least in part responsible for a functional independence of cortical columns.

Cortical columns can therefore be regarded as modules that function largely independent of neighboring modules. The concept of a modular organization of the brain is based on a work by M. E. Scheibel and A. B. Scheibel (1958), in which the structure of the brainstem is described. In subsequent decades, further experiments were carried out by Hubel and Wiesel (1959), Mountcastle (1978), and Szentagothai (1975). The results of this and similar research (see Szentagothai, Hamori, & Palkovits, 1981, pp. 55–89) indicate that virtually the entire human cortex with its extraordinarily large surface area (due to its intensive folding) of approximately 2,500 cm^2 consists of approximately 2.5 million modules. There are about 10,000 million neurons in the cortex, so the number of neurons per module amounts to approximately 4,000. Thus, a single square centimeter of cortical surface contains approximately 1,000 modules with approximately 4 million neurons. One square millimeter comprises approximately 10 modules with about 40,000 neurons. One module therefore has a diameter of approximately .3 mm. The height amounts to approximately 3 mm.

Cortical modules are connected to each other according to the convergence/divergence principle. Each module sends axonal fibers to other modules and is itself the target of converging cortico-corticular connections stemming from modules of the same as well as from the contralateral hemisphere. This means that modules project in a completely overlapping manner to a certain number of other modules (Eccles, 1981). It is important to note that these projections are (a) bidirectional (i.e., each module sends axons to a connected module and at the same time receives axonal fibers from that module), are (b) established by axons of pyramidal cells that function excitatorily, and (c) also connect modules that are not adjacent to each other. Consequently, this interconnection principle must not be confused with the lateral inhibition principle of inhibitory stellate cells mentioned earlier, which functions "locally" and affects only adjacent modules.

11.1.2 Neural Signal Processing

There are excellent reviews on this topic (e.g., Amit, 1989; Kandel & Schwartz, 1985; Llinas, 1989; Thompson, 1985). Instead of attempting yet another review, we focus selectively on only those results important for evaluating the processing assumptions of the connectivity model.

Those parts of a nerve cell of crucial importance for signal processing are the dendrites (which receive incoming signals), the cell body (or soma, which integrates and "sums up" incoming signals), the point where the axon leaves the cell body (which is responsible for generating the "output signal," i.e., the action potential), and finally the axon (which enables the action potential to move to the presynaptic membrane). The length of an axon ranges from a few 10^{-2} mm up to several centimeters. Branchings of the axon are termed *collaterals*. Typically, synapses are to be found between axons and dendrites (axo-dendritic synapses) and between axons and cell bodies (axo-somatic synapses). But there are also synapses that exist between axons (axo-axonic synapses) and between dendrites (dendro-dendritic synapses).

The action potential is a large and rapid change in voltage across the axon membrane that travels down the axon. The voltage change is characterized by a quick rise from -70 to 50 mV (millivolts) and a subsequent decline to the level of the negative resting potential of -70 mV. This short lasting peak of 50 mV is also known as a "spike." The action potential originates at the axon hillock (i.e., the point where the axon leaves the cell body) and traverses the entire length of the axon up to the synaptic cleft, where it ends. The amplitude of the action potential remains constant, but the number of spikes per time unit, indicating the frequency of the action potential, varies in a wide range of approximately 1 Hz to 500 Hz. Thus, it is clear that it is the frequency and not the amplitude that carries the information of a signal. In sensory stimulation experiments it can be demonstrated that with an increase in stimulation strength the frequency of the action potential increases logarithmically. We are thus confronted with a discrete frequency modulated encoding.

Because the action potential terminates at the presynaptic membrane, another mechanism must be responsible for the signal transfer beyond the synaptic cleft to neighboring nerve cells. This mechanism is biochemical, not electric, in nature and basically consists of the action potential triggering a release of transmitter substance at the presynaptic membrane, which is then diffused over the synaptic cleft. At the postsynaptic membrane, special receptors respond to the release of transmitter substance and, by means of other mechanisms, lead to the generation of postsynaptic potentials. This process can by very fast and can be completed in a few milliseconds. It should be noted, however, that the synaptic delay differs for different transmitters. Depending on whether or not it is an excitatory or inhibitory synapse, we speak of an excitatory or inhibitory postsynaptic potential (EPSP or IPSP). The frequency of the action potential is one of the most important factors influencing the strength of a postsynaptic potential. The higher the frequency is, (a) the more transmitter substance is released per time unit at the presynaptic membrane, (b) the more receptors respond at the postsynaptic membrane, and (c) the stronger is the extent of (excitatory or inhibitory) postsynaptic potential change. In the case of EPSPs it is a summation of potential changes in the direction of positive depolarization, in the case of IPSPs the summation proceeds in a negative direction or "hyperpolarization." Because it is the frequency of the action potential that finally determines the extent of summation, we speak of the *principle of temporal summation.*

In considering the large number of axo-dendritic synapses, it becomes quite obvious that one or a few postsynaptic potentials will not suffice to trigger an action potential in the postsynaptic neuron. And indeed it is the sum of EPSPs and IPSPs entering through several synapses in different sites of the dendritic tree that determine (besides other factors) whether or not an action potential will be generated. This fact that postsynaptic potentials generated in different regions of the neuron are added together, is termed *principle of spatial summation.*

Both principles show that encoding is analogous at the input side of a nerve cell, and not discrete as it is at the output side. The transition between analogy and frequency coding takes place at the trigger zone, which is located at that point where the axon leaves the cell body. This trigger zone responds if an electric threshold value is exceeded. If the potential shifts from the resting potential of -70 mV toward depolarization and reaches a value of -60 mV, then the threshold for generating an action potential has been reached (Thompson, 1985). If, however, the potential shifts in a negative direction (hyperpolarization), then the generation of an action potential is inhibited. These two mechanisms of summing up excitatory and inhibitory inputs and of exceeding a certain threshold in order to generate an output underly the assumptions of "formal neurons" (McCulloch & Pitts, 1943) and connectionist models (see the review in J. A. Anderson & Rosenfeld, 1988).

11.1.3 Synaptic Modification

One of the most important rules of synaptic modification was postulated by Donald Hebb, a psychologist interested in a complex cognitive theory, at a time when mechanisms of synaptic modification were neurophysiologically neither documented nor examined. Those who question the utility of neurophysiologically based representational assumptions should remember this interesting fact. Hebb (1949, chap. 4) defined the mechanism of synaptic modification that was later taken up within the framework of connectionism and became known and quoted under the name of the "Hebb rule": "When an axon of cell A is near enough to excite a cell B and repeatedly or persistently takes part in firing it, some growth process or metabolic change takes place in one or both cells such that A's efficiency, as one of the cells firing B, is increased" (p. 67).

It took about 25 years before the Hebb rule could be experimentally confirmed by Bliss (Bliss & Gardner-Medwin, 1973; Bliss & Lömo, 1973). In neurophysiology, this mechanism became known as *long-term synaptic potentiation* (LTP). It is characterized by the fact that short bursts of action potentials (in the frequency range of about 100–400 Hz and lasting approximately 50 ms), which are experimentally induced, lead to a long-term strengthening of persistent synaptic enhancement lasting several weeks or even months. The extent of LTP or synaptic strengthening is experimentally recorded by the increasing amplitude of the EPSP or by the frequency of postsynaptic spikes. There are different types or features of LTPs, but only two are mentioned here: the associative feature and the interactive dependence between afferent stimulation and postsynaptic excitation (see the review in T. H. Brown, Chapman, Kairiss, & Keenan, 1988). The associative feature is a function of the intensity of stimulation; only if an afferent input is sufficiently strong or if several weak but converging inputs meet simultaneously (and thus add up), will the EPSP be sufficiently large to generate a LTP. The principles of temporal and spatial summation mentioned earlier also play a central role here. However, LTPs can be generated only if EPSPs can be triggered at the postsynaptic neuron. Voltage clamp experiments have shown that while simultaneously suppressing postsynaptic excitation, presynaptic stimulation alone fails to generate LTPs. It can therefore be concluded that the occurance of both the presynaptic stimulation and the subsequent postsynaptic excitation is of crucial importance in generating LTPs (refer to Hebb's quotation). Finally, it should be mentioned that the opposing phenomenon of *long-term depotentiation* (LTD) has also been experimentally validated. This phenomenon is triggered by a short-lived afferent activation and leads to a long-term suppression of postsynaptic activation (Levy, 1985).

11.2 THE CONNECTIVITY MODEL AS A NEURAL MODEL

This section compares the assumptions and predictions of the connectivity model with the basic principles of neural information processing. We are aware that some of the following considerations are hypothetical and speculative. The justification for this attempt lies in the hope of arriving at a neuroscientific basis for psychological theories, if the possibilities available to us at the moment, albeit speculative, are used.

We have repeatedly emphasized that the avoidance of representational assumptions results in a variety of misconceptions and contradictions (chaps. 1 and 3). With respect to this fact, present-day memory psychology and its relation to neuroscience may find itself in a situation similar to the one Ebbinghaus faced about 100 years ago; in an attempt to arrive at a scientific foundation of psychology, he dismissed speculations on the encoding format (see section 1.2). Should we concern ourselves today with speculations on neurophysiological representational assumptions? We believe that such a concern is worthwhile. The logic of this book aims at exhausting all the possibilities that allow us to arrive at a more specific and detailed definition of representational assumptions. As a result of this approach, neuroscientific findings become an essential consideration.

11.2.1 Structural Assumptions: Their Possible Neural Basis

The central assumption of interconnectivity as a general principle for semantic encoding is entirely supported by the fact that individual neurons as well as cortical modules are intensely interconnected. It should also be noted that the connectivity principles of partially and completely interconnected codes (see section 8.3) correspond to the well-known divergence/convergence principle. In order to explain this fact, consider the three stages of activation in interconnected codes: During the first stage, the activated pathways diverge from the source node to the $n - 1$ feature nodes. At the beginning of the second stage activation diverges further to the remaining $n - 2$ feature nodes. But at the end of the second stage activation converges at each of the $n - 2$ feature nodes. The maximum extent of convergence is reached in the third stage, when activation from all of the $n - 1$ feature nodes accumulates at the source node.

In a functional sense, divergent circuits are seen as an indication of specialization and segregation. Convergent circuits, on the other hand, are interpreted in terms of integration (Zeki & Shipp, 1988). This notion is in accordance with the encoding principles of interconnected codes. The divergence in the first activation stage means specialization, as the different specific and diverging meanings of semantic features are retrieved from the source node. The convergence in the third stage means the integration of the different meanings of semantic features into a holistic conceptual meaning, which is represented by the entire code.

Does a node in the semantic network of the connectivity model correspond to an individual neuron in the neural network? The answer to this question is no, whereby the following reasons appear decisive:

1. A feature node stands for complex information, which can hardly be represented by an individual neuron. This reason makes it seem plausible to assume cortical modules (columns) as a possible neural basis for feature nodes.

2. Source nodes are responsible for complex monitoring processes (refer back to Assumptions C2 and C3 in sections 8.6.2 and 8.6.3). Thus, for a similar reason, cortical modules must also be taken into consideration here.

Once we assume that nodes correspond to modules, it becomes evident that the links in the network are not represented by individual axons but instead by a large set of different axons. Because cortical modules are connected with approximately 1,000 axons (in every direction), it is easy to accept the postulated bidirectionality that each link can be activated simultaneously in every direction (Assumption 4).

It should be noted that connectionist models proceed from the assumption that a node is represented by a single neuron. Thus, in contrast to most connectionist approaches, the connectivity model refers to the macrolevel of cortical modules, where a node stands for several groups of 1,000 neurons, and a link for approximately 1,000 axonal connections.

11.2.2 Processing Assumptions: Their Possible Neural Basis

Although we proceed from the assumption that nodes are represented by modules, we refer back to the functioning principles of individual neurons in the analysis of processing assumptions. This appears justified, because modules mirror the processing characteristics of individual neurons.

Assumption 1, the assumption of unlimited capacity of spreading activation, postulates that each node transmits the entire activation amount. This is actually the case in excitatory synapses, as we have seen in section

11.1.2. Furthermore, there is no evidence that a systematic weakening of the neural signal occurs with increasing length of the neural pathway (cf. the booster zones mentioned earlier) or with an increasing number of traversed synapses. These considerations therefore support the validity of the central processing assumptions of the connectivity model and speak against the assumption of a systematic weakening as it is postulated, for example, by ACT or ACT*.

Assumption 2 states that a node remains active only during a critical time span $t(k)$ and that its activity is set to zero if no activation arrives within $t(k)$. This is in accordance with the principle of temporal summation and the way in which an action potential is triggered. Synaptic potentials have particular time constants. The potentials add up only if they fall within a critical time span. Only then will they sum up and they can trigger an action potential. If, however, the amount of activation does not suffice to reach the threshold for triggering an action potential, its strength will fade and will not play any further role. Accordingly, we may assume that in this case activity is "set to zero." As a result, temporal factors play a decisive role in the process of triggering an action potential.

Assumption 3 simply states that within $t(k)$ different sources of activations sum up to a single activation value. This assumption, which is an addition to Assumption 2, is supported by the different summation principles and by the fact that the trigger zone responds only if a certain threshold value is reached.

Assumption 4 states that each link can be activated in both directions. Because we assume that a node in a semantic network does not correspond with a single neuron, but with larger units such as cortical modules, a link between nodes does not correspond with an individual axon connecting different neurons. Instead we assume that a link is represented by a set of axons connecting two cortical modules. As a result, Assumption 4 is in accordance with neural processing principles.

Assumption 5 rejects the notion of reverberating activation. The reason behind this assumption was to enable the prediction of a particular spreading activation pattern, which is based on three separate stages. As suggested in chap. 10, we may assume that a module is an intelligent unit that monitors the flow of activation of its neighboring modules. According to Assumption 5 then, a module sends activation only to those neighboring nodes from which (in a certain stage) activation was not received. Although it is easy to imagine that cortical modules are capable of taking over this task, the neural implementation suggested here is highly speculative.

According to Assumption 6, the time needed to activate a node is reciprocal to the strength of activation. This principle is in good agreement with the fact that the frequency of the action potential is an important factor influencing not only the strength of an EPSP but also the speed with which the potential change occurs. The higher the frequency, the faster the postsynaptic potential change takes place.

Assumption 7 states that in a neutral condition the nodes and links are functionally of equal importance. It is surely justified to proceed from the idea that different modules and their axonal interconnections are potentially of equal importance.

The assumption that nodes do not correspond to single neurons is of crucial importance, as the following considerations show: Assumption 7 would inevitably lead to contradictions if nodes would have been interpreted in terms of individual neurons. Different neurons may well differ in their function. Pyramidal cells, for example, have different functional and structural properties as inhibitory interneurons. Thus, it can be seen that Assumption 7 is consistent only when nodes are represented by modules and not by individual neurons. A similar conclusion holds for Assumption 4, which postulates bidirectionality of activation. This assumption is only consistent if nodes correspond to modules and not to neurons. Axons do not function bidirectionally but have a preferred direction of activation. Modules, on the other hand, are connected to axonal fibers in both directions.

Thus, given the assumptions of the connectivity model, we are forced to associate nodes with cortical modules and not with individual neurons. This is a compelling conclusion and not a more or less plausible assumption. We thus see that comparing the assumptions of psychological theories with neurophysiological findings is not only rewarding and promising but also not as speculative as had been assumed.

Finally, consider the central prediction of the connectivity model that the speed of spreading activation increases as the degree of interconnectedness and/or the complexity of the network increases. When evaluating this prediction, the following time critical processes are of importance. The principle of temporal summation confirms the basic notion that processing speed increases as the amount of activation increases. More importantly, however, is the effect of spatial summation. According to the connectivity model, the predicted accelerating effect is only reached, if the strengths of converging branches are summed up (Equations 8.4 and 8.5). It is precisely this effect, discussed in detail in section 8.3.2, which corresponds to the principle of spatial summation outlined in section 11.1.2. The more afferent inputs that converge at the dendrites of a neuron, the more rapidly the threshold for triggering an action potential can be exceeded and the higher is the speed of signal processing.

We have repeatedly emphasized that preactivation and inhibition are important concepts that explain dynamic processes in complex networks. It goes without saying that the mechanisms of LTP and LTD described in section 11.1.3 are of primary importance not only for learning processes, but also for priming phenomena and for the dynamic processes described repeatedly in chap. 9. Because they can be established rapidly, LTPs and LTDs offer an almost ideal explanation for the creation of new codes or the modification of existing codes in human memory. The importance of synaptic modification for learning and memory processes is also documented and described in detail in experiments with invertebrates (Alkon, 1987; Kandel, 1987).

11.3 ON THE LOCALIZATION OF MEMORY PROCESSES

The question of which regions of the brain store memory codes has a long tradition and is closely related to the concept of *engrams*, first proposed by Richard Semon and thoroughly examined by Lashley (see the excellent historical review in Orbach, 1982). Strongly influenced by behaviorism, Lashley proceeded from the then generally accepted notion that memory processes are localized in cortical association areas. One reason for this assumption was the general idea that memory performance can be interpreted in terms of associations established between sensory input (provided by the sensory cortex) and motor output (provided by the motor cortex). According to this view, it was quite obvious to see that engrams are represented in the association fields, which were understood as the mediators between sensory input and motor output. When Lashley began his lesion studies in the 1920s, he was convinced that removing significantly large parts of association fields would hamper learning and memory performance, but not sensory or motor functions. His results, however, did not confirm this view. Instead, they suggested that the decline in memory performance observed after the lesion depends only on its size, not on its area within the cortex.

These and similar findings made Lashley a radical critic of the classical view, which held that particular areas in the cortex are specialized for particular functions. He questioned the usefulness of the distinction between sensory, motor, and association fields and suggested that any site in the cortex has the potency of performing any type of task. This extreme position can best be characterized by his principles of equipotency (each area of the cortex can take on any function) and mass action (the entire mass of neurons participates in carrying out a task).

The research done in recent decades has shown that Lashley's principles of equipotency and mass action cannot be applied to sensory, motor, and linguistic processes (especially the results achieved by the brain stimulation technique of Ojeman & Whitaker, 1978). Some of the clearest evidence against Lashley's view comes from the research carried out by Hubel and Wiesel. But as justified as the critique of Lashley's theories with regard to sensory, motor, and linguistic information processes is, his opinion about the localization of long-term memory traces remains unchallenged. In his famous essay entitled "In Search of the Engram" (1950) Lashley wrote: "It is not possible to demonstrate the isolated localization of a memory trace anywhere within the nervous system. Limited regions may be essential for learning or retention of a particular activity, but within such regions the parts are functionally equivalent. The engram is represented throughout the region" (p. 478).

Lashley's view about the localization of memory codes (or engrams) is still a timely issue (e.g., Braitenberg & Schüz, 1991; Edelman & Mountcastle, 1978; John, Tang, Brill, Young, & Ono, 1986). Are memory codes represented in a distributed way (i.e., in a variety of different sites throughout the cortex) or are they represented in a localized form in particular sites? With respect to these questions the following facts are important: First, we see that in neuropsychology and physiology assumptions underlying the encoding format play a similarly crucial role as in cognitive psychology. Second, and even more important, the controversy between a distributed and a localized representation of memory codes shows many similarities with the controversy between holistic and component codes. The notion of looking for isolated and locally represented engrams originated in all probability from an incorrect memory conception: The concept of engrams misleadingly suggests a holistic coding format. If we were to accept the idea of a holistic format, we would inevitably also have to assume that codes are clearly localized in particular cortical areas. However, we have attempted to show (especially chaps. 3 and 8) that codes consist of an interconnected structure of different components. If we proceed from the idea that these components, which of course can also comprise information from different sensory systems, are stored in different regions of the cortex, then it becomes obvious that codes are represented in a distributed way. We thus arrive at the conclusion that memory codes cannot be clearly localized, because its components are represented in numerous but different regions of the cortex.

Some aspects of the controversy outlined here can be put down to the insufficient distinction made between complex semantic codes (representing symbolic information) and elementary codes (representing nonsymbolic information). Researchers like Alkon (1988) and Kandel (1987), who traced elementary learning and memory processes (e.g., the formation of conditioned responses in invertebrates) to specific processes of synaptic modification, seem to place the assumption of a localized representation on a sound empirical basis. In contrast to this, researchers like John (John et al., 1986), who use higher mammals and comparatively complex tasks, arrive at the conclusion that memory information is represented throughout the entire brain.

For a better evaluation of this controversy, however, it is also necessary to take note of the distinction made between encoding processes within the domain of STM and retrieval processes from LTM. It is well accepted that the hippocampal formation (the famous case of patient HM see Scoville & Millner, 1957) like other regions of the limbic system (see the reviews in Markowitsch, 1983, 1988; Markowitsch & Pritzel, 1985; Mishkin & Appenzeller, 1987) are of particular importance for encoding processes. However, for the assumption that the storage of long-term memory information takes place in clearly defined cortical sites, there is no convincing evidence.

Section 8.1 suggested that integrated, that is, intensively interconnected codes are stored in LTM. Because the development of interconnections can be interpreted as a long-term and learning-dependent process, it seems plausible to assume that LTM codes are, by far, more complex and, therefore, more distributed than STM codes. This interpretation may contribute to the explanation of the fact that, in contrast to LTM, encoding processes can be localized to some extent. Yet another interpretation could be based on the notion that attentional and monitoring processes — which also are needed to initiate search processes in LTM — converge in that site of the brain where encoding processes are localized (refer to the hippocampal indexing theory by Teyler & DiScienna, 1986). According to this view, the hippocampal formation — the integrity of which is of crucial importance for encoding — may be one of the sites, where pathways responsible for vital control mechanisms converge. A lesion in this site or the disruption of the pathways leading to this site thus lead to particularly obvious symptoms and, therefore, suggest a clear localizability of encoding processes.

11.3.1 The Possible Localization of Monitoring Processes

Complex monitoring processes were discussed in sections 8.6.3 and 8.7. Their task does not lie in directing spreading activation — which follows automatically by local mechanisms — but in the selection of access points, when initiating a search process, and the retrieval of information (see the distinction made between general and specific search processes in section 8.7.1). The result of a search process can be judged by the activation strength of a node (a module) or a code (assembly of modules): The node or code that reveals the highest activation value represents the relevant information to be retrieved. Those mechanisms that identify the relevant nodes or codes cannot be explained by activation processes described in chap. 8, but only by a special monitoring system.

In the identification of the relevant nodes or codes, feedback loops may play a decisive role. During the course of spreading activation the activation status of the searched network is constantly transmitted to a monitoring system by means of feedback loops. Because the source nodes are informed not only about the activation stage but also about the activation strength of all nodes, it would suffice if the monitoring network is connected with the source nodes. According to this view, the source nodes serve as interface between the storage and monitoring network.

When considering in which region of the brain the monitoring network is localized, we proceed from the following assumptions: The storage network is represented in the cortex and the links of the monitoring network converge in a particular monitoring system. Consequently, the monitoring system should be connected with the cortex by a dense network of axonal connections. Besides the basal ganglia, the thalamus with its thalamocortical projections to virtually all different cortical regions (e.g., Höhl-Abrahao & Creutzfeldt, 1991) is one of those brain structures that fulfills this requirement. Because the dorso-medial nucleus of the thalamus is closely linked to the hippocampus, we can imagine that encoding and retrieval are prominent functions of the monitor network that converges at thalamic nuclei and the hippocampus.

Some researchers have suggested that the EEG frequency within the alpha band (of about 8–13 Hz) stems from the thalamus and induces synchronized neural activity in the cortex (Andersen & Andersson, 1968). If we proceed from the aforementioned notion that memory codes are retrieved via longitudinal pathways linking thalamic nuclei with the cortex, and that alpha is the predominant rhythm reflecting the activity of these pathways, we arrive at the hypothesis that alpha frequency should be related to memory performance. We have tested this hypothesis (Klimesch, Schimke, Ladurner, & Pfurtscheller, 1990; Klimesch, Schimke, & Pfurtscheller, 1993) and found that alpha frequency increases significantly as memory performance increases.

12 Concluding Remarks

The rather complex nature of the preceding chapters warrants a reminder of the basic ideas guiding our discussion. Therefore this chapter summarizes the most important aspects of our arguments.

We entered this discussion with the aim of arriving at a comprehensive memory theory and we believe to have found such a theory in the connectivity model. Initially we had to deal with two difficulties: the assumption of holistic codes (chaps. 1–4) and the assumption of linear hierarchical structures (chaps. 5–7). Both assumptions inevitably result in contradictions, which were discussed in chaps. 4 and 8. We have replaced the assumption of holistic codes with that of component codes, and the assumption of a hierarchical coding format with that of an interconnected coding format. These new assumptions have formed the basis of the connectivity model developed in chap. 8. The quantitative analysis of the connectivity model, however, has shown that a third assumption, the assumption of partially or unlimited capacity of spreading activation, is necessary to support its predictions.

In chap. 9 we applied the connectivity model to semantic memory and confronted the experimental evaluation of its predictions. As a result, we have seen that the connectivity model was capable of explaining the following issues in semantic memory:

1. The representation of the meaning of a concept by an interconnected structure of semantic features.
2. Context effects that modify the meaning of a concept.
3. The effects of typicality on reaction time.

4. The representation of conceptual hierarchies.
5. The representation of basic concepts.
6. Complex search processes, such as the discovery, retrieval, and evaluation of semantic relations.
7. Priming effects.
8. The improved memory performance for codes rich in semantic features.

The connectivity model was capable of predicting the following experimental findings:

1. The more rapid processing of concepts rich in semantic features.
2. The more rapid processing of subordinate concepts in comparison to superordinate concepts.
3. The more rapid processing of basic concepts in comparison to other concepts.
4. The more rapid processing of typical concepts in comparison to untypical concepts.
5. The reaction time differences between yes and no responses in semantic decision and priming experiments.
6. The more rapid processing of pictures in comparison to words.
7. The improved memory performance of pictures in comparison to words.
8. Other findings connected to the picture effect.

12.1 THE CONNECTIVITY MODEL AND CONNECTIONIST APPROACHES

We have compared the connectivity model with the assumptions of Anderson's ACT and ACT* models, but also to the network theories of semantic memory. As a result, we have seen that the central assumptions of the connectivity model are incompatible with those of all other models. Is this claim still valid when considering connectionist and other neural network models?

When comparing the connectivity model with connectionist models (Rumelhart, McClelland, & the PDP research group, 1986) and other models within the domain of neural networks (J. A. Anderson & Rosenfeld, 1988; Hinton & J. A. Anderson, 1989), we see both striking differences and similarities. The similarities refer to the idea of a distributed storage, which is based on intense interconnections between elementary coding units and to the fact that the assumptions of both types of models can be related to basic findings in neuroscience. However, the basic architecture of the models and the representational assumptions are radically different. Connectionist models focus on dynamic processing characteristics such as learning, pattern recognition, and classification. To our knowledge, there is not a single connectionist or neural network model that is concerned with the prediction of time-critical processes in memory, such as search and retrieval time in semantic memory.

As an example, consider a typical connectionist network. It consists of an encoding, pattern processing, and a decoding network. Each of these three networks shows two partially overlapping processing layers, an input and output layer. The output layer of the encoding network is the input layer of the pattern processing network; its output layer, in turn, forms the input layer of the decoding network. With respect to the connectivity model, the following facts are important: First, each node in the input layer is connected with each node of the output layer. Second, the individual nodes within a layer are not connected to each other, as is the case in hierarchical networks. Thus, the representation of a code at the input layer consists of a list of not interconnected elements. We already know that this form of representation strongly contradicts the connectivity model. A list of elements indicates a linear code that is a special case of a hierarchical code (section 5.2). All arguments against hierarchical representational assumptions (introduced in chap. 8) also apply, at least in principle, to connectionist models. However, in contrast to ACT and ACT*, these models assume that all the components of a code can be processed in parallel and largely independently of each other. As a result, the complexity of a code (or the number of its elements) is not a suitable predictor of processing time in memory: Codes of differing complexity are processed at a constant speed. Without additional assumptions, therefore, these models will not be in a position to explain time-critical processes such as search and retrieval time.

Another peculiarity of connectionist and neural network models is the avoidance of explicit representational assumptions that go beyond a list or set of code elements. This is reminiscent of the discussion in chap. 3 and 4 in which we attempted to show that the avoidance of specific representational assumptions inevitably leads to contradictory memory theories. This fact also shows that the assumptions of connectionist models are incompatible with those of the connectivity model.

Another result of this avoidance of more explicit representational assumptions is the question of how connectionist models can describe semantic and syntactic structures. It is therefore not surprising that the connectionist approach is seen as a challenge to psycholinguistic theories. In reference to this, Fodor and Pylyshin (1988) wrote: "What's deeply wrong with connectionist architecture is this: because it acknowledges neither syntactic nor semantic structure in mental representations, it perforce treats them not as a generated set but as a list. But lists, qua lists, have no structure; any collection of items is a possible list" (p. 49).

12.2 REPRESENTATIONAL ASSUMPTIONS AND THEIR IMPORTANCE FOR THE FUTURE OF COGNITIVE PSYCHOLOGY

One of the basic arguments of this book purports that cognitive psychology cannot succeed without the explicit consideration of certain representational assumptions. One could undoubtedly object to this challenging claim by stating that the empirical testability of representational assumptions is only possible in part and the approach outlined here is only one of the many different approaches within cognitive and memory psychology.

It is certainly true that one single representational assumption in itself (e.g., Assumption 4 of the connectivity model) can hardly be tested. However, the predictions that result from a certain set of representational assumptions can be tested empirically (as shown in chap. 9) or evaluated theoretically (as shown in chaps. 10 and 11). This fact leads to the important conclusion that representational assumptions may only be tested within the framework of theories which, on the basis of differing representational assumptions, formulate mutually exclusive predictions. In other words, if different theories based on different representational assumptions arrive at the same predictions, then the validity of the representational assumptions underlying these theories cannot be empirically tested. The goal of cognitive research should therefore consist of contrasting theories that proceed from distinctive representational assumptions and are capable of making distinctive and empirically testable predictions. A good example is the assumptions and predictions of ACT, ACT*, and the connectivity model detailed in chap. 8. In this way it is possible to test certain sets and combinations of representational assumptions.

The more recent development in the area of neuroscience may be used as a guideline for the future research in cognitive psychology. Ideally, representational assumptions should also refer to the physical basis of memory and thus to the neurophysiological level of explanation. In discussing this approach in chap. 11, we wanted to show that neurophysiological knowledge is a valuable tool in testing and evaluating representational assumptions. Another promising aspect of this approach lies in the fact that neurophysiological knowledge is capable of spurring the development of comprehensive cognitive theories that can be tested with the help of psychophysiological experiments (Klimesch, Pfurtscheller, & Lindinger, 1986; Klimesch, Pfurtscheller, & Mohl, 1988).

References

Adams, M. J. (1979). Models of word recognition. *Cognitive Psychology, 11*, 133–176.

Alkon, D. L. (1987). *Memory traces in the brain*. Cambridge, England: Cambridge University Press.

Allport, D. A., Tipper, S. P., & Chmiel, N. R. J. (1985). Perceptual integration and postcategorical filtering. In M. I. Posner & O. S. Marin (Eds.), *Attention and performance* (Vol. XI, pp. 107–132). Hillsdale, NJ: Lawrence Erlbaum Associates.

Amit, D. J. (1989). *Modeling brain function: The world of attractor neural networks*. New York: Cambridge University Press.

Andersen, P., & Andersson, A. A. (1968). *Physiological basis of alpha rhythm*. New York: Century Crofts.

Anderson, J. A., & Hinton, G. E. (1981). Models of information processing in the brain. In G. E. Hinton & J. A. Anderson (Eds.), *Parallel models of associate memory* (pp. 213–236). Hillsdale, NJ: Lawrence Erlbaum Associates.

Anderson, J. A., & Rosenfeld, A. E. (Eds.). (1988). *Neurocomputing. Foundations of research*. Cambridge, MA: MIT Press.

Anderson, J. R. (1974). Retrieval of propositional information from long-term memory. *Cognitive Psychology, 5*, 451–474.

Anderson, J. R. (1975). Item-specific and relation-specific interference in sentence memory. *Journal of Experimental Psychology: Human Learning and Memory, 104*, 249–260.

Anderson, J. R. (1976). *Language, memory, and thought*. Hillsdale, NJ: Lawrence Erlbaum Associates.

Anderson, J. R. (1978). Arguments concerning representations for mental imagery. *Psychological Review, 85*, 249–277.

Anderson, J. R. (1981). Effects of prior knowledge on memory for new information. *Memory and Cognition, 9*, 237–246.

Anderson, J. R. (1983a). *The architecture of cognition*. Cambridge, MA: Harvard University Press.

Anderson, J. R. (1983b). Retrieval of information from long-term memory. *Science, 220*, 25–30.

Anderson, J. R. (1983c). A spreading activation theory of memory. *Journal of Verbal Learning and Verbal Behavior, 22,* 261–295.

Anderson, J. R. (1985a). *Cognitive psychology and its implications.* New York: W. H. Freeman.

Anderson, J. R. (1985b). Ebbinghaus's century. *Journal of Experimental Psychology: Learning, Memory, and Cognition, 11,* 436–438.

Anderson, J. R. (1987). Methodologies for studying human knowledge. *Behavioral and Brain Sciences, 10,* 467–505.

Anderson, J. R., & Bower, G. H. (1972). Recognition and retrieval processes in free recall. *Psychological Review, 79,* 97–123.

Anderson, J. R., & Bower, G. H. (1973). *Human associative memory.* Washington, DC: V. H. Winston.

Anderson, J. R., & Pirolli, P. L. (1984). Spread of activation. *Journal of Experimental Psychology: Learning, Memory, and Cognition, 10,* 791–798.

Anderson, J. R., & Reder, L. M. (1987). Effects of number of facts studied on recognition versus sensibility judgements. *Journal of Experimental Psychology: Learning, Memory, and Cognition, 13,* 355–367.

Anderson, R. E. (1976). Short-term retention of the where and when of pictures and words. *Journal of Experimental Psychology: General, 105,* 378–402.

Armstrong, S. L., Gleitman, L. R., & Gleitman, H. (1983). What some concepts might not be. *Cognition, 13,* 263–308.

Atkinson, R. C., & Shiffrin, R. M. (1968). Human memory: A proposed system and its control processes. In K. W. Spence & J. T. Spence (Eds.), *The psychology of learning and motivation: Vol. 2. Advances in research and theory* (pp. 89–195). New York: Academic Press.

Atkinson, R. C., & Shiffrin, R. M. (1971). The control of short term memory. *Scientific American, 225,* 82–90.

Averbach, E., & Coriell, A. S. (1961). Short-term memory in vision. *Bell Systems Technical Journal, 40,* 309–328.

Baddeley, A. (1981). The concept of working memory: A view of its current state and probable future development. *Cognition, 10,* 17–23.

Baddeley, A., Lewis, V., Eldridge, M., & Thomson, N. (1984). Attention and retrieval from long-term memory. *Journal of Experimental Psychology: General, 113,* 518–540.

Baddeley, A., Scott, D., Drynan, R., & Smith, J. C. (1969). Short-term memory and the limited capacity hypothesis. *British Journal of Psychology, 60,* 51–55.

Bahrick, H. B. (1984). Associations and organization in cognitive psychology: A reply to Neisser. *Journal of Experimental Psychology: General, 113,* 36–37.

Bahrick, H. B. (1985). Associationism and the Ebbinghaus legacy. *Journal of Experimental Psychology: Learning, Memory, and Cognition, 11,* 439–443.

Barsalou, L. W. (1985). Ideals, central tendency, and frequency of instantiation as determinants of graded structure in categories. *Journal of Experimental Psychology: Learning, Memory, and Cognition, 11,* 629–654.

Bartlett, F. C. (1932). *Remembering.* Cambridge, England: Cambridge University Press.

Bierwisch, M. (1977). Sprache und Gedächtnis: Ergebnisse und Probleme [Language and memory: Results and problems]. In F. Klix & H. Sydow (Eds.), *Zur Psychologie des Gedächtnisses* (pp. 117–149). Berlin: VEB Deutscher Verlag der Wissenschaften.

Bleasdale, F. (1983). Paivio's dual-coding model of meaning revisited. In J. C. Yuille (Ed.), *Imagery, memory and cognition.* (pp. 183–209). Hillsdale, NJ: Lawrence Erlbaum Associates.

Bliss, T. V. P., & Gardner-Medwin, A. R. (1973). Long-lasting potentiation of synaptic transmission in the dentate area of the unanaesthetized rabbit following stimulation of the perforant path. *Journal of Physiology, 232,* 357–374.

Bliss, T. V. P., & Lömo, T. (1973). Long-lasting potentiation of synaptic transmission in the dentate area of the unanaesthetized rabbit following stimulation of the perforant path. *Journal of Physiology, 232,* 331–356.

Bolinger, D. (1965). The atomization of meaning. *Language, 41,* 555–573.

Bond, C. F., Jr. (1985). The next-in-line effect: Encoding or retrieval deficit? *Journal of Personality and Social Psychology, 48,* 853–862.

Bond, C. F., Jr., & Kirkpatrick, C. K. (1982). Distraction, amnesia, and the next-in-line effect. *Journal of Experimental Social Psychology, 18,* 307–323.

Boring, E. (1950). *A history of experimental psychology* (2nd ed.). Englewood Cliffs, NJ: Prentice-Hall.

Bower, G. H. (1970). Organizational factors in memory. *Cognitive Psychology, 1,* 18–46.

Braitenberg, V., & Schüz, A. (1991). *Anatomy of the cortex.* New York: Springer.

Breitmeyer, B. G. (1984). *Visual masking: An integrative approach.* New York: Oxford University Press.

Broadbent, D. E. (1958). *Perception and communication.* London: Pergamon Press.

Broadbent, D. E. (1975). The magic number seven after fifteen years. In A. Kennedy & A. Wilkes (Eds.), *Studies in long-term memory* (pp. 3–18). London: Wiley.

Broadbent, D. E. (1977). Levels, hierarchies, and the locus of control. *Quarterly Journal of Experimental Psychology, 29,* 181–201.

Broadbent, D. E. (1985). A question of levels: Comment on McClelland and Rumelhart. *Journal of Experimental Psychology: General, 114,* 189–192.

Brown, A. S. (1991). A review of the tip-of-the-tongue experience. *Psychological Bulletin, 109,* 224–241.

Brown, G. D. (1987). Resolving inconsistency: A computational model of word naming. *Journal of Memory and Language, 26,* 1–23.

Brown, J. (1958). Some tests of the decay theory of immediate memory. *Quarterly Journal of Experimental Psychology, 10,* 12–21.

Brown, R., & McNeill, D. (1966). The "tip of the tongue" phenomenon. *Journal of Verbal Learning and Verbal Behavior, 5,* 325–337.

Brown, T. H., Chapman, P. F., Kairiss, E. W., & Keenan, C. L. (1988). Long-term synaptic potentiation. *Science, 242,* 724–727.

Bruder, K. J. (1984). Behaviorismus [Behaviorism]. In H. E. Lück, R. Miller, & W. Rechtien (Eds.), *Geschichte der Psychologie. Ein Handbuch in Schlüsselbergriffen* (pp. 74–81). München: Urban & Schwarzenberg.

Calkins, M. W. (1898). Short studies in memory and association from the Wellesley College Laboratory. *Psychological Review, 5,* 451–462.

Cattell, J. M. (1886). The time it takes to see and name objects. *Mind, 11,* 63–65.

Chow, S. L. (1985). Iconic store and partial report. *Memory and Cognition, 13*(3), 256–264.

Chumbley, J. I. (1986). The roles of typicality, instance dominance and category dominance in verifying category membership. *Journal of Experimental Psychology: Learning, Memory, and Cognition, 12,* 257–267.

Collins, A. M., & Loftus, E. F. (1975). A spreading-activation theory of semantic processing. *Psychological Review, 82,* 407–428.

Collins, A. M., & Quillian, M. R. (1969). Retrieval time from semantic memory. *Journal of Verbal Learning and Verbal Behavior, 8,* 240–248.

Collins, A. M., & Quillian, M. R. (1970). Does category size effect categorization time? *Journal of Verbal Learning and Verbal Behavior, 9,* 432–438.

Coltheart, M. (1980). Iconic memory and visible persistence. *Perception and Psychophysics, 27,* 183–228.

Craik, F. I. M., & Lockhart, R. S. (1972). Levels of processing: A framework of memory research. *Journal of Verbal Learning and Verbal Behavior, 11,* 671–684.

Crowder, R. G. (1978). Sensory memory systems. In E. C. Carterette & M. P. Friedman (Eds.), *Handbook of perception: Vol. 8. Perceptual coding* (pp. 343–373). New York: Academic Press.

Daneman, M., & Carpenter, P. A. (1980). Individual differences in working memory and reading. *Journal of Verbal Learning and Verbal Behavior, 19,* 450–466.

Dell, G. S. (1986). A spreading-activation theory of retrieval in sentence production. *Psychological Review, 93,* 283–321.

Donders, F. C. (1868). On the speed of mental processes. In W. G. Koster (Ed.), *Attention and performance II: Acta Psychologica, 30,* 1969, 412–431.

Duncan, J. (1985). Visual search and visual attention. In M. I. Posner & O. S. Marin (Eds.), *Attention and performance* (Vol. XI, pp. 85–104). Hillsdale, NJ: Lawrence Erlbaum Associates.

Ebbinghaus, H. (1885). *Über das Gedächtnis* [About memory]. Leipzig: Veith.

Eccles, J. C. (1981). Modular organization principles in the central nervous system: Opening remarks. In J. Szentagothai, J. Hamori, & M. Palovits (Eds.), *Regulatory functions of the CNS subsystems* (pp. 55–57). New York: Pergamon Press.

Edelman, G. M., & Mountcastle, V. B. (1978). *The mindful brain: Cortical organization and the group selection theory of higher brain function.* Cambridge, MA: MIT Press.

Engelkamp, J. (1987). Modalitätsspezifische Gedächtnissysteme im Kontext sprachlicher Informationsverarbeitung [Modality specific memory systems for the processing of linguistic information]. *Zeitschrift für Psychologie, 195,* 1–28.

Engelkamp, J. (1991). *Das menschliche Gedächtnis* [Human memory]. Göttingen: Hogrefe.

Erdelyi, M. H. (1982). A note on the level of recall, level of processing, and imagery hypotheses of hypermnesia. *Journal of Verbal Learning and Verbal Behavior, 21,* 656–661.

Erdelyi, M. H., & Becker, J. (1974). Hypermnesia for pictures: Incremental memory for pictures but not words in multiple recall trials. *Cognitive Psychology, 6,* 159–171.

Erdelyi, M. H., Buschke, H., & Finkelstein, S. (1977). Hypermnesia for socratic stimuli: The growth of recall for an internally generated memory list abstracted from a series of riddles. *Memory and Cognition, 5,* 283–286.

Erdelyi, M. H., Finkelstein, S., Herrell, N., Miller, B., & Thomas, J. (1976). Coding modality versus input modality in hypermnesia: Is a rose a rose a rose? *Cognition, 4,* 311–319.

Erdelyi, M. H., & Kleinbard, J. (1978). Has Ebbinghaus decayed with time? The growth of recall (hypermnesia) over days. *Journal of Experimental Psychology: Human Learning and Memory, 4,* 275–289.

Evans, S. H. (1967). A brief statement of schema theory. *Psychonomic Science, 8,* 87–88.

Evans, S. H., & Arnoult, M. D. (1967). Schematic concept formation: Demonstration in a free sorting task. *Psychonomic Science, 9,* 221–222.

Evans, S. H., & Edmonds, E. M. (1966). Schema discrimination as a function of training. *Psychonomic Science, 5,* 303–304.

Finke, R. A. (1980). Levels of equivalence in imagery and perception. *Psychological Review, 87,* 113–132.

Finke, R. A. (1986). Mental imagery and the visual system. *Scientific American, 254,* 76–83.

Flores d'Arcais, G. B., & Schreuder, R. (1987). Semantic activation during object naming. *Psychological Research, 49,* 153–159.

Flugel, J. C. (n.d.). *Probleme und Ergebnisse der Psychologie* [Problems and results of psychology]. Stuttgart: Ernst Klett.

Fodor, J. A. (1983). *The modularity of mind.* Cambridge, MA: MIT Press.

Fodor, J. A. (1985). Precis of "the modularity of mind." *The Behavioral and Brain Sciences, 8,* 1–42.

Fodor, J. A., Garrett, M. F., Walker, E. C. T., & Parkes, C. H. (1980). Against definitions. *Cognition, 8,* 263–367.

Fodor, J. A., & Pylyshyn, Z. W. (1988). Connectionism and cognitive architecture: A critical analysis. *Cognition, 28*, 3–72.

Gabriel, R. G. (1986). Massively parallel computers: The connection machine and non-von. *Science, 231*, 975–978.

Garner, W. R. (1962). *Uncertainty and structure as psychological concepts.* New York: Wiley.

Gentner, D. (1975). Evidence for the psychological reality of semantic components: The verbs of possession. In D. A. Norman & D. E. Rumelhart (Eds.), *Explorations in cognition* (pp. 211–246). San Francisco, CA: W. H. Freeman.

Gentner, D. (1981). Verb semantic structures in memory for sentences: Evidence for componential representation. *Cognitive Psychology, 13*, 56–83.

Glass, A. L., & Holyoak, K. J. (1975). Alternative conceptions of semantic theory. *Cognition, 3*, 313–339.

Graumann, C. F. (1983). Theorie und Geschichte [Theory and history]. In G. Lüer (Ed.), *Bericht über den 33. Kongreß der Deutschen Gesellschaft für Psychologie in Mainz 1982* (Vol. 1, pp. 64–75). Göttingen: Hogrefe.

Guenther, R. K., & Klatzky, R. L. (1977). Semantic classification of pictures and words. *Journal of Experimental Psychology: Human Learning and Memory, 3*, 498–514.

Hayes-Roth, B. (1977). Evaluation of cognitive structures and processes. *Psychological Review, 84*, 260–278.

Hebb, D. O. (1949). *The organization of behavior.* New York: Wiley.

Hillis, W. D. (1985). *The connection machine.* Cambridge, MA: MIT Press.

Hinton, G. E., & Anderson, J. A. (Eds.). (1989). *Parallel models of associative memory.* Hillsdale, NJ: Lawrence Erlbaum Associates.

Hintzman, D. L. (1986). "Schema Abstraction" in a multiple-trace memory model. *Psychological Review, 93*, 411–428.

Hintzman, D. L., & Ludlam, G. (1980). Differential forgetting of prototypes and old instances: Simulation by an exemplar-based classification model. *Memory and Cognition, 8*, 378–382.

Höhl-Abrahao, J. C., & Creutzfeldt, O. D. (1991). Topographical mapping of the thalamocortical projections in rodents and comparison with that in primates. *Experimental Brain Research, 87*, 283–294.

Hoffmann, J. (1982). Representation of concepts and the classification of objects. In F. Klix, J. Hoffmann, & E. van der Meer (Eds.), *Cognitive research in psychology* (pp. 72–89). Berlin: VEB Deutscher Verlag der Wissenschaften.

Hoffmann, J. (1986). *Die Welt der Begriffe* [The "universe" of concepts]. Berlin: VEB Deutscher Verlag der Wissenschaften.

Hoffmann, J., & Klimesch, W. (1984). Die semantische Kodierung von Worten und Bildern [The semantic encoding for words and pictures]. *Sprache und Kognition, 3*, 1–25.

Hoffmann, J., & Zießler, M. (1982). Begriffe und ihre Merkmale [Concepts and their features]. *Zeitschrift für Psychologie, 190*, 46–77.

Hoffmann, J., & Zießler, M. (1986). The integration of visual and functional classifications in concept formation. *Psychological Research, 48*, 69–78.

Hoffmann, J., Zießler, M., & Grosser, U. (1984). Psychologische Gesetzmäßigkeiten der begrifflichen Klassifikation von Objekten [Psychological principles for the conceptual classification of objects]. In F. Klix (Ed.), *Gedächtnis, Wissen, Wissensnutzung* (pp. 52–86). Berlin: VEB Deutscher Verlag der Wissenschaften.

Hollan, J. D. (1975). Features and semantic memory: Set-theoretic or network model? *Psychological Research, 82*, 154–155.

Homa, D., & Cultice, J. (1984). Role of feedback, category size, and stimulus distortion on the acquisition and utilization of illdefined categories. *Journal of Experimental Psychology: Learning, Memory, and Cognition, 10*, 83–94.

Hubel, D. H. (1988). *Eye, brain, and vision*. New York: W. H. Freeman.

Hubel, D. H., & Wiesel, T. N. (1959). Receptive fields of single neurons in the cat's striate cortex. *Journal of Physiology, 148*, 574–591.

Hubel, D. H., Wiesel, T. N., & Stryker, M. P. (1978). Anatomical demonstration of orientation columns in Macaque monkey. *Journal of Comparative Neurology, 177*, 361–379.

Humphrey, G. (1963). *Thinking: An introduction to its experimental psychology*. New York: Wiley.

John, E. R., Tang, Y., Brill, A. B., Young, R., & Ono, K. (1986). Double-labeled metabolic maps of memory. *Science, 233*, 1167–1175.

Johnson, M. K., & Hasher, L. (1987). Human learning and memory. *Annual Review of Psychology, 38*, 631–668.

Johnson-Laird, P. N. (1987). The mental representation of the meaning of words. *Cognition, 25*, 189–212.

Johnson-Laird, P. N., Gibbs, G., & de Mowbray, J. (1978). Meaning, amount of processing, and memory for words. *Memory and Cognition, 6*, 372–375.

Johnson-Laird, P. N., Herrmann, D. J., & Chaffin, R. (1984). Only connections: A critic of semantic networks. *Psychological Bulletin, 96*, 292–315.

Jolicoeur, P., Gluck, M. A., & Kosslyn, S. M. (1984). Pictures and names: Making the connection. *Cognitive Psychology, 16*, 243–275.

Jones, G. V. (1979). Multirate forgetting. *Journal of Experimental Psychology: Human Learning and Memory, 5*, 98–114.

Jost, A. (1897). Die Assoziationsfestigkeit in ihrer Abhängigkeit von der Verteilung der Wiederholungen [The strength of association as a function of the intervals between repetitions]. *Zeitschrift für Psychologie, 14*, 436–472.

Kahneman, D., Treisman, A., & Burkell, J. (1983). The cost of visual filtering. *Journal of Experimental Psychology: Human Perception and Performance, 9*, 510–522.

Kandel, D. L. (1987). *Memory traces in the brain*. Cambridge, England: Cambridge University Press.

Kandel, E. R., & Schwartz, J. H. (Eds.). (1985). *Principles of neural science*. New York: Elsevier.

Katz, J. J., & Fodor, J. A. (1963). The structure of a semantic theory. *Language, 39*, 170–210.

Keppel, G., & Underwood, B. J. (1962). Proactive inhibition in short-term retention of single items. *Journal of Verbal Learning and Verbal Behavior, 1*, 153–161.

King, D. R. W., & Anderson, J. R. (1976). Long-term memory search: An intersecting activation process. *Journal of Verbal Learning and Verbal Behavior, 15*, 587–606.

Kintsch, W. (1974). *The representation of meaning in memory*. Hillsdale, NJ: Lawrence Erlbaum Associates.

Kintsch, W. (1980). Semantic memory: A tutorial. In R. S. Nickerson (Ed.), *Attention and performance* (Vol. VII, pp. 595–620). Hillsdale, NJ: Lawrence Erlbaum Associates.

Kintsch, W. (1985). Reflections on Ebbinghaus. *Journal of Experimental Psychology: Learning, Memory, and Cognition, 11*, 461–463.

Kirkpatrick, E. A. (1894). An experimental study of memory. *Psychological Review, 1*, 602–609.

Klatzky, R. L., & Stoy, A. M. (1978). Semantic information and visual information processing. In J. W. Cotton & R. Klatzky (Eds.), *Semantic factors in cognition* (pp. 71–101). New York: Wiley.

Klimesch, W. (1974). *Informationstheoretische Indikatoren der Intelligenz*. Unpublished doctoral dissertation, University of Salzburg, Austria.

Klimesch, W. (1979a). Ansätze zu einer Theorie des Vergessens [Elements of a theory of forgetting]. In H. Ueckert & D. Rhenius (Ed.), *Komplexe menschliche Informationsverarbeitung* [Complex human information processing] (pp. 28–37). Bern: Hans Huber.

Klimesch, W. (1979b). Reminiszenz bei visuellen Merkaufgaben: Implikationen für die Art des Vergessensprozesses [Reminiscence in visual memory tasks: Implications for the type of forgetting processes]. *Psychologische Beiträge, 21*, 40–48.

Klimesch, W. (1979c). Vergessen: Interferenz oder Zerfall? Über neuere Entwicklungen der Gedächtnispsychologie [Forgetting: Interference or decay? Aspects of new approaches in memory psychology]. *Psychologische Rundschau, 30*, 100–131.

Klimesch, W. (1981). Die Encodierung von Begriffen auf der Basis von Merkmalsstrukturen [The encoding of pictures on the basis of features]. *Zeitschrift für Experimentelle und Angewandte Psychologie, 28*, 609–636.

Klimesch, W. (1982a). Die semantische Encodierung von Bildern [The semantic encoding of pictures]. *Zeitschrift für Experimentelle und Angewandte Psychologie, 29*, 472–504.

Klimesch, W. (1982b). Verbal processes in visual short- and long-term memory: Evidence against the hypothesis of independent visual and verbal codes? *International Journal of Psychology, 17*, 9–17.

Klimesch, W. (1982c). Visual coding processes and semantic classification. In F. Klix, J. Hoffmann, & E. van der Meer (Eds.), *Cognitive Research in Psychology* (pp. 90–97). Amsterdam: North Holland.

Klimesch, W. (1986a). Codierung und kognitive Struktur: Das Repräsentationsproblem [Coding and cognitive structure: The representational problem]. In K. Daumenlang & J. Sauer (Eds.), *Aspekte psychologischer Forschung* (pp. 277–292). Zürich: Hogrefe.

Klimesch, W. (1986b). The structure of memory codes. In F. Klix & H. Hagendorf (Eds.), *Human memory and cognitive capabilities* (pp. 245–252). North Holland: Elsevier Science

Klimesch, W. (1987). A connectivity model for semantic processing. *Psychological Research, 49*, 53–61.

Klimesch, W. (1989). Bewußtsein und Gedächtnis: Zur Neuropsychologie kognitiver und emotionaler Kontrollprozesse [Consciousness and memory: Toward a neuropsychology of emotional control processes]. In E. Roth (Ed.), *Denken und Fühlen* (pp. 146–163). Heidelberg: Springer.

Klimesch, W., Pfurtscheller, G., & Lindinger, G. (1986). Das corticale Aktivierungsmuster bei verbalen Gedächtnisaufgaben [The pattern of cortical activation in verbal memory tasks]. *Sprache und Kognition, 3*, 140–154.

Klimesch, W., Pfurtscheller, G., & Mohl, W. (1988). ERD-mapping and long-term memory: The temporal and topographical pattern of cortical activation. In G. Pfurtscheller & F. H. Lopes da Silva (Eds.), *Functional brain imaging* (pp. 131–141). Toronto: Huber.

Klimesch, W., Schimke, H., & Ladurner, G. (1988). Die Suchzeit für episodische und semantische Information [Retrieval time for episodic and semantic information]. *Sprache und Kognition, 7*, 129–143.

Klimesch, W., Schimke, H., Ladurner, G., & Pfurtscheller, G. (1990). Alpha frequency and memory performance. *Journal of Psychophysiology, 4*, 381–390.

Klimesch, W., Schimke, H., Pfurtscheller, G. (1993). Alpha frequency, cognitive load, and memory performance. *Brain Topography, 5, 241–251.*

Klix, F. (1977a). Strukturelle und funktionelle Komponenten des Gedächtnisses [Structural and functional components of memory]. In F. Klix & H. Sydow (Eds.), *Zur Psychologie des Gedächtnisses* (pp. 59–80). Bern: Hans Huber.

Klix, F. (1977b). Über die Repräsentation von Bedeutungsträgern im menschlichen Gedächtnis [On the representation of meaning in human memory]. In W. Reulecke (Ed.), *Strukturelles Lernen* (pp. 162–176). Hamburg: Hoffmann & Kampe.

Klix, F., Kukla, F., & Klein, R. (1976). Über die Unterscheidbarkeit von Klassen semantischer Relationen im menschlichen Gedächtnis [The differentiation between different classes of semantic relations in human memory]. In F. Klix (Ed.), *Psychologische Beiträge zur Analyse kognitiver Prozesse* (pp. 302–314). München: Kindler.

Knapp, A. G., & Anderson, J. A. (1984). Theory of categorization based on distributed memory storage. *Journal of Experimental Psychology: Learning, Memory, and Cognition*, *10*, 616–637.

Kosslyn, S. M. (1981). The medium and the message in mental imagery: A theory. *Psychological Review*, *88*, 46–66.

Kosslyn, S. M., & Shwartz, St. P. (1981). Empirical constraints on theories of visual mental imagery. In J. Long & A. Baddeley (Eds.), *Attention and performance* (Vol. IX, pp. 241–259). Hillsdale, NJ: Lawrence Erlbaum Associates.

Kroll, N. E. A., & Klimesch, W. (1992). Semantic memory: Complexity or connectivity? *Memory and Cognition*, *20*, 192–210.

Kroll, N. E. A., & Ramskov, C. B. (1984). Visual memory as measured by classification and comparison tasks. *Journal of Experimental Psychology: Learning, Memory, and Cognition*, *10*, 395–420.

Kroll, N. E. A., Bee, J., & Gurski, G. (1973). Release of proactive interference as a result of changing presentation modality. *Journal of Experimental Psychology*, *98*, 131–137.

Külpe, O. (1904). Versuche über Abstraktion [Attempts on the explanation of abstraction]. In F. Schuhmann (Ed.), *Bericht über den 1. Kongreß für experimentelle Psychologie, Gießen 1904* (pp. 56–88). Leipzig: Barth.

LaBerge, D. (1981). Automatic information processing: A review. In J. Long & A. Baddeley (Eds.), *Attention and performance* (Vol. IX, pp. 173–186). Hillsdale, NJ: Lawrence Erlbaum Associates.

Lashley, K. S. (1950). In search of the engram. *Society for Experimental Biology, Symposium No.4*, 454–482.

Levy, W. B. (1985). Associative changes at the synapse: LTP in the hippocampus. In W. B. Levy, J. A. Anderson, & S. Lehmkuhle (Eds.), *Synaptic modification, neuron selectivity, and nervous system organization* (pp. 5–33). Hillsdale, NJ: Lawrence Erlbaum Associates.

Lindsay, P. H., & Norman, D. A. (1972). *Human information processing*. New York: Academic Press.

Llinas, R. R. (1989). *The biology of the brain: From neurons to networks*. New York: W. H. Freeman.

Loftus, G. R. (1985). Observations: Evaluating forgetting curves. *Journal of Experimental Psychology: Learning, Memory, and Cognition*, *11*, 397–406.

Loftus, G. R., & Loftus, E. F. (1976). *Human memory: The processing of information*. Hillsdale, NJ: Lawrence Erlbaum Associates.

Long, G. M. (1980). Iconic memory: A review and critique of the study of short-term visual storage. *Psychological Bulletin*, *88*, 785–820.

Lück, H. E., Miller, R., & Rechetien, W. (Eds). (1984). *Geschichte der Psychologie. Ein Handbuch in Schlüsselbegriffen* [History of Psychology. A handbook in basic terms]. München: Urban & Schwarzenberg.

Madigan, St. (1976). Reminiscence and item recovery in free recall. *Memory and Cognition*, *4*, 233–236.

Madigan, St. (1983). Picture memory. In J. C. Yuille (Ed.), *Imagery, memory and cognition* (pp. 65–89). Hillsdale, NJ: Lawrence Erlbaum Associates.

Malt, B. C., & Smith, E. E. (1984). Correlated properties in natural categories. *Journal of Verbal Learning and Verbal Behavior*, *23*, 260–269.

Mandler, J. M., & Johnson, N. S. (1976). Some of the thousand words a picture is worth. *Journal of Experimental Psychology: Human Learning and Memory*, *2*, 529–540.

Markowitsch, H. J. (1983). Transient global amnesia. *Neuroscience and Biobehavioral Reviews*, *7*, 35–43.

Markowitsch, H. J. (Ed.). (1988). *Information processing by the brain*. Toronto: Hans Huber.

Markowitsch, H. J., & Pritzel, M. (1985). The neuropathology of amnesia. *Progress in Neurobiology*, *25*, 189–288.

Marr, D. (1982). *Vision*. San Francisco: W. H. Freeman.

Martin, J. M. (1985). Cortical neurons, the EEG, and the mechanisms of epilepsy. In E. R. Kandel & J. H. Schwartz (Eds.), *Principles of neural science* (pp. 636–647). New York: Elsevier.

Massaro, M. (1975). *Experimental psychology and information processing*. Chicago: Rand McNally

McClelland, J. L., & Rumelhart, D. E. (1985). Distributed memory and the representation of general and specific information. *Journal of Experimental Psychology: General, 114*, 159–188.

McCloskey, M., & Bigler, K. (1980). Focused memory search in fact retrieval. *Memory and Cognition, 8*, 253–264.

McCloskey, M., & Glucksberg, S. (1978). Natural categories: Well defined or fuzzy sets? *Memory and Cognition, 6*, 462–472.

McCulloch, W. S., & Pitts, W. (1943). A logical calculus of the ideas immanent in nervous activity. *Bulletin of Mathematical Biophysics, 5*, 115–133.

McGeoch, J. A. (1932). Forgetting and the law of disuse. *Psychological Review, 39*, 352–370.

McGeoch, J. A. (1942). *The psychology of human learning*. New York: Longman.

MacGregor, J. N. (1987). Short-term memory capacity: Limitation or optimization? *Psychological Review, 94*, 107–108.

McNamara, T. H. P., & Sternberg, R. J. (1983). Mental models of word meaning. *Journal of Verbal Learning and Verbal Behavior, 22*, 449–474.

Medin, D. L., & Smith, E. E. (1984). Concepts and concept formation. *Annual Review of Psychology, 35*, 113–138.

Medin, D. L., Altom, M. W., & Murphy T. D. (1984). Given versus induced category representations: Use of prototype and exemplar information in classification. *Journal of Experimental Psychology: Learning, Memory, and Cognition, 10*, 333–352.

Medin, D. L., Wattenmaker, W. D., & Hampson, S. E. (1987). Family resemblance, conceptual cohesiveness, and category construction. *Cognitive Psychology, 19*, 242–279.

Melton, A. W. (1963). Implications of short-term memory for a general theory of memory. *Journal of Verbal Learning and Verbal Behavior, 2*, 1–21.

Melton, A. W., & Martin, E. (Eds.). (1972). *Coding processes in human memory*. Washington, DC: V. H. Winston.

Mervis, C. B., & Pani, J. R. (1980). Acquisition of basic object categories. *Cognitive Psychology, 12*, 496–522.

Mervis, C. B. & Rosch, E. (1981). Categorization of natural objects. *Annual Review of Psychology, 32*, 89–115.

Messer, A. (1924). *Empfindung und Denken* [Sensation and thinking]. Leipzig: Quelle & Meyer.

Miller, G. (1956). The magical number seven, plus or minus two: Some limits on our capacity for processing information. *Psychological Review, 63*, 91–97.

Mishkin, M., & Appenzeller, T. (1987). The anatomy of memory. *Scientific American, 6*, 62–71.

Moeser, S. D. (1977). Recognition processes in episodic memory. *Canadian Journal of Psychology, 31*, 41–70.

Moeser, S. D. (1979). The role of experimental design in investigations of the fan effect. *Journal of Experimental Psychology: Human Learning and Memory, 5*, 125–134.

Mountcastle, V. B. (1978). An organizing principle for cerebral function: The unit module and the distributed system. In G. M. Edelman & V. B. Mountcastle (Eds.), *The mindful brain* (pp. 7–50). Cambridge, MA: MIT Press.

Moyer, R. S (1973). Comparing objects in memory: Evidence suggesting an internal psychophysics. *Perception & Psychophysics, 13,* 180–184.

Moyer, R. S., & Landauer, T. K. (1967). Time required of judgements of numerical inequality. *Nature, 215,* 1519–1520.

Müller, G. E. (1917). *Zur Analyse der Gedächtnistätigkeit und des Vorstellungsverlaufes* [Contributions to the analysis of memory and imagery processes]. Leipzig: Barth.

Müller, G. E., & Pilzecker, A. (1900). *Experimentelle Beiträge zur Lehre vom Gedächtnis* [Experimental approaches to the theory of memory]. Leipzig: Johann Ambrosius Barth.

Munzert, R. (1984). Würzburger Schule [The Würzburg school]. In H. E. Lück, R. Miller, & W. Rechtien (Eds.), Geschichte der Psychologie. Ein Handbuch in Schlüsselbegriffen (pp. 82–87). München: Urban & Schwarzenberg.

Murdock, B. B., Jr. (1964). Proactive inhibition in short-term memory. *Journal of Experimental Psychology, 68,* 184–189.

Murdock, B. B., Jr. (1974). *Human memory: Theory and data.* Potomac, MD: Lawrence Erlbaum Associates.

Murdock, B. B., Jr. (1980). Short-term recognition memory. In R. S. Nickerson (Ed.), *Attention and performance* (Vol. VIII, pp. 497–519). Hillsdale, NJ: Lawrence Erlbaum Associates.

Murphy, G. L., & Medin, D. L. (1985). The role of theories in conceptual coherence. *Psychological Review, 92,* 289–316.

Murphy, G. L., & Smith, E. E. (1982). Basic-level superiority in picture categorization. *Journal of Verbal Learning and Verbal Behavior, 21,* 1–20.

Myers, J. L., O'Brien, E. J., Balota, D. A., & Toyofuku, M. L. (1984). Memory search without interference: The role of integration. *Cognitive Psychology, 16,* 217–242.

Neisser, U. (1967). *Cognitive psychology.* New York: Appleton-Century-Crofts.

Nelson, D. L. (1979). Remembering pictures and words: Appearance, significance, and name. In L. S. Cermak & F. I. M. Craik (Eds.), *Levels of processing in human memory* (pp. 45–76). Hillsdale, NJ: Lawrence Erlbaum Associates.

Nelson, D. L., Reed, V. S., & McEvoy, C. L. (1977). Learning to order pictures and words: A model of sensory and semantic encoding. *Journal of Experimental Psychology: Human Learning and Memory, 3,* 485–497.

Nelson, D. L., Reed, V. S., & Walling, J. R. (1976). Picture superiority effect. *Journal of Experimental Psychology: Human Learning and Memory, 2,* 523–528.

Nelson, T. O. (1978). Detecting small amounts of information in memory: Savings for non-recognized items. *Journal of Experimental Psychology: Human Learning and Memory, 4,* 453–468.

Nelson, T. O., Metzler, J., & Reed, D. (1974). Role of details in the long-term recognition of pictures and verbal descriptions. *Journal of Experimental Psychology, 102,* 184–186.

Newell, A., & Simon, H. (1972). *Human problem solving.* Englewood Cliffs, NJ: Prentice-Hall.

Norman, D. A., & Rumelhart, D. E. (1975). *Explorations in cognition.* San Francisco: W. H. Freeman.

Ojeman, G., & Whitaker, H. (1978). Language localization and variability. *Brain and Language, 6,* 239–260.

Orbach, J. (Ed.). (1982). *Neuropsychology after Lashley.* Hillsdale, NJ: Lawrence Erlbaum Associates.

Paivio, A. (1971). *Imagery and verbal processes.* New York: Holt, Rinehart & Winston.

Paivio, A. (1976). Imagery in recall and recognition. In J. Brown (Ed.), *Recall and recognition* (pp. 103–129). New York: Wiley.

Paivio, A., & Csapo, K. (1973). Picture superiority in free recall: Imagery or dual coding? *Cognitive Psychology, 5,* 176–206.

Palmer, St. E. (1977). Hierarchical structure in perceptual representation. *Cognitive Psychology*, *9*, 441-474.

Payne, D. G. (1986). Hypermnesia for pictures and words: Testing the recall level hypothesis. *Journal of Experimental Psychology: Learning, Memory, and Cognition*, *12*, 16-29.

Payne, D. G. (1987). Hypermnesia and reminiscence in recall: A historical and empirical review. *Psychological Bulletin*, *101*, 5-27.

Pellegrino, J. W., Rosinski, R. R., Chiesi, H. L., & Siegel, A. (1977). Picture-words differences in decision latency: An analysis of single and dual memory models. *Memory and Cognition*, *5*, 383-396.

Peterson, L. R., & Peterson, M. G. (1959). Short-term retention of individual items. *Journal of Experimental Psychology*, *58*, 193-198.

Poetzl, O. (1917). Experimentell erregte Traumbilder in ihren Beziehungen zum indirekten Sehen [Experimentally evoked images during dreaming and their relationship to normal vision]. *Zeitschrift für Neurologie & Psychiatrie*, *37*, 278-349.

Posner, M. (1978). *Chronometric explorations of mind*. Hillsdale, NJ: Lawrence Erlbaum Associates.

Posner, M., Boies, S. J., Eichelman, W. H., & Taylor, R. L. (1969). Retention of visual and name codes of single letters. *Journal of Experimental Psychology Monograph*, *79*, 1-16.

Postman, L., & Underwood, B. J. (1973). Critical issues in interference theory. *Memory and Cognition*, *1*, 19-40.

Potter, M. C., & Faulconer, B. A. (1975). Time to understand pictures and words. *Nature*, *253*, 437-438.

Potter, M. C., So, K., von Eckardt, B., & Feldman, L. B. (1984). Lexical and conceptual representation in beginning and proficient bilinguals. *Journal of Verbal Learning and Verbal Behavior*, *23*, 23-38.

Pylyshyn, Z. W. (1981). The imagery debate: Analogue media versus tacit knowledge. *Psychological Review*, *88*, 16-45.

Ratcliff, R., & McKoon, G. (1981). Does activation really spread? *Psychological Review*, *88*, 454-462.

Reder, L. M. (1987). Strategy selection in question answering. *Cognitive Psychology*, *19*, 90-138.

Reder, L. M., & Anderson, J. R. (1980). A partial resolution of the paradox of interference: The role of integrated knowledge. *Cognitive Psychology*, *12*, 447-472.

Reder, L. M., & Ross, B. H. (1983). Integrated knowledge in different tasks: The role of retrieval strategy on fan effects. *Journal of Experimental Psychology: Learning, Memory, and Cognition*, *9*, 55-72.

Reder, L. M., & Wible, C. (1984). Strategy use in question-answering: Memory strength and task constraints on fan effects. *Memory and Cognition*, *12*, 411-419.

Reitman, J. S. (1971). Mechanisms of forgetting in short-term memory. *Cognitive Psychology*, *2*, 185-195.

Reitman, J. S. (1974). Without surreptitious rehearsal, information in short-term memory decays. *Journal of Verbal Learning and Verbal Behavior*, *13*, 365-377.

Rips, L. J., Shoben, E. J., & Smith, E. E. (1973). Semantic distance and the verification of semantic relations. *Journal of Verbal Learning and Verbal Behavior*, *12*, 1-20.

Roediger, H. L. (1974). Inhibiting effects of recall. *Memory and Cognition*, *2*, 261-269.

Roediger, H. L., Knight, J. L., & Kantowitz, B. H. (1977). Inferring decay in short-term memory: The issue of capacity. *Memory and Cognition*, *5*, 167-176.

Roediger, H. L., & Payne, D. G. (1982). Hypermnesia: The role of repeated testing. *Journal of Experimental Psychology: Learning, Memory, and Cognition*, *8*, 66-72.

Roediger, H. L., & Payne, D. G. (1985). Recall criterion does not affect recall level or hypermnesia: A puzzle for generate/recognize theories. *Memory and Cognition*, *13*, 1-7.

Roediger, H. L., & Thorpe, L. A. (1978). The role of recall time in producing hypermnesia. *Memory and Cognition*, *6*, 296–305.

Rolfes, E. (1918). *Aristoteles: Topik*. Leipzig: Verlag Meiner.

Rosch, E. (1975). Cognitive representations of semantic categories. *Journal of Experimental Psychology: General*, *104*, 192–233.

Rosch, E. (1978). Principles of categorization. In E. Rosch & B. Lloyd (Eds.), *Cognition and categorization* (pp. 27–48). Hillsdale, NJ: Lawrence Erlbaum Associates.

Rosch, E., & Mervis, C. B. (1975). Family resemblances: Studies in the internal structure of categories. *Cognitive Psychology*, *7*, 573–605.

Rosch, E., Mervis, C. B., Gray, W. D., Johnson, D. M., & Boyes-Braem, P. (1976). Basic objects in natural categories. *Cognitive Psychology*, *8*, 382–439.

Rubin, D. C. (1980). 51 properties of 125 words: A unit analysis of verbal behavior. *Journal of Verbal Learning and Verbal Behavior*, *19*, 736–755.

Rumelhart, D. E., & McClelland, J. L. (1985). Levels indeed! A response to Broadbent. *Journal of Experimental Psychology: General*, *114*, 193–197.

Rumelhart, D. E., McClelland, J. L., & PDP research group. (1986). *Parallel distributed processing: Explorations in the microstructure of cognition: Vol. 1. Foundations*. Cambridge, MA: Bradford Books/MIT Press.

Runquist, W. N. (1983). Some effects of remembering on forgetting. *Memory and Cognition*, *11*, 641–650.

Sanders, A. F. (1971). *Psychologie der Informationsverarbeitung* [Psychology of information processing]. Bern: Hans Huber.

Sattath, S., & Tversky, A. (1987). On the relation between common and distinctive feature models. *Psychological Review*, *94*(1), 16–22.

Scheibel, M. E., & Scheibel, A. B. (1958). Structural substrates for integrative patterns in the brain stem reticular core. In H. H. Jasper, L. D. Proctor, R. S. Knighton, W. C. Noshay, & R. T. Costello (Eds.), *Reticular formation of the brain* (pp. 31–68). Boston: Little, Brown.

Schneider, W., & Shiffrin, R. M. (1977). Controlled and automatic human information processing: I. Detection, search, and attention. *Psychological Review*, *84*, 1–66.

Scoville, W. B., & Milner, B. (1957). Loss of recent memory after bilateral hippocampal lesions. *Journal of Neurology, Neurosurgery, and Psychiatry*, *20*, 11–21.

Shepard, R. N. (1967). Recognition memory of words, sentences, and pictures. *Journal of Verbal Learning and Verbal Behavior*, *6*, 156–163.

Shepard, R. N., & Podgorny, P. (1978). Cognitive processes that resemble perceptual processes. In W. K. Estes (Ed.), *Handbook of learning and cognitive processes* (pp. 189–237). Hillsdale, NJ: Lawrence Erlbaum Associates.

Shiffrin, R. M. (1970a). Forgetting: Trace erosion or retrieval failure? *Science*, *168*, 1601–1603.

Shiffrin, R. M. (1970b). Memory search. In D. A. Norman (Ed.), *Models of human memory* (pp. 375–447). New York: Academic Press.

Shiffrin, R. M. (1973). Information persistence in short-term memory. *Journal of Experimental Psychology*, *100*, 39–49.

Shiffrin, R. M., & Geisler, W. S. (1973). Visual recognition in a theory of information processing. In R. L. Solso (Ed.), *Contemporary issues in cognitive psychology* (pp. 53–101). Washington: The Loyola Symposium.

Shiffrin, R. M., & Schneider, W. (1977). Controlled and automatic human information processing: II. Perceptual learning, automatic attending, and a general theory. *Psychological Review*, *84*, 127–190.

Shiffrin, R. M., & Schneider, W. (1984). Theoretical note: Automatic and controlled processing revisited. *Psychological Review*, *91*, 269–276.

Slamecka, N. J. (1985a). Ebbinghaus: Some associations. *Journal of Experimental Psychology: Learning, Memory, and Cognition, 11*, 414–435.

Slamecka, N. J. (1985b). Ebbinghaus: Some rejoinders. *Journal of Experimental Psychology: Learning, Memory, and Cognition, 11*, 496–500.

Slamecka, N. J. (1985c). Observations: On comparing rates of forgetting: Comment on Loftus (1985). *Journal of Experimental Psychology: Learning, Memory, and Cognition, 11*, 812–816.

Slamecka, N. J., & McElree, B. (1983). Normal forgetting of verbal lists as a function of their degree of learning. *Journal of Experimental Psychology: Learning, Memory, and Cognition, 9*, 384–397.

Smith, E. E. (1978). Theories of semantic memory. In W. K. Estes (Ed.), *Handbook of learning and cognitive processes* (Vol. 1, pp. 1–56). Hillsdale, NJ: Lawrence Erlbaum Associates.

Smith, E. E., Adams, N., & Schorr, D. (1978). Fact retrieval and the paradox of interference. *Cognitive Psychology, 10*, 438–464.

Smith, E. E., Balzano, G. J., & Walker, J. (1978). Nominal, perceptual, and semantic codes in picture categorization. In J. W. Cotton & R. L. Klatzky (Eds.), *Semantic factors in cognition* (pp. 137–168). Hillsdale, NJ: Lawrence Erlbaum Associates.

Smith, E. E., & Medin, D. L. (1981). *Categories and concepts.* Cambridge, MA: Harvard University Press.

Smith, E. E., Shoben, E. J., & Rips, L. J. (1974). Structure and process in semantic memory: A featural model for semantic decisions. *Psychological Review, 81*, 214–241.

Smith, S. M. (1982). Enhancement of recall using multiple environmental contexts during learning. *Memory and Cognition, 10*, 405–412.

Smith, S. M. (1984). A comparison of two techniques for reducing context-dependent forgetting. *Memory and Cognition, 12*, 477–482.

Smith, S. M., Glenberg, A. M., & Bjork, R. A. (1978). Environmental context and human memory. *Memory and Cognition, 6*, 342–353.

Snodgrass, J. G. (1984). Concepts and their surface representations. *Journal of Verbal Learning and Verbal Behavior, 23*, 3–22.

Sperling, G. (1960). The information available in brief visual presentations. *Psychological Monographs, 74*, 498, 1–29.

Spring, C. (1968). Decay and interference theories of short-term forgetting. *Psychomonic Sciences, 12*, 373–374.

Standing, L. (1973). Learning 10,000 pictures. *Quarterly Journal of Experimental Psychology, 25*, 207–222.

Stern, L. D. (1981). A review of theories of human amnesia. *Memory and Cognition, 9*, 247–262.

Sternberg, S. (1969). Memory scanning: Mental processes revealed by reaction-time experiments. *American Scientist, 57*, 421–457.

Szentagothai, J. (1975). The "module-concept" in the cerebral cortex architecture. *Brain Research, 95*, 475–496.

Szentagothai, J., Hamori, J., & Palkovits, M. (Eds.). (1981). *Regulatory functions of the CNS subsystems.* New York: Pergamon Press.

Tabossi, P., & Johnson-Laird, P. N. (1980). Linguistic context and the priming of semantic information. *Quarterly Journal of Experimental Psychology, 32*, 595–603.

Tanenhaus, M. K., & Lucas, M. M. (1987). Context effects in lexical priming. *Cognition, 25*, 213–234.

Te Linde, D. J. (1982). Picture-word differences in decision latency: A test of common-coding assumptions. *Journal of Experimental Psychology: Learning, Memory, and Cognition, 8*, 584–598.

Teyler, T. J., & DiScienna, P. (1986). The hippocampal memory indexing theory. *Behavioral Neuroscience, 100*, 147-154.

Thompson, R. F. (1985). *The brain. An introduction to neuroscience.* New York: W. H. Freeman.

Toglia, M. P., & Battig, W. F. (1978). *Handbook of semantic word norms.* Hillsdale, NJ: Lawrence Erlbaum Associates.

Treisman, A. (1986a). Features and objects in visual processing. *Scientific American, 255*, 106-115.

Treisman, A. (1986b). Properties, parts, and objects. In K. Boff., L. Kaufman, & J. Thomas (Eds.), *Handbook of perception and performance* (Vol. 2, pp. 123-146). New York: Wiley.

Treisman, A., & Gelade, G. (1980). A feature-integration theory of attention. *Cognitive Psychology, 12*, 97-136.

Treisman, A., & Kahneman, D. (1985). Addendum: A reply to Duncan. In M. I. Posner & O. S. Marin (Eds.), *Attention and performance* (Vol. XI, pp. 105-106). Hillsdale, NJ: Lawrence Erlbaum Associates.

Treisman, A., & Paterson, R. (1984). Emergent features, attention, and object perception. *Journal of Experimental Psychology: Human Perception and Performance, 10*, 12-31.

Tulving, E. (1972). Episodic and semantic memory. In E. Tulving & W. Donaldson (Eds.), *Organization of memory* (pp. 381-403). New York: Academic Press.

Tulving, E. (1974). Cue-dependent forgetting. *American Scientist, 62*, 74-82.

Tulving, E. (1983). *Elements of episodic memory.* New York: Oxford University Press.

Tulving, E. (1984). Precis of elements of episodic memory. *Behavioral and Brain Sciences, 7*, 223-268.

Tulving, E. (1986). What kind of hypothesis is the distinction between episodic and semantic memory. *Journal of Experimental Psychology: Learning, Memory, and Cognition, 2*, 307-311.

Tulving, E., & Pearlstone, Z. (1966). Availability versus accessibility of information in memory for words. *Journal of Verbal Learning and Verbal Behavior, 5*, 381-391.

Tversky, A. (1977). Features of similarity. *Psychological Review, 84*, 327-352.

Tversky, B., & Hemenway, K. (1984). Objects, parts, and categories. *Journal of Experimental Psychology: General, 113*, 169-193.

Underwood, B. J. (1964). Forgetting. *Scientific American, 210*, 91-99.

Watkins, M. J., Watkins, O. C., Craik, F. I. M., & Mazuryk, G. (1974). Effect of nonverbal distraction on short-term storage. *Journal of Experimental Psychology, 101*, 296-300.

Weber, R. J., Hochhaus, L., & Brown, W. D. (1981). Equivalence of perceptual and imaginal representation: Developmental changes. In J. Long & A. Baddeley (Eds.), *Attention and performance* (Vol. IX, pp. 295-309). Hillsdale, NJ: Lawrence Erlbaum Associates.

Welford, A. T. (1960). The measurement of sensory-motor performance: Survey and reappraisal of twelve years' progress. *Ergonomics, 3*, 189-230.

Wellek, A. (1955). *Ganzheitspsychologie und Strukturtheorie* [Holistic psychology and structural theory]. Bern: Francke.

Wender, K. F., Colonius, H., & Schulze, H. H. (1980). *Modelle des menschlichen Gedächtnisses* [Models of human memory]. Stuttgart: Kohlhammer.

Wickens, D. D. (1970). Encoding categories of words: An empirical approach to meaning. *Psychological Review, 77*, 1-15.

Wickens, D. D. (1972). Characteristics of word encoding. In A. W. Melton & E. Martin (Eds.), *Coding processes in human memory* (pp. 191-215). Washington, DC: V. H. Winston.

Wiener, N. (1968). *Kybernetik* [Cybernetics]. Reinbek/Hamburg: Rowohlt.

Wimmer, H., & Perner, J. (1979). *Kognitionspsychologie* [Psychology of cognition]. Stuttgart: Kohlhammer.

Winkler, F. G. (1991). *Das Vernetzungsmodell von Klimesch - eine Simulation* [The connectivity model of Klimesch — a simulation]. Unpublished master's thesis, University of Vienna, Austria.

Whitney, P., & Kellas, G. (1984). Processing category terms in context: Instantiation and the structure of semantic categories. *Journal of Experimental Psychology: Learning, Memory, and Cognition*, *10*, 95–103

Yuille, J. C. (Ed.). (1983). *Imagery, memory, and cognition*. Hillsdale, NJ: Lawrence Erlbaum Associates.

Zeki, S., & Shipp, S. (1988). The functional logic of cortical connections. *Nature*, *355*, 311–319.

Zießler, M., & Hoffman, J. (1985). Continuous information processing in conceptual identifications. *Psychological Research*, *47*, 109–118.

Author Index

Note: "f" means "and following page"; "ff" means "and following two pages."

A

Adams, M. J., 134
Adams, N., 57, 60, 62, 85
Alkon, D. L., 199f
Allport, D. A., 34
Altom, M. W., 139, 143ff
Amit, D. J., 192
Andersen, P., 202
Anderson, J. A., 81, 144f, 189, 194, 204
Anderson, J. R., 6f, 9, 11, 13, 19, 35, 41f,
    44, 46, 48, 52ff, 56, 60f, 63f, 66–70, 82,
    85, 103ff, 109, 168f, 188
Anderson, R. E., 168
Andersson, A. A., 202
Appenzeller, T., 201
Armstrong, S. L., 140
Arnoult, M. D., 5
Atkinson, R. C., 7, 33, 35
Averbach, E., 33

B

Baddeley, A., 35, 125
Bahrick, H. B., 1, 7
Balota, D. A., 60
Barsalou, L. W., 143
Bartlett, F. C., 5
Battig, W. F., 132, 148, 152, 155, 157, 169
Becker, J., 18

Bee, J., 15
Bierwisch, M., 50
Bigler, K., 57f, 60, 139
Bleasdale, F., 48, 171
Bliss, T. V. P., 194
Boies, S. J., 1
Bolinger, D., 73
Balzano, G. J., 146
Bjork, R. A., 11
Bond, C. F., Jr., 17
Boring, E., 1, 4
Bower, G. H., 6f, 18f, 44, 48
Boyes-Braem, P., 139, 143, 146
Braitenberg, V., 190, 200
Breitmeyer, B. G., 33
Brill, A. B., 200
Broadbent, D. E., 33, 35, 37, 188
Brown, A. S., 29, 135
Brown, G. D., 134
Brown, J., 11ff
Brown, R., 18, 29, 135
Brown, T. H., 194
Brown, W. D., 35
Bruder, K. J., 9
Burkell, J., 33f
Buschke, H., 19

C

Calkins, M. W., 2, 170
Carpenter, P. A., 35

Stryker, M. P., 33
Szentagothai, J., 191

T

Tabossi, P., 138
Tanenhaus, M. K., 138
Tang, Y., 200
Taylor, R. L., 1
Te Linde, D. J., 171
Teyler, T. J., 201
Thomas, J., 19
Thompson, R. F., 192f
Thomson, N., 125
Thorpe, L. A., 19
Tipper, S. P., 34
Toglia, M. P., 132, 148, 152, 155, 157, 169
Toyofuku, M., 60
Treisman, A., 33f
Tulving, E., 18, 35, 42, 48, 72, 158
Tversky, A., 145
Tversky, B., 146

U, V

Underwood, B. J., 11, 13
von Eckardt, B., 171

W

Walker, E. C. T., 79, 131, 137
Walker, J., 146
Walling, J. R., 168
Watkins, M. J., 11
Watkins, O. C., 11
Wattenmaker, W. D., 140, 145, 162
Weber, R. J., 35
Welford, A. T., 36
Wellek, A., 8
Wender, K. F., 49
Whitaker, H., 199
Wible, C., 60
Wickens, D. D., 15
Wiener, N., 5
Wiesel, T. N., 33, 190f
Whitney, P., 143
Wimmer, H., 7
Winkler, F. G., 174

Y, Z

Young, R., 200
Yuille, J. C., 168
Zeki, S., 196
Zießler, M., 74, 138, 146, 172

Subject Index

Note: "f" means "and following page"; "ff" means "and following two pages."

A

ACT, 44ff, 48, 51f, 54ff, 66f, 69f, 77, 81, 83, 86, 90, 97–100, 104, 109f, 124ff, 129, 189, 197, 204ff

ACT*, 46, 48, 66, 70, 77, 82, 86, 97–100, 104ff, 109f, 110, 125f, 129f, 189, 197, 204ff

Action potential, 192ff, 197f

Activation
  amount, 55, 59, 67, 85, 87, 92–95, 97, 99, 104ff, 109, 112ff, 116ff, 123, 126–129, 165f, 196ff
  capacity of spreading, 45, 83, 93, 98ff, 103f, 106, 109, 119f, 125f, 196, 203
  convergent, 86f, 110f
  dampening, 94, 109f, 195
  decay, 93, 98
  direct, 67
  duration, 87f, 113, 122
  indirect, 62f, 67, 82f, 85–91, 93, 95ff, 99f, 102ff, 106, 109–119, 121ff, 126–129, 159, 164f
  input, 56, 83, 98, 100f, 125
  output, 56, 98, 100f, 125
  preactivation, 46, 87, 93, 109–114, 116–119, 121, 137, 158f, 163–167, 175f, 182, 198
  reverberating, 69, 82, 86f, 90, 93ff, 98, 104f, 109, 111, 197
  speed, 56, 60, 63, 66, 75, 81ff, 85, 88, 97, 104, 117, 129, 175, 198

spread, 45f, 55f, 63, 67, 69, 85, 90, 93f, 98, 104ff, 108ff, 115–118, 121–124, 126, 134, 159, 163, 166, 175ff, 183, 198, 201

stage, 93–97, 110–125, 174–182

strength, 46, 56, 58f, 67, 92f, 100, 106, 113, 116, 118, 125, 179ff, 197, 201f

time, 56, 90, 97, 103, 108, 129

Activation process, *see* search process

Address, *see also* access node, 25–28, 134f

Artificial intelligence, 6, 187

Associationism, 4, 5, 10

Attention, *see also* distractor activity/task
  capacity, 16f, 33
  span, 1, 6

Axon, 191–194, 196ff, 202

B

Brown-Peterson paradigm, 11f, 14f

C

Code
  binary, 43f
  completely interconnected, 48, 90ff
  component, *see also* semantic feature, 25, 27ff, 37–41, 44, 51, 74f, 86f, 89f, 114, 117f, 128f, 131f, 134f, 156, 168, 170, 200, 203, 205
  definition, 3, 45, 86, 90ff